Development
Fieldwork

Development Fieldwork

A Practical Guide

Edited by **Regina Scheyvens and Donovan Storey**

SAGE Publications
London • Thousand Oaks • New Delhi

First published 2003

SAGE Publications Ltd
6 Bonhill Street
London EC2A 4PU

SAGE Publications Inc
2455 Teller Road
Thousand Oaks, California 91320

SAGE Publications India Pvt Ltd
B-42, Panchsheel Enclave
Post Box 4109
New Delhi 100 017

British Library Cataloguing in Publication data

A catalogue record for this book is available from the British Library

ISBN 0 7619 4889 9
ISBN 0 7619 4890 2 (pbk)

Library of Congress Control Number 2002112348

Printed and bound in Great Britain by TJ International, Padstow, Cornwall

Contents

Notes on contributors

Dan Brockington works on environmentalisms, environmental change and inequality, particularly in Africa. He has examined the consequences of coercive conservation policies in Tanzania, and the politics and ethnography of environmentalism, again in rural Tanzania. He is an anthropologist by training and now works at the School of Geography and the Environment at the University of Oxford.

Julie Cupples has a long standing interest in Nicaragua and has conducted development fieldwork here and in other parts of Central America. She is particularly interested in constructions of masculinity and femininity, gendered responses to war, disaster and neoliberalism, and the negotiation of competing multiple identities. Julie currently works as a lecturer in human geography at the University of Canterbury in New Zealand.

Sara Kindon is a senior lecturer in human geography and development studies at Victoria University of Wellington. She has been active in feminist and participatory research since 1990 and has carried out development fieldwork in Costa Rica, Indonesia and Aotearoa/New Zealand. She is currently exploring the politics and practices of using participatory video with indigenous peoples, drawing on collaborative fieldwork with a Maori *iwi*(tribe) over the last four years.

Helen Leslie is a lecturer in sociology at the University of the South Pacific, Fiji. She has conducted fieldwork in New Zealand, El Salvador and more recently, Fiji, where she is researching the disempowering impacts of the May 2000 coup on Indo Fijian and Indigenous Fijian women. Her research and teaching interests include, feminist research methods, gender and development, gender and conflict, and the sociology of development and underdevelopment.

Warwick E. Murray is a lecturer in human geography and development studies at Victoria University of Wellington, New Zealand. He holds a PhD from the University of Birmingham, and has worked at Brunel University and the University of the South Pacific. His research interests span the social and economic geography of inequality and development, specialising particularly in the globalisation of agriculture and its local impacts in Latin America (especially Chile), the Pacific Islands (especially Fiji, Tonga and Niue) and Pacific Asia (especially Malaysia). In August 2002 he was appointed Managing Editor of the journal Asia Pacific Viewpoint.

Barbara Nowak is programme coordinator and senior lecturer in the Institute of Development Studies at Massey University. She carried out anthropological fieldwork while living for over two years with Btsisi', an Orang Asli people of Malaysia, and began to recognise the importance of issues surrounding fieldwork ethics while doing her research and writing on this small indigenous community. Barbara's work includes articles on research ethics, human rights, changing land tenure, reservation systems, and gender issues among both Btsisi' and the Iroquois of New York State.

John Overton is a geographer by training who now devotes most of his energies to development studies. Having done his doctoral research in Kenya, his subsequent fieldwork has included Fiji and Malaysia and combined pouring over dusty archives with village-based surveys. His particular interests are in land tenure, rural socio-economic transformations and changing concepts of development throughout the Asia-Pacific region. John is the Professor of Development Studies at Massey University.

Henry Scheyvens has recently completed his PhD at Monash University, Australia, after conducting fieldwork in Bangladesh and the Philippines on aid and poverty alleviation. His research focused in particular on the nexus between aid politics, practice, evaluation and policy reform in Japan's official development assistance programme. Henry also enjoys whitewater kayaking, growing his own vegetables and other outdoor adventure pursuits.

Regina Scheyvens is a senior lecturer in geography and development studies at Massey University, New Zealand. She has conducted fieldwork in Southern Africa and the Pacific Islands on sustainable livelihood strategies for local communities, including ecotourism initiatives and eco-timber production. A recent publication arising from this research is *Tourism for Development: Empowering Communities* (Prentice Hall, 2002). She also has strong interests in gender issues and debates surrounding sustainable development.

Donovan Storey is a lecturer in Development Studies, Massey University. He joined Massey University in 1999 after three years also teaching Development Studies at the University of the South Pacific, Suva. His work has especially focused on urban issues, particularly governance, citizenship, the environment and housing in South East Asia and the Pacific. Other research interests include politics and development; Non Government Organisations; and development theory/practice. He has conducted fieldwork in the Philippines and throughout the South Pacific. Donovan's greatest ambition is to integrate his passion for wine into future research and fieldwork.

Sian Sullivan is a research fellow in the Centre for the Study of Globalisation and Regionalisation at Warwick University, UK (www.csgr.org). Her current research focuses on the phenomenology of protest politics in what has become known as the anti-capitalist and pro-justice movement. Previously her work explored disjunctions between discourses regarding 'the environment' held at local, national and transnational levels, focusing on wildlife conservation and desertification, and with fieldwork conducted over an eight-year period in Namibia. A number of publications have arisen from this work including *Political Ecology: Science, Myth and Power* (co-edited with Philip Stott, Edward Arnold, 2000). Sian also dances.

Peter van Diermen is a senior lecturer at the School of Resources, Environment and Society, The Australian National University. Peter's research is in the field of economic policy and development studies, including fieldwork in Indonesia, Sri Lanka and Thailand. He also continues to work as a policy advisor for the World Bank and Asian Development Bank.

List of boxes

Preface and Acknowledgements

An increasing demand from our postgraduate students for guidance in conducting development fieldwork was the main motivating factor behind this book. While some were well versed in methods, they had never travelled abroad and needed advice on practical and logistical hurdles they might have to overcome. Others were all too eager to launch themselves into a foreign community to begin their fieldwork, yet they lacked a full appreciation of ethical concerns associated with their research. Many of our international students going home to do research, meanwhile, were not aware of conflicts of interest which could arise from them conducting critical academic research on particular topics. Thus we decided to draw on our own experiences and call on those of a number of friends and colleagues in order to put together a book which addressed methodological, practical and ethical issues which often present challenges to those conducting development research.

All of the contributing authors have benefited from being able to utilise the wealth of material published by other researchers. Our main concern is that in attempting to bring together this massive and diverse range of ideas we have really only been able to scratch the surface of the available literature.

Personal stories have also added an important dimension to this book. Through regular boxed examples we give readers a taste of the experiences of both first time and more practiced researchers. In this regard we would like to thank in particular our students who readily agreed to share stories of their fieldwork highs and lows with us.

As the writing of the book came to a close we realised how great it would be to get feedback from actual users of the book, rather than relying on the usual reviews in academic journals. We have set up a web site especially for this purpose (http://fieldwork.massey.ac.nz), so if you happen to be reading this book while in the field, please consider sending in stories of your own which either back up, or refute, the ideas presented herein. You may also have tips for others planning fieldwork in your region. We will organise this site according to the contributions that are sent in, hopefully including sections on geographical regions as well as on broader issues, such as ethical dilemmas and the application of different data collection techniques.

Producing this book was a lot of fun thanks to the great team of authors and support

Development Fieldwork

people we have worked with. We would particularly like to acknowledge our research and technical assistants, Mike Hull and Shelley Guy, who frequently put other work aside in order to help us out of one crisis or another. We could employ Mike and Shelley thanks to funding from the Massey University Research Fund and the Institute of Development Studies at Massey, whose support we gratefully acknowledge. Karen Puklowski kindly redrew the diagram in Box 10.9 'Leaving strategies', for us. We would also like to thank our families, especially Craig and Helen.

Our main debt of gratitude, however, is due to all of those who have participated in research that we or our students have conducted in past years. It is your tolerance of us that makes fieldwork possible, and your knowledge and skills which are the basis of our findings, and it is therefore to you that we dedicate this book. Our hope is that all development researchers will keep the needs and interests of research participants foremost in their minds and act with sensitivity and sincerity in their fieldwork relationships.

1 Introduction

Regina Scheyvens and Donovan Storey

Purpose

The purpose of this book is to assist researchers, especially postgraduate students, to prepare for fieldwork on development issues in the Third World. A broad approach is taken to allow ample attention to be paid to practical, methodological, and ethical issues. We endeavour to show that where researchers are well-prepared for 'the field' and sensitive to the local context and culture, research in Third World locations can be a valuable experience for both the researcher and their research participants.[1]

The contributors to this book are well aware of the mixture of excitement, apprehension and even self-doubt, which commonly faces researchers who are preparing for fieldwork. The advice they need to prepare well for their field experience extends beyond practical tips to guidance on ethical issues and personal/psychological preparation for the difficulties they may encounter in the field. Often it is these issues that determine the success or otherwise of fieldwork – at least as much as methodological challenges. However, unless students have a supervisor who has experience in their particular field site, they may receive little of the guidance they need. The main sources of published information available to research students, for example, are books detailing methods or those dedicated to anthropological enquiry. While publications on methodology are essential, they often overlook the range of personal, social and logistical issues faced by researchers entering Third World contexts. As Devereux and Hoddinott (1992:2) have concurred 'Anyone who has done research outside his or her home community knows that questions relating to lifestyle and personal relationships loom as large as narrowly defined technical issues'. Similarly, while anthropological texts offer some deep insights into cross-cultural interactions, they are usually limited to a very specific type of enquiry (e.g. participant observation in one location for an extended period of time). They are thus not always helpful for researchers using a multi-method approach, or where time and resources for fieldwork are very limited.

We have therefore aimed to provide a text which:

- firstly, provides practical information for researchers entering 'the field' and wishing to effectively engage with research questions and respondents, specifically in Third World contexts;

- secondly, prepares researchers for some of the ethical and personal challenges they may face and also makes supervisors aware of these issues; and

- thirdly, overviews issues of research design and the selection of appropriate research methods.

This allows the book to cover a wide range of critical issues facing researchers in the field, from managing relationships with the 'host' community and avoiding cross-cultural misunderstanding, to staying on track with data collection and keeping up morale while facing unanticipated obstacles.

Concerns over appropriateness of doing fieldwork in the Third World

An important concern about fieldwork needs to be raised at the outset. Prior to discussing *how* to do fieldwork there is the ethical dilemma of whether to do fieldwork in the Third World. This is an issue which has stimulated much debate in recent years, primarily from those concerned about the power gradients inherent in events such as a relatively privileged Western researcher travelling to a Third World country to study people living in poverty. Some have referred to such research as 'academic tourism' (Mowforth and Munt, 1998:101), while Clifford (1997:67) simply sees fieldworkers as 'research travelers'. Relationships between researchers and the researched can seem particularly skewed when the country being studied is a former colony of the Western country from which the researcher derives. Madge (1993:297) thus argues that academics, 'have not yet adequately explored the power relations, inequalities and injustices' upon which differences between ourselves and those we research are based.

Since the early 1980s, challenging questions have been directed at geographers, social anthropologists, sociologists and others who carry out social research in Third World contexts. England (1994: 85), for example, warns us that 'fieldwork might actually expose the researched to greater risk and might be more intrusive and potentially more exploitative than more traditional methods', even suggesting that 'exploitation and possibly betrayal are endemic to fieldwork'. Further, post-development commentators such as Escobar (1995), criticise the way in which development discourse has been constructed so as to legitimate the voices of Western 'experts' while undermining those of local people. More specifically, England (1994:81) asks 'can we incorporate the voices of "others" without colonizing them in a manner that reinforces patterns of domination?' While there are no simple answers to such questions, they have forced Western researchers to be more accountable, especially in the light of past experiences in which much research has been of no benefit at all for the country or communities concerned, bringing into question its relevance (Edwards, 1989). According to Lather (1988:570), in the worst cases, 'rape research' has occurred whereby exploitative methods of inquiry have been used exclusively in the interests of the researcher's own career. As a consequence of this many researchers are being encouraged to engage in some serious self-reflection. As Jolly and Macintyre (1989:17) report with respect to research in the Pacific region:

> Leaders of Pacific states and Aboriginal movements are concerned to monitor and restrict foreign researchers and to ensure the research benefits more than the researchers themselves. There is a prevalent resentment of what is seen as a cultural imperialism persisting past decolonisation...[thus] Pacific scholars have been forced to re-examine both the relevance of their work and their right to do it.

In some Third World contexts local voices are seldom heard commenting on development policy or contributing to mainstream development planning. Debates which have consequently emerged over power relations between the researcher and the researched, and the dominance of Westerners as researchers of 'other' people's cultures, have thus been long overdue. Such debates have drawn attention to the voices of more marginalised people and 'dislodged the smugness of much feminist and anti-racist scholarship' (Kobayashi, 1994:74). For example, post-colonial feminist writers including Mohanty (1988) and Spivak (1987) have been particularly vigilant in drawing attention to issues concerning the politics of representation of women of the Third World in texts produced by Western researchers. Wolf (1996:32), talks about the 'discomfort' that researchers have consequently felt during fieldwork and in the post-fieldwork context. Such discomfort is demonstrated by Katz's (1994:70) use of the term 'the arrogance of research' when reflecting on her own early motivation for fieldwork and behaviour in the field.

Efforts to highlight the need for 'greater consideration of the role of the (multiple) "self", showing how a researcher's positionality (in terms of race, nationality, age, gender, social and economic status, sexuality) may influence the "data"' (Madge, 1993:294), have served to make researchers more aware of themselves. In so doing they have challenged the notion of fieldwork as being 'no more than the application of relevant techniques to problems' (Clarke, 1975:96).

This has created somewhat of a crisis of legitimacy affecting both male and female researchers from Western countries who have been forced to reconsider their role in the research process in Third World contexts in recent years. We see this as a constructive shift along the lines that Clarke (1975:104) outlined almost three decades ago when he noted that even with an emerging interest in fieldwork experiences 'the personal consequences of fieldwork are still secluded in separate papers, mimeographed informal journals, semi-fictional accounts and appendices', rather than as the fundamental contents of academic papers and theses.

Responses to the crisis of legitimacy facing Western researchers

Perhaps the most dramatic way in which researchers have chosen to respond to the crisis of legitimacy is to simply abandon development research altogether. As noted by Kobayashi (1994:74), debates over who has the right to research whom, and therefore who has the right to speak for whom, have 'led some academic women – and men – to withdraw completely from research that might place them in territory to which they have no social claim, or that might put in question their credentials for social representation'.

A second response, often associated with the first, has been to adopt a relativist perspective which privileges the knowledge and understanding of those from Third World countries. This sometimes involves the sorts of claims identified by Wolf (1996:13), for example, that 'only those who are of a particular race or ethnic group can study or understand others in a similar situation, or that only those who are women of color or lesbian can generate antiracist or antihomophobic insights'.

This viewpoint has also been criticised, however, on the basis that it is excessively romantic to posit that only indigenous people are competent to speak on the social issues affecting their countries (Goodman, 1985), or that only a woman, a person of colour or a homosexual can carry out justice-inspiring research on, respectively, other women, people of colour or homosexuals: 'To assume that "insiders" automatically have a more sophisticated and appropriate approach to understanding social reality in "their" society is to fall into the fallacy of Third Worldism, and a potentially reactionary relativism' (Sidaway, 1992:406). This debate even applies to historical/archival research (see Munro, 1994).

Romanticising or privileging Third World knowledge does not solve the ethical problems of cross-cultural research because it allows the Western researcher to ignore their own responsibilities as well as introducing problems of 'gatekeeping' (see Chapter 8). As Radcliffe (1994:28) explains, 'disclaiming the right to speak about/with Third World women [and men] acts…to justify an abdication of responsibility with regard to global relations of privilege and authority which are granted, whether we like it or not, to First World women [and men]'.

Also, it should not be assumed that Third World students based in Western universities will be able to return 'home' to do research immune to issues of power relations and ethics. It is likely, for example, that even if they speak the same language as their research participants they are separated from them by way of class and ethnic differences. Both Back (1993) and Amadiume (1993) have noted that when studying their cultures of origin, their supposed shared backgrounds with their participants did not prevent them from often feeling emotionally and politically set apart from the people they studied. These 'native' researchers may also face reverse culture shock which is all the more difficult to deal with because it is unexpected. Thus we explicitly consider examples of 'home-based' research in the Third World in many chapters of this book.

McDowell (1992:413) further warns researchers against adopting the postmodern position whereby 'any viewpoint is as valid as another'. As argued by Sayer and Storper (1997:5), this type of relativism 'licenses dogmatism while appearing to let a hundred flowers bloom, for it allows each to disqualify the criticism of others by claiming that there are no common grounds for argument'.

Another response to the crisis of legitimacy has been for researchers to continue with development fieldwork as always, while adopting non-traditional research methodologies such as Participatory Rural Appraisal (PRA) and Participatory Learning and Action (PLA), which supposedly allow participants more power in the research process (Smith et al. 1997). Similarly, Nast (1994:58) suggests using methodologies 'that promote mutual respect and identification of commonalities and differences between researcher and researched in non-authoritative ways...[that] allow for "others" to be heard and empowered'. Others have sought to redress inequities in the post-fieldwork stage by, for example, sharing authorship with local people or giving them editorial power over final works (Staeheli and Lawson, 1994, Wolf, 1996). Finally, the idea has also been pursued that Western researchers should support publication of the writing of marginalised groups within Third World countries by, for example, assisting them to obtain the necessary funding (Reinharz, 1992).[2]

The suggestion that research between Western and Third World people is always exploitative, however, is based on the assumption that Third World people have no power. Power though is rarely an either/or phenomenon and is best understood as existing along a continuum. The reality is that researchers rarely hold all of the control in the research process and that individuals and communities may well be very effective in forms of 'research resistance'. Respondents can, for example, exercise control by withholding information from the researcher, failing to cooperate or refusing to answer questions (Cotterill, 1992). In addition, they may use language as a means of controlling the responses they give to the researcher. For example, in the Solomon Islands where there are approximately 70 local languages, Scheyvens (1995) typically used the lingua franca, *pigin*, to ask questions of groups of women. Women would then discuss their response in their own language, often for several minutes, before delivering back their 'official', often one line, answer in *pigin*. In such cases, it may be that the women actually felt some comfort that Scheyvens did not speak their language, as this allowed them to express themselves freely without their views being officially recorded. Then, if they wished, they could deliver a sanitised, or otherwise altered, version of their ideas.

The potential value of research with 'others'

We take it as given that most readers of this book will be convinced that there is value in conducting research, even after reading the entertaining view of researchers which a research participant put to an Indian anthropologist working in India (see Box 1.1). Though research can become obsessive and defy logic at times, and criticisms of particular types of fieldwork certainly hold validity, field research still plays a central role in most postgraduate degrees and in the careers of many academics and development professionals. Gupta and Ferguson's (1997) ideas on the value of anthropological fieldwork are cited in Box 1.2, while more general reasons as to why fieldwork is likely to remain a central feature of thesis-related degrees and development work are considered below.

Box 1.1 A lesson about obsessive researchers

'Suppose you and I are walking on road', said Swamiji. 'You've gone to University. I haven't studied anything. We're walking. Some child has shit on the road. We both step in it. "That's shit!" I say. I scrape my foot; it's gone. But educated people have doubts about everything. You say, "what's this?!" and you rub your foot against the other.' Swamiji shot up from his prone position in the deckchair, and placing his feet on the linoleum, stared at them with intensity. He rubbed the right sole against the left ankle. 'Then you reach down to feel what it could be,' his fingers now explored the ankle. A grin was breaking over his face. '"Something sticky!" You lift some up and sniff it. Then you say, "Oh! This is *shit*." ...

'Educated people always doubt everything. They lie awake at night thinking, "What was that? Why did it happen? What is the meaning and the cause of it?" Uneducated people pass judgement and walk on. They get a good night's sleep'.

Source: Narayan (1998:178)

Most responses to the crisis of legitimacy facing Western researchers fail to consider the potential value of cross-cultural research, instead focusing on potentially harmful aspects of such research. It is important that social science students and academics conducting research in the Third World realise there can be considerable merit in research which crosses the bounds of one's own culture, sex, class, age and other categories of social positioning. Heggenhougen (2000:269) refers to the value of being 'touched by a different reality'. One reason for this, as noted by Shaw (1995:96), is that 'there is much to be gained through cross-cultural exchange, in that structural problems between North and South cannot be solved by the South alone'. Potter (1993:294) takes this point further: 'The value of Third World research should be clear for all to see in an interdependent world in which rich and poor, rural and urban, formal and informal are the opposite sides of the same coin...there is vast potential for enlightened outsider research'.

Reinharz (1992) comments on the way that a lack of cross-cultural research impedes our understanding of complex development issues. She feels that the limited vision presented in past accounts by Western feminists should not mean that only Third World women should study their own society, as this would 'legitimise Western feminist ethnocentrism by stating that women should study their own society only rather than learn about other societies' (Reinharz, 1992:121). Similarly, Sidaway (1992:406-7) claims that, 'Research in/of "other" cultures and societies...offers a counter to universalistic and ethnocentric views. It is the enemy of parochialism...[and it] may pose challenges to frameworks and assumptions developed in the core'.

> **Box 1.2 The value of anthropological fieldwork**
>
> 1. The fieldwork tradition counters Western ethnocentrism and values detailed and intimate knowledge of economically and politically marginalised places, peoples, histories, and social locations
> 2. Fieldwork's stress on taken-for-granted social routines, informal knowledge, and embodied practices can yield understanding that cannot be obtained either through standardised social science research methods (e.g. surveys) or through decontextualised reading of cultural products (e.g. text-based criticism)
> 3. Fieldwork reveals that a self-conscious shifting of social and geographical location can be an extraordinarily valuable methodology for understanding social and cultural life, both through the discovery of phenomena that would otherwise remain invisible and through the acquisition of new perspectives on things we thought we already understood.
>
> *Source: Gupta and Feguson (1997: 36-7)*

Other commentators have noted there may be value in presenting a diversity of perspectives on a particular problem (Amadiume, 1993). Tixier y Vigil and Elsasser, for example, proved that when interviewing Chicana subjects, a Chicana woman had access to certain information not available to an outside woman, but that the reverse was also true (cited in Wolf, 1996:15). In addition, Pratt and Loizos (1992) have rejected the argument that only lower class people can research issues impacting on the poor. Walsh (1996) also carried out an interesting study in Fiji, noting that the ethnicity of the research assistants (either ethnic Fijians or Fijian Indians) skewed survey results considerably.

If we support the logic that a multiplicity of perspectives can be valuable in developing a detailed understanding of complex development issues, we should also attempt to even up the imbalance which has seen Third World peoples positioned as guinea pigs to be examined in Western research projects, with little interaction occurring in the opposite direction. Thus, according to McDowell (1992:407), it is not sufficient that researchers are 'reflexive', acknowledging their situatedness in relation to the research project and how, for example, their relative privilege may influence the research process and outcomes. Rather, researchers should actively promote opportunities for the less privileged to undertake research with the privileged. Supporting such a stance is Sidaway (1992:407), who argues that the vitality of geography as a discipline would be 'enhanced in a world where Third World geographers came in large numbers to conduct research of "exotic" and "different" European and North American societies'. Doubtless his comments could be extended to include Social Anthropology, Sociology, Economics, Development Studies and other disciplines concerned with development issues.

As Sayer and Storper (1997:5) argue, criticism of 'others' is only a bad thing if the criticism is based on a lack of understanding of the 'other'. External criticism can be both relevant and helpful. What is essential is that those studied should not merely be seen as a source of data through which a researcher can further his or her career; the researcher should be accountable, reflexive, and research should be a two-way process of interaction (Elson, 1991).3 Further, Kobayashi asserts that:

> the question of 'who speaks for whom?' cannot be answered upon the slippery slope of what personal attributes – what color, what gender, what sexuality – legitimise our existence, but on the basis of our history of involvement, and on the basis of understanding how difference is constructed and used as a political tool. (1994:78)

Issues such as how well informed, how politically aware and how sensitive the researcher is to the topic in question and to the local context, would therefore seem a more pertinent means of judging suitability to conduct research with people in the Third World than an essentialising characteristic such as sex or nationality.

The criticisms of fieldwork outlined above have contributed to healthy debates and reflections on fieldwork which have helped us to move beyond positivist assumptions about the neutral role of the researcher to more nuanced understandings of ways in which one's positionality, relationships and personality affect the research process. This book then represents an effort to contribute to raising awareness of such issues, as well as offering some strategies to deal with them, and should be considered alongside other texts which focus on purely methodological concerns.

'The field'

So, what is 'the field', this locus of 'fieldwork'? Spatial differences are inherent in dominant conceptualisations of 'the field':

> When one speaks of working in the field, or going into the field, one draws on mental images of a distinct place with an inside and outside, reached by practices of physical movement. (Clifford, 1997:54)

In addition, 'the field' encapsulates cultural difference in that traditionally, fieldwork was about a search for the 'exotic other'. Such differences added to the mystique of fieldwork and also made adjustment difficult for first time fieldworkers:

> 'being there' demands at the minimum hardly more than a travel booking and permission to land; a willingness to endure a certain amount of loneliness, invasion of privacy, and physical discomfort; a relaxed way with odd growths and unexplained fevers; a capacity to stand still for artistic insults, and the sort of patience that can support an endless search for invisible needles in infinite haystacks. (Geertz, 1988:23-4)

Academics have been busy querying the binary oppositions suggested by common understandings of 'the field', including 'home' versus 'away' or 'here' versus 'there', and 'staying' or 'moving', 'insider' and 'outsider' (Clifford, 1997:84), terms which are embedded with the notion of spatiality. Gupta and Ferguson suggest we should conceptualise field sites as 'political locations' rather than 'spatial sites':

> Ethnography's great strength has always been in its explicit and well-developed sense of location, of being set here-and-not-elsewhere. This strength becomes a liability when notions of 'here' and 'elsewhere' are assumed to be features of geography, rather than sites constructed in fields of unequal power relations. (Gupta and Ferguson, 1997:35)

Their views are supported by contributors to a special edition of the *Professional Geographer* devoted to 'Women in the field', who supported the idea of the 'field' being a 'social terrain' where there is considerable overlap between the realms of the personal and the political. The coordinator of this special edition, Nast, noted the following similarities in the contributions:

> Most strikingly, the 'field' is not naturalized in terms of 'a place' or 'a people'; rather it is located and defined in terms of specific political objectives that…cut across time and space…. The objectives ideally work toward critical and liberatory ends, which are not formulated in terms of altruistically saving an exoticized 'other'. The authors instead stress the importance of identifying objectives based upon concerns to overcome shared experiences of oppression levied, for example, through patriarchy, racism, and capitalism. (Nast, 1994:57)

Another reason why it is useful to move beyond a spatialised sense of the field is that this 'continues to uphold an evaluative hierarchy regarding the kinds of fieldwork and subjects of research that are deemed "appropriate"' (Caputo, 2000:19). Thus some people still hold on to the notion of 'a *hierarchy of purity* of field sites' (Gupta and Ferguson, 1997:13), with the more exotic and distant the site, the more difficult or dangerous the experience (Passaro, 1997), and the longer it is endured for, the more valuable it is:

> 'Exotic' fieldwork pursued over a continuous period of at least a year has, for some time now, set the norm against which other practices are judged. Given this exemplar, different practices of cross-cultural research seem less like 'real' fieldwork. (Clifford, 1997:55)

When compared to the diverse experiences of fieldwork practice today, however, such traditional conceptions of fieldwork can seem largely fictional (Amit, 2000:2). Much valuable research is being conducted in cosmopolitan, urban centres rather than in remote villages, and work among the powerful is being seen as increasingly important. For example, examining the experience of western mining company employees working as expatriates in Third World countries (Cannon, 2002) can be just as valuable as intensive research at grassroots level among the supposed 'victims' of mining activity.

It is also important to note that while this book focuses on the Third World, we do not support the view that fieldwork in the Third World is any more legitimate than fieldwork within Western societies. Rather, we take a Third World focus because: a) many researchers still choose to conduct research there; b) quality research on pressing development issues is needed to both question dominant discourses about 'progress' in the Third World (e.g. as seen in the almost universal endorsement of structural adjustment programmes, or the newer poverty 'consensus') and to search for appropriate ways forward; and c) researchers working in Third World contexts are often faced with specific challenges – physical, logistical and ethical – in doing their fieldwork.

Gupta and Ferguson (1997:2) note that the mystique of fieldwork is preserved in many anthropology departments in the United States where no provision is made for critical reflection on choice of field sites, and no training on methods is provided. We are not particularly supportive of the idea of throwing students into unknown field situations to see if they will sink or swim. Rather, we feel they should carefully choose their field sites and examine their motivations for doing so (see Chapter 6), be meticulous when selecting an appropriate methodology, and conscientiously consider ethical issues. If they do these things, while seeking out information about the communities, cultures and organisations they will be working with, they should be able to formulate well-planned research projects which will, hopefully, maximise the benefits of their research while minimising the likelihood of harm to themselves or their participants.

Scope and limitations

This book is not intended to be a manual which addresses or answers all problems encountered in the field. Indeed, as Burgess (1982:9) notes, there is not one successful formula for doing effective fieldwork. Rather, it adheres to the conviction that much can be learned from reading others' experiences and problems and how they were dealt with.

This book is primarily aimed at both qualitative and quantitative researchers and research students based in Western universities who are planning fieldwork in the Third World. Their disciplinary backgrounds include Political Science, Geography, Economics, Sociology, Development Studies and Social Anthropology, and topics of interest could range from tourism to natural resource management to urban development. There is a very strong participation in social science fieldwork in the Third World by graduate students from both Third World and Western societies. Third World researchers planning research in their home societies will thus find regular mention of specific issues which they may face, and a number of boxed examples derive from the experiences of African, Pacific Island, Latin American and Asian students.

While this book is primarily intended for students undertaking postgraduate thesis work, it is also likely that development practitioners, who are increasingly expected to conduct ongoing research as part of their work, will find this a useful and accessible reference book. Similarly, while we focus on social science research, this book may also be of interest to those from more technical or scientific backgrounds (e.g. geologists or botanists) who are planning fieldwork in the Third World and want to be cognisant of relevant issues surrounding ethics, cross-cultural interaction and the logistics of working in foreign settings.

This is not a book of methods, but it does have chapters which document a range of qualitative and quantitative methods used in the social sciences and how they might be applied to different research topics and settings. Students and others planning their research will find it useful to consult other sources on fieldwork methods and techniques, including those listed at the end of Chapters 2, 3 and 4.

The term 'development fieldwork' used in our title is not restricted to the Third World, as mentioned in the section above, although this is our focus. This book can be of general relevance to researchers working in any cross-cultural context in which issues of social development are of primacy, from the hill tribes of Thailand to the reclaimed tribal lands of Maori in New Zealand, from the rural poverty of Burkino-Faso to the urban decay of Brixton.

Format

The tone of this book is intentionally informal, sometimes even irreverent. While we are dealing with some serious issues such as ethics and relationships between researchers and the researched, we also know from first hand experience that things can and do go wrong during fieldwork, and the best way to deal with these matters is to have an open mind and a sense of humour. This is confirmed by the following email which we received while writing this chapter. It was sent to us by a Masters student who was two weeks into a 10 week field visit to a Polynesian island.

> My participants are proving hard to find, or get to.... I had a really good contact arranged to take me to a rural area. Today I rang him to reconfirm our meeting and trip to the village this week, to find he was in Japan – he went last night. So what the heck I think I will go to McDonalds today instead. My computer also won't work; it has worked twice since being here. Moisture apparently. So as you can see all is going just as I hoped. (pers. comm., December 2001)

We have ensured that such anecdotal accounts of the experiences of chapter authors and other researchers are included in text boxes throughout the book. These boxed examples demonstrate both positive and negative fieldwork experiences, and demonstrate how fieldwork rarely goes as smoothly as we may anticipate. Van Maanan (1988) refers to these as 'confessional tales' and this style has also been used in DeVita (2000).

At the end of each chapter, the authors provide annotated lists of recommended readings which students may wish to pursue to delve more deeply into specific ideas or issues.

Overview

The chapters of this book draw on the rich and diverse experiences of a range of researchers. The chapter authors are either academic staff or PhD candidates who have conducted fieldwork on topics ranging from the effectiveness of NGOs in aid delivery to the social impacts of logging operations, from women's mental health in a post-conflict zone to ecotourism as a livelihood option for rural communities. They have worked in both urban and rural settings in geographical regions which include Africa, Asia, the Pacific, and Latin America. Frequently the ideas we present in individual chapters are complemented by issues raised in other chapters of this book, so readers will find frequent cross-references to follow up on.

Eleven chapters, divided into four parts, follow this introductory piece. Part I 'Methodology', provides material to assist students in planning for field research and as such it has chapters on Designing Development Research (Chapter 2), Using Quantitative Techniques (Chapter 3), and Qualitative Research (Chapter 4).

Part II 'Preparation for the Field', includes Chapter 5 on Practical Issues, which considers matters such as funding, research permission, health preparations and what to pack. This is followed by Chapter 6 on Personal Issues which examines what motivates people to do research and how this influences attitudes and behaviour in the field, and it also considers relative merits of taking family or a partner to the field versus leaving them behind.

Part III 'In the Field', launches the reader into fieldwork proper, with three chapters examining Entering the Field (Chapter 7), Ethical Issues (Chapter 8), and Working with Marginalised, Vulnerable and Privileged Groups (Chapter 9). The first of these chapters contemplates issues such as culture shock (including reverse culture shock for Third World researchers going home) and hiring research assistants, while the second and third chapters address a number of 'big questions', including who should sanction fieldwork, how to manage power relations between researchers and the researched, and whether men should do research on women.

Part IV 'Leaving the Field', begins with Chapter 10 which reflects on the experience of leaving the field, from saying farewell to new friends and colleagues, to what one 'owes' the research participants, and is followed by Chapter 11 on Returning to University and Writing the Field. Finally, Chapter 12 provides an Afterword, summarising the main themes and findings of the book, with an emphasis on reasserting the importance of fieldwork. The Afterword will also identify the factors which are most likely to lead to a successful and fulfilling research experience for researchers, and a valuable experience for the research participants.

Recommended reading

Corbridge, S. and Mawdsley, E. (2003) Special issue: fieldwork in the 'tropics': power, knowledge and practice. *Singapore Journal of Tropical Geography.*
This special issue had not been published as we went to print with this book but it promises to provide

an exciting range of papers dealing with practical issues that arise when carrying out fieldwork in 'the tropics' as well as addressing concerns associated with power and positionality.

Devereux, S. and Hoddinott, J. (eds) (1992) *Fieldwork in Developing Countries* Harvester Wheatsheaf, New York.
This edited book has some good critical essays and case studies on the realities of fieldwork.

Robson, E. and Willis, K. (eds) (1997) *Postgraduate Fieldwork in Developing Areas: A Rough Guide* Monograph No.9, Developing Areas Research Group of the Royal Geographical Society, with the Institute of British Geographers, London.
This edited collection brings together insights on fieldwork in 'developing areas' based on the first hand experiences of Geography students and academics. There are some very useful contributions on methodology, ethics and the practicalities of fieldwork.

Notes

1. Cognizant of the debates surrounding understandings of many Development Studies terms, we decided that the terms 'Third World' and 'Western' would be used throughout this book. Undoubtedly these terms can be contested, and we regret that there are no uncontested terms in current usage. Our understanding of 'Third World' is based on the meaning accorded to it by Alfred Sauvy, a French economist and demographer who coined the term in 1952. He used the word 'third' to suggest that it was 'excluded from its proper role in the world by two other worlds', not to suggest that it was inferior (Hadjor, 1993:11). While the term 'Third World' lumps together a diverse range of countries into one category and thus is in danger of oversimplifying their socio-economic circumstances, there are also undeniable similarities among many Third World countries. These similarities stem largely from their histories of colonialism and imperialism, and are represented in their current economic dependency and in their disadvantaged political position in the world. The term 'Third World' thus draws attention to inequities in the world; it '…helps to emphasise the ways in which power, resources and development are unequally and unevenly shared globally' (Mowforth and Munt, 1998:6). While the term 'Third World' is thus used in preference to a term such as 'Less Developed World' which implicitly infers inferiority, 'First World' is not used because of the notions of superiority it implies. Similarly, the increasingly popular use of 'North' versus 'South' in writing on development issues is rejected as this makes a geographical division out of what is really a social, economic and political division (Hadjor, 1992:11). Instead 'Western' will be used as the alternative to 'Third World' countries as this term has come to represent those societies exhibiting the economic systems, consumer culture and individualism characteristic of North American, Australasian and European countries.

2. Chapter 10 provides further ideas as to how researchers can acknowledge the input of research participants and ensure they give something back which is valuable to the community they have worked with.

3. These issues will be expanded upon in Chapter 8, which examines ethical issues in detail.

PART I

METHODOLGY

2 Designing Development Research

Warwick E. Murray and John Overton

Introduction

Good research requires good design yet the process of research design is fraught with difficulties and frustration. Fortunately, there is a wide literature on the principles of research design in social and economic studies that offers both theoretical and practical guidance (Blaxter et al., 1996; Kitchen and Tate, 2000; Robinson, 1998; Robson, 1993). Research design is an enormous theme. It covers three broad overlapping areas which are crucial to the genesis and initiation of a viable and relevant research topic. Firstly, research *philosophy* covers issues of ontology (theories of what the world is) and epistemology (theories of what it is possible to know about the world and how we might come to know it). Secondly, research philosophy flows into *methodologies* (theories of how the world can be interpreted) and methods (sets of techniques for interpreting the world). Finally and crucially, 'design' also incorporates issues of research *logistics and practice* which include site selection, proposal writing, research timing, budgetary issues, and planning for ethical research.

For new researchers the design phase is often daunting, coming at the beginning of the investigation period with the expectation that it should be made watertight, within a neat time frame, before flying-off to 'do' the real research. This conception of the process can be unhelpful. Design is a fundamental and integral part of actually *doing* research, and in most social research at least, design is likely to evolve as the subsequent phases of the project unfold and the perspectives of the researcher almost invariably shift. This does not imply that design should not be thoroughly worked out before 'fieldwork' begins – it should. Using a 'building' analogy, Kitchen and Tate echo this point:

> We are moving from the choice of what type of building we want to construct to decisions regarding the process of construction. To take the analogy further, if we miss out this stage and progress straight to constructing the building without adequate planning then there is a good chance we will run into problems at a later date. (2000:34)

It is important to reiterate, however, that design should be seen as an essential part of the on-going research process requiring, as does every other component of research activity, flexibility and reflexivity. To extend the analogy, this means that you may have to be prepared for some walls to falter and buckle as the ground shifts during construction. Ultimately, it is the balance between rigidity and flexibility which is likely to determine the success or otherwise of the project. Those who live in earthquake zones know well that architecture which is too rigid can be disastrous.

Given the wide literature which already exists, why include a chapter on design in a book such as this? We argue that a range of issues particular to development research design often sets it apart from design in other areas of social science. Although all research is built from fundamentally similar (albeit highly contested) foundations, it is important to understand something of the difference of development field research.

What makes development research different?

A number of points can be offered in order to support our claim that development research is somehow different. Firstly, research often takes place in localities and cultures that are relatively unfamiliar to the researcher. This is not always the case of course, and 'foreignness' lies on a continuum which is influenced by cultural, life-cycle, gender and geographical factors. Consider a female Londoner from high-income Hampstead Heath conducting research into male rural labour markets in low-income Herefordshire in the United Kingdom – is this any less 'foreign' than an urban New Zealander doing urban research in the Philippines? In practical terms, however, it is often the case that both the territorial geographies and cultural traits of the research 'site' are relatively unknown to the development researcher. Related to the first point is a second, which concerns language. Despite the rapid globalisation of English it is likely that the researcher will undertake his/her work in a foreign or second language. Particularly if the research is socio-cultural in nature, it can be argued that, without a high level of proficiency, or excellent assistance, whole worlds will remain unexplored, misinterpreted and, ultimately, poorly conveyed. Thirdly, development research by researchers from Western institutions often necessarily involves a discrete period of research activity in the field with little chance of returning to 'fill the gaps'. Finally, as Sidaway (1992) reminds us, development researchers from the 'first world' will often enter local society further up the hierarchy than their respective position at 'home' – it has been increasingly argued that the consideration of this should not only influence the practice of doing research but should be explicitly fed into design (see Chapter 9).

In the increasingly common case of foreign students from the Third World doing home-based development research, some of the above discussion remains pertinent. Doing development research away from home is distinct to doing research on one's own society and culture while based there indefinitely. For example, the researcher is likely to have a discrete fieldwork period available and will thus face all the same problems of limited piloting, distance from supervisors whilst in the field, and the perils of the return phase. Also, the fact that the student is work-ing in a Western university implies that they are relatively privileged. Even if this is not the case, it is likely to be perceived as such during fieldwork and will undoubt-edly influence data collection and the outcome of research. Finally, the foreign stu-dent doing home-based research is likely - or may be bound - to take something of the philosophical and methodological baggage picked up from the foreign insti-tutions and supervisors with whom they are working. Just as the distinction between 'foreign' and 'home-based' research is far from watertight, research can never be free of 'external' influences however 'local' it may appear.

This chapter makes the case that successful development research - whilst not inherently different from social research in general - does require a special set of skills and sensitivities. The development researcher needs to be more eclectic than is the case with research in more familiar terrains, more sensitive to cultural and eth-ical issues, and more willing to re-design research strategy as the research project evolves. Nevertheless there are a range of generic issues in social science research design which we deal with first.

Design - the ideal field research project

The business of research design is about putting philosophy into practice and oper-ationalising ways of exploring theoretical ideas. As the 'bridge' between the con-ceptual and the logistical, it involves both abstract and practical issues and the lines between them are not always clearly demarcated. The following section touches on both of these areas moving in general from philosophy to practice. We are mindful that the reader may well be embarking on his or her first research project, and thus we have attempted to keep the following as jargon-free as possible. For those who wish to pursue these generic themes in greater depth please refer to the reading list at the end of the chapter and follow-up the references utilised in the text.

Is philosophy important to research?

Before beginning your design it is worth considering the philosophy and nature of research in general and the various types of research that can be undertaken. You may wonder, understandably, what on earth philosophy has to do with the practi-cal business of undertaking a sound field research project. Indeed some people do ignore such questions - but always at their peril. There is a common misconception outside of academia that research is a value-free, objective process, often undertak-en by men and women with white coats, thick-rimmed glasses and untidy hair. Whilst this may be true of some types of research, and perhaps some researchers, such generalisations are less relevant in the post-modern world. In the social sci-ences and Development Studies in particular, there has been a flowering in the range of alternative philosophies and methodologies resulting partly from the 'cul-tural turn' of the 1980s (see Cloke et al., 1991). Lamentably, research and the term 'science' have long been colonised by one approach which has assumed the mantle of 'scientific-method' - the empirical-analytical perspective. This approach, generally built on positivistic epistemological assumptions, is more often associated with the natural sciences. However, an on-going debate concerning whether or not social science can be approached using similar philosophies and methods (the naturalist/anti-naturalist debate) continues to rage. As with all examples of contesting paradigms (Kuhn, 1970; Lakatos and Musgrave, 1970) proponents of opposing factions are active in research in Development Studies, often in the same departments! It has to be said that there is now widespread recognition that social science is somehow different and requires differentiated foundations and tools from the natural sciences (Sayer, 1988).

In fact, there are a number of different types of science. It is important to have a basic grasp of these essentially different 'worldviews' as no research can take place in a philosophical vacuum. It is important to know something about where you fit in as this makes design, practice and the defence of your arguments far easier. In this context Graham argues:

> Philosophy is to research as grammar is to language, whether we immediately recognise it or not. Just as we cannot speak a language successfully without following certain grammatical rules, so we cannot conduct a successful piece of research without making certain philosophical choices. (1997:8)

Different types of science and Development Studies

Habermas (1978) divides science into three types; *empirical-analytical, historical-hermeneutic, and critical* (Box 2.1). Each of these branches is host to a range of approaches and it is perhaps best to see the three as lying on a continuum given the considerable overlap which exists. The first is comprised of approaches where it is largely believed that facts speak for themselves, that science should concern itself with observable entities and that there is no room for 'normative' or value judgement based research.[1] The most influential branch of this approach is positivism which seeks to verify or falsify propositions through the collection of empirical data and argues for the construction of laws based on its findings. It is this branch of science which has come to dominate the public imagination and, to some erroneously, define intellectual endeavour or progress.

Historical-hermeneutic science lies at the other end of the spectrum and rejects the empirical view of the world. Facts do not exist independently of experience and individual perception is paramount. As such, outcomes are not predictable, laws are not derivable and the objective becomes the *interpretation* of patterns and processes. Examples of such approaches include humanism, phenomenology and, arguably, post-modernism and post-structuralism (see Kitchen and Tate, 2000, for a useful summary of these approaches).

In between these two views lie critical sciences - of which Marxism, realism and (some types of) feminism are three very different examples (see Johnston, 1997).

Box 2.1 Different types of science

Empirical–analytical
Essential elements – Facts speak for themselves; science should seek facts about observable objects; normative and moral questions are avoided as they cannot be measured scientifically; proposes that processes and patterns can be predicted.
Most common methods – Surveys, closed questionnaires, some cartographic analysis, secondary data can be important, although primary data central also.
Development Studies example – The devaluation of the Chilean peso and its impacts on open urban unemployment in Santiago.

Historical–hermeneutic
Essential elements – Rejects the empirical view of the world; facts do not exist independently of experience; interpretation of process and pattern rather than prediction.
Common methods – Interviews, open questionnaires, visual texts, participatory methods including participant observation and ethnography; primary data generally more important.
Development Studies example – Social identity formation among the unemployed in the squatter settlements of Peñalolen, Santiago de Chile.

Critical
Essential elements – The uncovering of non-explicit processes and relations; the communication of these findings to promote progressive social change; the explicit incorporation of moral questions.
Main approaches – A broad range of methods are utilised depending on the nature of the critical science being utilised. Mixed methods are often appropriate for such studies.
Development Studies example I– Structural adjustment and the role of military-labour relations in Chile during the 1980s.

What these approaches have in common – although some would argue that the differences are greater than the similarities – is that they have a moral dimension. The purpose of critical research is to uncover non-explicit processes and relations (including the nature of previous research findings) and communicate these to people so that they may act upon them in order to improve society, a process referred to as emancipation.

Changes in Development Studies over the 50 or so years of its disciplinary history illustrate the shifts and tides of changing paradigms in the social sciences in general. Early Development Studies was generally more empirical-analytical, especially given its preoccupation with economic growth and modernisation which it was felt could be 'measured' in objective ways (Lewis, 1954; McClelland 1970; Rostow, 1960; Soja 1968). The 1960s, and in particular the rise of dependency analysis, saw a flourishing of critical approaches in Development Studies – some of which were explicitly action-oriented and policy based (Dos Santos, 1970; Frank, 1967; Prebisch, 1962). More recently, development has been contested by more reflexive, explicitly subjective philosophies. The post-modern and post-colonial critiques have been particularly influential in academic (if not policy) circles as totalising strategies and the research used to generate them has been heavily criticised. In particular the 'value free' nature of modernisation research was labelled a façade (Brohman, 1995; Chambers, 1983; Esteva, 1992; Rahnema and Bawtree, 1997). There are, of course, major exceptions to the neat chronology described above - modernisation was often researched from a hermeneutic viewpoint (as in some forms of Anthropology and Sociology); some of the dependency theory of the 1960s and 1970s was based on an empirical-analytical worldview (especially structuralist influenced versions), some of the more recent post-turns are heavily critical, while others are highly conservative given their almost complete relativism (see Corbridge, 2000 for an introductory critique). This illustrates the danger of stereotyping different types of research and different worldviews.

What should you do about all the above philosophical debates? Is it essential that you have your theoretical colours nailed onto the mast before you begin? We would sound a note of warning here. It is possible to get too deeply, sometimes painfully, involved in such considerations. However, unless your project is specifically about the application of philosophy, try not to become too tied up in it.[2] The nature of your training to date and your intellectual character will partly pre-determine which of the 'worldviews' you most closely identify with. While in the field it will quickly become quite apparent where you best 'fit'. It is quite possible that you may hold two worldviews at the same time (especially if you believe that opposing worldviews are incommensurable as some post-modernists do), or you may find that the research process changes how you feel about competing philosophies. Very few academics have fully resolved where they sit in this respect and are constantly evolving their theoretical lenses to interpret and understand what they observe. If you think you know the answer in its entirety then clearly you do not fully understand the question!

Considering your position - what kind of research?

Flowing from the idea of different types of science comes the recognition that there are therefore many different 'types' of research (Box 2.2) in which one can become engaged. There are a number of continuums which are likely to apply to all projects.

Every individual project will be located somewhere along each of these continuums, making each unique. You may decide that you wish to locate yourself at specific points along these planes. In this case it will be fruitful to consider *positionality* early on. Where are you coming from? Whose side are you on? Are you a pragmatist or an idealist? It is impossible not to have a position and for your individuality to not influence the research process in some way. How does the avowed 'positivist' who undertakes a regression analysis of causal variables in economic growth decide which variables to include, and how does he

Box 2.2 Research types

Pure ——— Applied
Descriptive ——— Explanatory
Market ——— Academic
Exploratory ——— Problem solving
Covert ——— Collaborative
Value free ——— Action based
Subjective ——— Objective

Source: Blaxter et al. (1996:5)

or she arrive at this research topic in the first place? All research, however positivist in appearance, has value-judgements at its root. Soja (1979), for example, has written a stinging self-critique on the application of positivism in his research on modernisation in Kenya.

Considerable academic debate surrounds the issue of positionality and other linked themes and this has been greatly amplified since it was first considered by feminist researchers in the late 1970s and 1980s (Cloke et al., 1991; Dear, 1988;). Your position, however, may 'fall-out' naturally as the research project and the questions which you will address become clearer. Despite the myriad possibilities, based to a large extent on the differential philosophical foundations;

(T)he basic characteristics shared by all of these different kinds or views of research is that they are, or aim to be, planned, cautious, systematic and reliable ways of finding out or deepening understanding. (Blaxter et al., 1996:5)

It should be made very clear that non empirical-analytical science is equally as rigorous as its counterparts. Indeed, it could be argued that in order to convince, other types of science have to be even more rigorous in their analysis as they swim against the popular tide of what is considered really 'scientific'. This has certainly been the case in Development Studies where modernisation approaches continue to dominate in the policy-sphere. Those who adopt 'alternative' approaches, beware, as in some ways you have an extra responsibility to be diligent and systematic. While there are some excellent examples of research in this vein to which you can turn to for guidance, it is, however, advisable to consult your supervisor on which examples would be relevant to your particular topic.

How can I think of a project?

Robson (1993) likens research design to crossing a river, whereby with each step you move between the stones which represent focus, questions, strategy, methods. Before questions or hypotheses can be set-up, it is necessary then to cross the first stone and come up with a focus for the study. This period can be both stressful and enjoyable, involving a fair bit of dreaming and drifting through the literature. Some may already have the general area of their project decided for them if they choose to study with a supervisor that only offers postgraduate study in areas of his or her expertise. Although this might seem like an easy option at the time and the student may be flattered that the academic wants to have him/her working on a pet theory or topic, in the long run (and the research period feels like a very long run at times) it may not be a good idea. The student should choose a topic that rings bells and sets off fireworks in the mind. Being very interested in the matter you are going to invest a significant part of your life in is a bare minimum (see Chapter 6 on issues of personal motivation). How then do you decide on a topic that has these qualities? The suggestions in Box 2.3 may be useful.

Box 2.3 Suggestions for thinking of a research topic

• Pick up some of the current development journals such as Third World Quarterly, Development and Change, or World Development and see what published researchers are doing. You will be amazed how much of the material that is published comes from post-graduate or post-doctoral work.
• Think of a country you are interested in, and have perhaps studied or travelled in to some extent before. Find a journal for that country or the region in which it is located like The Contemporary Pacific, Asia Pacific Viewpoint, Journal of Modern African Studies or Bulletin of Latin American Studies. Consider what is being studied in the region of your choice and whether it would excite you to do more, or take another angle, on these issues.
• Talk to people about development issues in the department where you are working or plan to work. Find out what the strengths of the department are if you don't already know them. Talk to both staff and previous students. Try also to talk to people outside the department about what are perceived as the strengths from their vantage point.
• Look at previous postgraduate work that has been deposited in the library. Most departments will store their theses in some form. Build from these ideas, while taking care to distinguish the better quality theses.
• You could consider developing some of your previous research. You may have done an undergraduate research essay or an honours dissertation on a development topic of interest to you.
• You might like to relate it to other interests you have. You may have done charity work, or you may have travelled. If you are from the Third World you may have worked for a government department focused on a particular aspect of development. You might consider incorporating this experience.
• Drawing a diagram may also be useful. Place the very general area of interest to you in the centre (e.g. urbanisation) and draw linking topics from it, creating a spider-like effect.
• Consider what puzzles and/or 'bugs' you in terms of development issues. Is there anything that you feel very strongly about? You may take every opportunity to educate friends and family about the moral outrage associated with Third World trade and European and US protectionism - do a

> project on some aspect of it then! You are likely to have to hone it down considerably from the initial flash of inspiration however (see later section).
> • Enjoy the freedom of not knowing exactly what you are doing at this point. This won't always be the case. Don't be scared to follow wild ideas – it is your supervisor's job to help you make them manageable. Just dream a little bit.
>
> *Source: Adapted from Blaxter et al. (1996)*

Don't be scared about being confused at the early stages of research: it can even be useful. Reading and thinking widely helps push out our intellectual boundaries and, though it might threaten to confuse and overwhelm you at first, out of that broadness of view, with all its contradictions, blind alleys and unresolved issues, comes a good appreciation of the breadth of your topic and its possibilities. Having been confused and then (hopefully) having found some clarity, you can be a lot more confident about proceeding.

When deciding what to focus upon a number of things should be borne in mind. As previously mentioned, your motivation is very important. The project will have to sustain your interest for one or two and possibly many more years – so you need something you are passionate about. It is not hard to find such issues in Development Studies – although we would like to point out that the most unlikely of topics (such as the social and economic impacts of pumpkin exports from Tonga) may often turn out to be fascinating. You will also need to consider the regulations of the department you are working in; the size and manageability of the project in the time period that you have to complete it; the cost and any sources of funding you may need to find; the resources available in and around the department and your project's demand for support. Finally, and this may be especially relevant for development research, you will need to consider access issues – it may not be automatic that research permits are granted (see Chapter 5). This may be the case if the research is around sensitive issues (see Chapter 9). This is not to say that such issues should be avoided, however, as with all aspects of research a fine balance between pragmatism and idealism needs to be struck.[3]

Robson (1993:26) offers a useful categorisation of the roots of successful and unsuccessful research – although these ideas will not apply in every case (see Box 2.4). Arguably, research does not have to have 'real world value' to be successful. How is real world value measured? What of pure research which pushes back academic and theoretical boundaries? Look particularly at the roots of unsuccessful research. You should avoid taking the 'easy options' – such as relying on secondary data – as they often involve hidden pitfalls. Resist attempting to build a research project around a method you believe you are particularly adept at; methods are tools and are only as good as their suitability to the job.

> **Box 2.4 Successful and unsuccessful research**
>
> *Successful research begins from:*
> a. **Activity and involvement** – good and frequent contacts in the field and with colleagues
> b. **Convergence** – coming together of two or more activities or interest
> c. **Intuition** – feeling the work is important, timely, right
> d. **Theory** – concern for theoretical understanding
> e. **Real world value** – work leading to tangible and useful ideas
>
> *Unsuccessful research begins from:*
> a. **Expedience** – undertaken because it is easy, cheap, quick or convenient
> b. **Method or technique** – using it to try out a specific method or technique
> c. **Motivation by publication, money or funding** – research done for publication interest rather than interest in the issue
> d. **Lack of theory** – without this research is easier, but will be of less value
>
> *Source: Robson (1993:26)*

How can I narrow it down?

Thinking widely helps to inspire, extend and contextualise your research topic but it can also overwhelm you and distract you from conducting well-focused field-work. In any research, there comes a time when the exploring of the boundaries has to finish and commitment must be made to a specific topic and design. Such a process is also mirrored in the structure of many research reports.

We can think of a piece of research (and a thesis or academic paper) as being shaped like an hour glass. It starts wide at the top. Here we have a broad scope to explore and encompass existing knowledge: knowledge about the philosophy and methodology of study, the themes for the study, and the region being studied. Out of this, as the hour glass begins to narrow, we should identify gaps or debates in existing knowledge or aspects that you think are inadequate or wrong. These define our key general research questions, which we then refine to develop specific questions that we seek to answer in our research. This takes us to the start of the narrow section of the hour glass, analogous to the focused field work we undertake. This done, and our data collected, we then begin our analysis, at first narrow and specific but gradually widening out to re-address more general issues and debates as we see our contribution to knowledge across a broad base.

Of course, this is much easier said than done and rarely in practice do we follow this neat path from broad to narrow to broad again. Indeed, we should always, even when focused most narrowly on our field work, be aware of the broad issues and reflect on them. However, there are some ways in which we can try to narrow our ideas down from the general to the specific:

- *Talk*: Talking to others (rather than being buried in our own thoughts) helps to articulate ideas more clearly. Issues that seemed muddy in your mind often become clearer when you have to express them to others.
- *The aunty/uncle sentence*: This is a refinement of the talking strategy. Imagine you are at home with your relatives on holiday and you are asked by Auntie Flo or Uncle Fred 'what are you studying at university?' You have one sentence to offer a reply about your research topic. Because Flo/Fred are not academics, you must not use any jargon or language that cannot be understood by a non-expert ('It is an examination of the socio-psychological parameters underpinning the construction of meta-narratives relating to the incremental impoverishment of a selected sub-section of a marginalised population') but, because you don't want to patronise them by offering a glib response ('I'm going to free the world from poverty'), you must give a sense of what the research is about. It is a tough exercise but well worth doing. If you can construct such a sentence that you are happy with, write it down in large letters, pin it to your wall, show others and keep it in mind throughout your work.
- *Draw a picture*: Just as we suggested above using a diagram to begin to explore a possible project, a drawing can help you identify the key elements of a research project and their linkages. See what the central issue is, what the main components are to support this central issue, and identify linkages among them. Your drawing could be a neat box-and-line type or a more free-form doodle that evolves as you add or emphasise different components. Again, if you are happy with the end result, store it away, discuss it and keep it in mind. Such a drawing might even pass as a 'conceptual framework' for your project and it can help later to inform the structure of what you write.
- *Ask questions*: Research usually involves finding answers to a series of questions. Sometimes these are big, earth-shattering questions ('what are the causes of poverty?'); other times they are more simple and specific ('why do children in this region suffer from malnutrition more than nearby?'). Think of research as having one central focusing question (the question you really want to answer and the one that will define your contribution to knowledge - this is rather like your auntie/uncle sentence) and a series of secondary questions that you need to answer first if you are to address the main one. Try writing these questions down and using them to direct your work thereafter, though you will need to return to and modify these questions as your research proceeds.

Which methods should I use?

Having defined your question and the approach you wish to take you will have a range of methods at your disposal. You need to decide on methods for generating data and methods for analysing the data you produce. Certain methods are often associated with particular approaches - however there is greater flexibility than some may think. Crang (1997) argues for a more realistic exploration of these links and questions whether particular philosophies necessitate certain methods. It is true that some methods are better suited to some approaches (e.g. textual analysis in hermeneutic research or chi-squared analysis in empirical-analytical studies). This need not be the case at all times however. In this context Giddens (1984, quoted in Wolfe, 1989:71) argues:

> However statistical a given study might be, however abstract and remote it is, it presumes some kind of ethnography of individuals involved in the context of what is being described.

There is something of an artificial distinction which has evolved concerning the use of qualitative and quantitative methods - the former for hermeneutic and the latter for empirical-analytical science. There is no reason why methods cannot be mixed - one shouldn't fall into the trap of being qualitative or quantitative and thinking that they are mutually exclusive. This idea of the applicability of mixed methods is taken up in greater detail in subsequent chapters.

Chapters 3 and 4 review some of the methods open to researchers but before making a choice about methods, it is important to remember the place of methods in research design. Methods are a means to an end, not an end in themselves. Your methods must be appropriate to what you seek to discover or answer and they must be appropriate to you as an individual: your abilities, values and preferences. Again, it is important to be flexible in research design. We suggest moving from philosophy to positionality to choice of topic and, thence, to method. However, in practice, this may be more reflexive. If you are an expert in multi-variate statistical analysis, there may be no point in locking yourself into a path that takes you only to qualitative participant observation as a method. Draw on your strengths - but do not be a prisoner to them.

In considering which methods to adopt, think of research as being like preparing a meal. You may start with an idea, you then explore the cookbooks to see if others have done this before, you eventually settle on a menu and, later, specific recipes. Your menu is like your research design and your recipes are like your methods (bearing in mind that you might favour recipes you have used before but which suit the overall menu). Your recipes then should specify a list of ingredients (your data needs). This shopping list is important: remember that you have defined what you need to get the job done and you do not need to buy up the whole market or cook the same dish six different ways. Yet, when you go to the market, you might find that not all the ingredients are available. This requires some quick thinking: you either have to find acceptable substitutes or, in the worst case, you have to revise your menu. In Box 2.7 we see how one of us had to make some quick changes to his research menu in Chile. Box 2.5 summarises our meal metaphor.

The market might also reveal some exciting ingredients that you had not thought of but which you can acquire and accommodate within your menu. Even in cooking and serving your meal, be prepared to make changes: some seasoning added near the end can make a big difference to the taste and good presentation of the meal will make its consumption more pleasurable!

Box 2.5 Cooking up research

1. Plan a research 'menu' (research design) but be prepared to revise it as you go.
2. Seek ideas and inspiration from the literature and others.
3. Find 'recipes' (methods) that are appropriate to what you want to achieve overall and which you can manage.
4. Draw up a shopping list of the 'ingredients' (data) you need: make sure you have enough to achieve your goals but don't acquire too much or there will be much wasted effort.
5. Plan your work to the time and resources available.
6. Be prepared to change and modify your plan according to what 'ingredients' (data) you can find.
7. A great result requires inspiration, organisation and hard work in equal measure.

Should the research process look like spaghetti?

In the above, we have outlined in a roughly chronological way the first steps of the research process, flowing from general philosophy to particular methods. In reality, research is very rarely ever like this. Three models of the research process sum up the options, linear, circular and spaghetti.

• The linear model, where the process flows in an ideal way from one completed task to the next rarely, if ever, happens, and yet most students expect that it will. This is a major source of frustration for them.
• The circular model shows the various components of research looping and linking into one another, re-enforcing and re-defining as projects progress. If your research process looks like this then you are doing well and there is a good chance you will be successful.
• In many cases however the research process looks more like a plate of spaghetti, with the various components becoming interlinked, tangled and of little form. This is not something that should be aspired to. However, when things go wrong there is no need to panic or start again – as the case study in a later section shows adjustments can often cater for unexpected turns in the research process.

Logistics - proposing and planning

We have considered overall research design but this broad planning process is not sufficient. There are some critical practical issues that flow from the general design and these, again, require both careful planning but also a flexible attitude that allows modification.

One of the most critical aspects of research design is the research proposal. Proposals may be drawn up at different stages and for different purposes, for example, requesting funds, immigration clearance, ethics approval, PhD programme application or confirmation, and the purpose and timing of the proposal affects the particular shape and length of what is written. Nonetheless, a good proposal must have certain elements (Box 2.6).

Keep the proposal as concise as possible: you are writing a statement of intent, not draft chapters. Unless you are required to produce something more substantial, a proposal should be able to cover the above aspects in 3000 words or less. However, more specific proposals, for example for an ethical approval process, may require a longer paper or a more specific format. In line with our overall theme about flexibility, treat the research proposal as a working document. It may meet a particular need and summarise your intent at one point in time but it should not put your project in a straightjacket. Review and, if necessary, revise your proposal as you go.

Box 2.6 Essential components of a good research proposal

• A research title or statement of intent: this should be concise and jargon-free (the auntie/uncle sentence helps here).
• Key research question(s).
• An acknowledgement of the wider literature and issues as they pertain to the topic: what do we know or not know already? Only the key references should be listed.
• The context of the research: the particular region or locality for the research and the way this shapes the topic.
• The methods to be used, including data needs, location, methods of collection and analysis.
• A discussion of ethical issues, and ethics procedures/permissions which may need to be obtained.
• A timetable: when will the main phases of the work be conducted?
• A budget: what are the anticipated costs and sources of income?

Within the proposal, several logistical issues may need to be covered. Furthermore, such issues may take on particular importance or shape in a piece of Development Studies research. Examples of such issues include:

• *Site selection*: What is the intended location for field research? Choose a site or sites that, from what you can find out, are likely to give you appropriate data. This can be difficult if you do not have first-hand knowledge of the place and you may have to modify your selection once in the field. Bear in mind practical issues of accessibility, health, safety and sustenance (can I find a place to stay?) as well as suitability for the topic of study. Do try to find out as much as possible about health and safety hazards beforehand and either avoid overly hazardous places or take reasonable steps to mitigate the hazards (such as anti-malarial measures or personal safety plans). Always have an emergency plan so you can get help and get to safety from the places you are in.

• *Pre-testing*: Ideally, it is desirable to test and refine your methods in the field before embarking on the full field project. Given the difficulties and expense of travelling overseas to a field site, this is not always possible. In some circumstances, some sort of virtual pre-testing might be tried, for example using friends or, if possible, expatriates from your intended country/region.

• *Language and cultural issues*: Are you going to be able to communicate effectively in the field and behave appropriately? If you have doubts, language courses should be looked at and/or enquiries made to arrange a field assistant and translator. A 'cultural mentor' - someone from the cultural group you intend to work in - can also help pave the way and educate you both before you enter the field and during your work. In addition, prior contact with key informants and gatekeepers (if possible) should be considered to ease the path to the field.

• *Ethics and immigration clearance*: Most research activity requires some form of official clearance to proceed. Many universities now have human ethics approval procedures that require prior application before a project can be approved. You need to find out about such principles see (Chapter 8), and procedures at an early stage and plan for this in your timetable. Similarly, if you are working in a country that you are not a citizen of, you will almost always need a special research visa. Investigate this early, for some countries have a very lengthy and difficult application process (see Chapter 5).

• *Budget*: Estimating the costs of research is not straightforward, especially if it is an unfamiliar location. Apart from the obvious costs of international travel and field equipment (tape recorders, etc.), you may need to add items such as visa and insurance costs, photocopying of documents, local travel, pay for translator/research assistant, gifts (if appropriate), and personal accommodation and sustenance. One of the best ways to estimate these latter costs is to consult an up-to-date backpacker guide (such as the *Lonely Planet* series) as they cover cheaper accommodation and travel better than official tourist guides. You often succeed in finding accommodation with local households but do not underestimate the costs of this and you should never exploit local hospitality. Be prepared to contribute to household expenses and give gifts above what may be asked for as 'rent'.

• *Timetable*: A good timetable is critical for guiding not just your time in the field but also your whole research project. It is often best to start at the end! Set a completion date for your work (this may be determined by funding etc.) and keep to it. To assist you in this, making a completion date public to friends, family and supervisors creates a disincentive to drag your research on too long. Within this outer time frame, set intermediate signposts: for example, finish literature review, leave for the field, finish fieldwork, complete data analysis, submit first draft etc. You may have to revise these as you go and, of course, disasters or mishaps may justify extensions but try to keep to your end date. Meeting intermediate targets might create pressures and panics along the way but they are better than leaving them all to the end. But also, when you meet those targets, reward yourself - have a (short) break – so you can maintain your energy and enthusiasm throughout the process. Some people, in preparing a timetable, also draw up a 'Plan B timetable': if things don't go according to Plan A, have a fall-back option that you can manage. Although you need to remain flexible, you can always find a reason to stay longer in the field. Use your data 'shopping list' to define the priorities of the data you see as essential (as opposed to that which is in the 'might be useful or interesting' category) and use the completion date to sharpen your decision when to stop.

Thus, research design is a critical process. You can plan what you have to do, you can anticipate what lies ahead and you can develop contingencies if things don't go quite as intended. Some degree of rigidity is necessary: keep a focus on your topic and don't be distracted by too many interesting cul-de-sacs; develop a budget and keep to it as much as possible; and set a timetable that allows for some latitude and down-time but sets an achievable end-date. But balance this rigidity with flexibility: be prepared to modify the plan as you go, for no piece of research ever goes exactly as anticipated. Expect shocks and disappointments. Be prepared to accommodate exciting and serendipitous opportunities. And always review throughout your research what you want to achieve, how you are going to achieve it and when you will have it done by.

Research practice - between rigidity and flexibility

The boxed case study below (Box 2.7) relates to the PhD design experience of one of the authors of this chapter – Warwick (Murray, 1997). It is intended to give heart to those who experience tectonic shifts – from tremors to full-blown earthquakes – in their research design structure over time.

Conclusion

Each field experience, like the places in which they unfold, will be totally different. However, a number of broad points can be offered, some of which may be of use to those about to start their fieldwork period. The study in Box 2.7 seems to suggest that a fine balance between rigidity and flexibility is required in fieldwork. It is important that the researcher has a clear idea of the purpose of his/her research aims and objectives. It is also advisable to have a clear idea of what methods will be employed in order to achieve these things. On the other hand, one must be pre-

> **Box 2.7 Rigid methodology melting in the Chilean sun**
>
> In April 1994, feeling scared and elated at the same time, I (Warwick) arrived in Chile to begin a year's PhD fieldwork. My only real comfort on arrival was the knowledge that my research objectives were clearly laid out with a neat methodology to suit. A lot of hard work had gone into developing the topic, which included regular meetings with my supervisor and a

set of progress review tutorials. By June of the same year, I had the feeling that these efforts had been of little worth as the rigid methodology had all but melted in the Chilean sun. In truth, this was far from the case. The research methodology and the nature of the project had 'evolved' considerably but, in retrospect, this was no bad thing. The shift in research objectives and methods was not only inevitable - it was desirable.

The main aim of my research in Chile was to assess the implications of neo-liberalism for small-scale fruit growers. In particular it aimed to analyse the relationship existing between such growers and multinational export companies. This would require a lot of qualitative and quantitative primary and secondary material, for which a detailed and timetabled plan had been devised. In the case of the small-scale growers, a questionnaire/semi-structured interview had been developed which would be used with at least one hundred growers in two localities where fruit exports were important. Two localities were pre-selected for study, El Palqui (in the 'Norte Chico' region) and West Curicó (Maule region). Both localities (reputedly) had large populations of small-scale growers, and exhibited major specialisations export fruits. In order to gain information as to the workings of the multinational exporters a postal questionnaire had been written. Further to this it was intended that a range of other informers in the field - including agronomists, packing-house managers, local agricultural input suppliers, labour agencies etc - would be interviewed. I planned to spend at least two months engaged in intensive research in each locality and return to Santiago to pick-up secondary data at the conclusion of the project. I even had a good idea about where I was going to stay and what bus company I was going to use to get about!

Hopes of sticking to this methodology soon evaporated. The first major problem lay in the selection of the study localities. El Palqui was fine, everything that was supposed to be there existed. However, in the case of West Curicó, I had clearly relied on rather outdated secondary information. Virtually no apple growers existed in the area. Furthermore, the agricultural roles obtained in Santiago detailing land ownership in the area were subject to errors. Many of the listed farms did not even exist! Those that did were invariably of a different size to that quoted. Eventually, a suitable area - East Curicó - was identified for study with the help of the local INDAP (Instituto Nacional de Desarrollo Agropecuario) office in Curicó and a pilot study was organised. By the time broad characteristics of the area had been collated and a specific focus area had been identified, two weeks had been knocked off the timetable.

I also encountered considerable problems getting to as many small-scale growers as I had hoped and getting the level of information required. A major shortcoming was linguistic. A three-month, once-a-week, course in Spanish was not sufficient preparation for Chilean Spanish in general, let alone the nuances of countryside Chilean. It was necessary to take an intensive course back in the capital and hang around a lot of cafes and bars talking, but mainly listening, to people. Of course, we would never suggest that you spend significant amounts of time drinking coffee or in bars, but it is extremely educational to just 'hang-out' at times.

There were further logistical impediments. First, there were problems with obtaining the 'random' sample hoped for. A number of 'gatekeepers' (Crang and Cook, 1994) had to be relied on for contacts within the communities. Clearly, this led to a bias, as the individuals would select those who they felt would be 'most interested' and 'interesting'. Second, the postal questionnaire was a failure (three responses from thirty, two of which were to inform me that they couldn't help!). Personal, pre-appointed visits were the only way that the export companies could be successfully approached, which all took time. Third, it was time consuming to track down individuals. The growers' work took place from sun-up until sun-down. More often than not I would attempt to locate them at their plots (parcelas) and these parcelas were sometimes very far apart. This was particularly the case in Curicó. Riding up to 50 km in the Chilean sun on mainly rough stone surface roads and with pockets full of stones to scare off mad dogs, was not envisaged during the research design phase.

A number of positive 'chance' discoveries also partly altered the direction of research. For example, whilst in a legal office in Ovalle (the major market town near to El Palqui) for another purpose, a large set of fruit sale contracts drawn up between export firms and farmers was stumbled upon. The analysis of these contracts formed a major section in the final thesis.

Surprise meetings with informed individuals also became increasingly important. A chance meeting occurred in a restaurant with one of Ovalle's lawyers; somebody who had worked in the defence of small farmers in disputes concerning the re-possession of their property by companies. Further meetings helped clarify the aims and objectives of the project in an important way. Of course, in cases where chance discoveries are made, one often has to rapidly alter tack and not become excessively concerned if the research timetable is altered.

The first few months in the field led to a large re-definition in the methodology of my project. Further, to a certain extent, the aims of the project were refined. Crucially, not as much time as originally hoped for could be spent in the field. At first, this created a problem as I really wished to avoid the worst excesses of researching as a 'visiting outsider' as Chambers (1983) would term it. However, it probably helped create a 'bigger picture'. Ambitions as to the number of farmers to be interviewed were cut and language difficulties meant that the information was not always as rich as I would have liked. This, however, forced me to think about and focus on the really important issues. Chance findings convinced me that there was a much greater role for qualitative elements in the research. Overall, as time went on, it became obvious that it was important to be as 'flexible' and 'eclectic' as possible in method and that learning by doing can be very constructive.

Source: Murray, doctoral research in Chile, 1994

pared to refine and, in some cases, let go of these plans once in the field - often at very short notice. In the same context, it may also be important to be prepared to think on one's feet. But the most important thing, perhaps, is not to give up - the authors know of very few researchers who have not experienced the above types of problems. Almost invariably they have managed to sort them out.

Research is not easy, but it is remarkably rewarding. Expecting the unexpected and undertaking contingency planning can help researchers cope with unforeseen outcomes, raising the quality of the final output and the undoubted joys associated with arriving at that point. Good researchers are those who can design their work well and organise their time and resources accordingly. But they are also those who can react, adapt and revise their plans so that they can retain an eye on their objectives yet, if necessary, re-draw the map in order to get there.

Recommended reading

Crang, M. and Cook, I. (1994) *Doing Ethnographies* University of East Anglia, Norwich.
For those engaged in intensive primary fieldwork this is an excellent, relatively jargon-free introduction covering theoretical and practical issues.

Creswell, J. W. (1994) *Research Design* Sage, London.
This book provides a broad-ranging introduction aimed at postgraduates to both qualitative and quantitative research design. In particular it deals with the possibility of combining approaches.

Graham, E. (1997) Philosophies underlying human geography research. In R. Flowerdew and D. Martin, (eds) *Methods in Human Geography* Longman, Harlow, pp. 6-30.
This is a comprehensive and jargon-free introduction to the philosophies underlying human geography research and is applicable across the social sciences.

Robson, C. (1993) *Real World Research* Blackwell, London.
Robson provides a non-specialist introduction to the practical and philosophical issues surrounding research in what he terms the 'real world'. Excellent for those who are doing 'applied' research.

Notes

1. Kitchen and Tate (2000:7) remind us that the term empirical should not be confused with the term empiricism. The latter refers to the research philosophy described in this chapter, whilst the former refers to the collection of data for testing - which can take place within many different philosophical frameworks.
2. Naturally this will vary according to the level of study you are involved in. For PhD research there is generally a requirement that you engage with philosophical and epistemological debates in a sound way. You must check with your supervisors regarding the expectations of your particular institution.
3. Chapter 8 on Ethical Issues includes a section on truth and deception.

3 Using Quantitative Techniques

John Overton and Peter van Diermen

Introduction

Quantitative techniques in the past have dominated most social science research. Such techniques can be a powerful aide to Development Studies research for they can give us precise and accurate results, they can allow us to gain a picture of broad patterns and phenomena and they can provide us with evidence to inform policy formulation. They have particular utility when firm answers are required. How many people do not have access to clean water? What is the likely monetary impact of a scheme to convert from subsistence to cash crops? How much income and employment are generated by street traders? Yet their use in developing countries, whilst essential in many aspects of research, does raise some particular problems and limitations.

Unfortunately the use of quantitative techniques tends to polarise researchers. Some, without sufficient training in statistics, go weak at the sight of a formula or a spreadsheet or talk of 'margins of error', or 'statistical significance'. Others have a deep suspicion of quantitative methods from a more philosophical post-modernist perspective: empiricism is seen as flawed because it seeks truth and objectivity from a research process, so it is suggested, that will always be subjective and contested. On the other hand, there are many researchers who rely on quantitative techniques because they believe that only these techniques allow us to uncover verifiable and meaningful 'facts' that have scientific validity. We suggest here that a common sense view of research will place us somewhere in between: quantitative techniques can be very useful – and are often essential – but they must be treated with caution and often supplemented by other techniques.[1]

In this chapter we explore some potential benefits and pitfalls in the use of quantitative techniques. We do not aim to present a detailed guide to the range or use of such techniques (see Recommended Reading at the end of the chapter to follow-up further). We start by discussing why we use these techniques before suggesting some basic approaches. We finish by stressing some problems commonly encountered and suggesting simple strategies for avoiding them.

What is quantitative data?

Almost all fieldwork generates quantitative data. In many cases this is done intentionally as either the main methodology or as a secondary technique to supplement and support other research strategies. The intentional collection of data by the fieldworker occurs through methods such as questionnaires, observations, structured interviews and the use of published data. The collection of data may also be incidental to the main fieldwork strategy. Where the researcher uses case studies or ethnographic fieldwork, informal quantitative data collection often occurs in the footsteps of the main methodology: in interviews we discuss how many people might live in a household, what rice prices are like at present, or how much land a household can access. Regardless of the reasons or methods for quantitative data collection, the discussion here is useful for those considering using quantitative analysis. The focus in this section is first on identifying the main characteristics of quantitative data before we move to discussing the techniques for collecting and analysing such data.

Quantitative data is characterised by many of its proponents as objective, representative and most important, specified in numbers. In contrast, qualitative data is often said to be subjective, not representative and prescribed in text. It is assumed that quantitative data are objective because they are collected as independent 'facts' and can be replicated by other researchers. Further, with careful sampling, it can be argued that the findings generated from such data can be representative of a larger population from which the sample was drawn or for other populations with the same characteristics. For example, if a sample survey in a village in Java, Indonesia showed 20 per cent of women in the village received some income from informal sector work, it can be assumed, with a certain degree of error, this is the same for the entire village and other similar villages in Java.

The representation of information by numbers is an important characteristic of quantitative data. The use of numbered data can be characterised into two types: discrete and continuous. Discrete data does not contain fractions and is usually associated with a count within a category. For example, counting family size provides discrete data - you cannot have 2.5 children! Continuous data, in contrast, comes mostly from measuring a variable. For example, age can be measured in years and fractions of a year. You *can* be 2.5 years old! Data collected through samples can be either discrete or continuous. However, data collected by observation is often qualitative, discrete and in categories (Bailey, 1987: 65).

Quantitative data has a particular strength because it can be verified and replicated. Because it is 'objective' and scientific - collected using specified (and putatively neutral) assumptions and techniques, other researchers can examine what one piece of research has done, repeat the methods and, hopefully, acquire the same results. In doing so, they replicate and verify the original work or, if they fail to replicate the results, they may begin to question the original work and its conclusions. Thus, when in 1999, the World Bank disputed the ILO and UNDP's poverty figures and predictions for Indonesia, it was possible for other researchers to revisit the quantitative data and comment authoritatively on the two different sets of figures and predictions (Manning and van Diermen, 2000). Thus the objectiveness of quantitative data analysis allows for confidence in predictions and policy recommendations. For example, from survey data it is often possible to predict quite accurately the changes in population and its requirements in terms of schools, hospitals and transport and telecommunication networks.

What techniques should be used?

Thus far we have considered important issues relating to the nature of quantitative data. The next step is to think about how to collect the data. In doing fieldwork the four primary means for collecting quantitative data are through observations, questionnaires, structured interviews and the use of secondary data.

1. Observations. Observations are used for both quantitative and qualitative data collection and provide a straightforward and seemingly accurate means of collecting data. Observations are one of the most crucial tools for researchers, whether they result in the generation of 'hard data' or merely impressions and surprises which help the way we shape and interpret our research. Observation may involve relatively simple techniques, such as counting the number of cars passing a certain point, or measuring the area of land under a certain crop. These result in, usually, precise measurements that are amenable to quantitative data analysis (see below). However, observations might also involve measurements and analysis of human behaviour and this may require more subjective assessments of what is actually happening and being measured, hence the need for qualititative methods such as participant observation (see Chapter 4).

2. Questionnaires. Questionnaires are the most common means for collecting quantitative data. They are widely used by a range of agents, including NGOs, government authorities, multilateral donors and academic researchers. The design of questions and the questionnaire is a well-developed science with most books on social science research methods dedicating one or two chapters to this alone (see Babbie, 2001; Bailey, 1987; de Vaus, 1991:80–105; Nichols, 1991:26,41; Wuelker, 1993:161). Therefore, since most of the technical information is readily available, what we do here is touch on some general points, particularly as they relate to doing fieldwork in the Third World. In general, questionnaires should begin with the basic and least intrusive questions and progress to the more complex and sensitive questions. All questions should be simple to understand and unambiguous. This is particularly important when your questionnaire will need to be translated into the local language. Complex and ambiguous language can be easily misinterpreted in the translation. To avoid this it is worthwhile having your questionnaire proof-read by several local people for accuracy and relevance. It is also important to avoid reference to concepts that are not common in the population to whom you will administer the questionnaire. Peter (one of the authors) once interviewed workers in the Indonesian informal sector asking questions about whether they were paid on a daily, weekly or monthly basis. However, it was soon discovered the concept was alien to them. Rather, they were usually paid when returning to their village. Piloting the questionnaire and afterwards asking the respondents to comment on the questionnaire can quickly identify such problems.[2]

How to deliver the questionnaire is also an important issue. In the Third World a mail out or telephone interview is unlikely to be successful. Even in the West, returns on postal questionnaires are usually low. An alternative is to administer the questionnaire directly by yourself or with the help of a local research assistant. If you conduct the questionnaire yourself you will need to be sufficiently fluent in the local language (see Chapter 7, 'Language issues'). If you use research assistants such as graduate students from a local university, you will need to thoroughly brief them and have a means to check quality. When conducting research on agricultural education in Papua New Guinea, Watson (1993) found that despite an intensive training session his 12 assistants were recording data incorrectly or simply neglecting some questions. While this meant his first data return after two weeks work was invalid, he was able to provide further guidance to his assistants at this early stage so that subsequent data was reliable.

Several other points can also be made when constructing and implementing questionnaires in the Third World:

• Present questions in an unbiased way as respondents will often look for prompts as to what kind of answer you want. Finishing a sentence with 'don't you agree' is an obvious cue as to the kind of response you are seeking.

• Conduct the questionnaire away from others, so the person being interviewed does not feel pressured by their peers in giving a particular response. Note that this is not always possible and it may be particularly difficult to speak with women or children without someone else such as a parent or husband overseeing the process (see Chapter 9). You must also maintain confidentiality and not divulge to other respondents what someone has said.

• Don't make the questionnaire too long. An hour is about the maximum time you can ask from someone for an open-ended questionnaire before it becomes an imposition. Try to make closed-answer surveys even shorter. Include only questions that are essential rather than everything you would like to get information on! Remember that respondents are doing you a favour by giving freely of their time and, in a Third World context, will often see outside researchers as someone to defer to and please with their answers regardless of how busy they are. Do not abuse their goodwill.

• Allow for notes to be made in the margin of the questionnaire, as these can help later in writing up the research. Note, for example, other comments that are made beyond what was asked in the questionnaire as well as things such as body language (for example, did the respondent look uncomfortable when asked a particular question, were they joking?) and others present. It is also important to put a date and location on each questionnaire. These notes are best made soon after the interview while these observations are still fresh in your mind.

• Obtain their informed consent. Make sure you explain to the respondent who you are and what the research is for. A covering letter from your institution usually helps (see Chapter 8).

• Construct the questionnaire in such a way that it is easy to later enter the quantitative data into a computer. This means that questions are often better framed as 'closed questions' (for example, a 'yes/no' answer or one that asks for a particular fact or figure) and often prescribed by a range of options ('tick the appropriate box'). However, note that such questions might not always be appropriate given either the objectives of your study or the possibility that yes/no answers do not always capture the subtlety of what a person might wish to express. Inclusion of more qualitative open-ended questions as part of the questionnaire can help deal with such problems.

3. Structured interviews. Structured interviews are less rigidly constructed than questionnaires, but nevertheless follow a set pattern in asking questions or bringing topics up for discussion. Much of the discussion on questionnaires above can also be applied to structured interviews. Structured interviews may be of the 'closed question' type but often they will involve more open-ended questions (for example, 'what is your view on…?') and they are sometimes designed to elicit data on opinions and behaviour as much as they are to get hard facts. Therefore they tend to cross the boundary between quantitative and qualitative techniques.

In conducting research in rural Fiji, John (one of the authors) used structured interviews to obtain data on village land tenure. He asked each interviewee how much land they had access to. This elicited standard quantitative data on land, allowing analysis of landholdings per household, but it also opened up wider and very useful open-ended discussion on where the land was and the processes by which people gained access to land (Overton, 1989). Although the quantitative material was important, and revealed some marked inequalities in land holding, it was open-ended questions that were of more value because they illuminated more about the issues and problems in Fijian land tenure.

In designing an interview schedule, it is important to balance the need to ask the same questions of each respondent (so that you have some standard frame for comparison and analysis) with the need to allow respondents to roam more freely with their answers (which can open up new possibilities for data but make analysis more difficult). In recording the data, you may need to consider taping the conversations (if appropriate and if you obtain consent) rather than relying on a tightly formatted questionnaire form. Whilst an interview form might allow you to record answers to the standard questions, lengthy answers to open-ended questions are often difficult to record by hand. As with questionnaires, accompany your interview record with notes that you write soon afterwards on aspects such as the respondent's attitude, the timing and condition of the interview and their attitude to you and the interview process.

4. Use of secondary data. Collecting secondary data is standard practice for doing fieldwork in the Third World, whether the researcher undertakes primarily quantitative or qualitative data collection. The range of secondary data is enormous, including published government statistics, local or regional government reports and collected data, local newspaper and magazine archives, universities, NGOs and other organisations' reports and data, local government maps and company reports to name just a few sources. Even when the published data is not directly applicable it is often useful for understanding the context of the more narrowly defined research topic.

Such data can be critical not just to analyse in its own right but also to supplement or triangulate your own primary research data. For example, it is common practice to compare the characteristics of a sample population (age and sex distribution, income, religion, etc.) with census data to see if the profile of your sample matches that of a wider population.

Beware, however, that just because data is published or official, it may not be necessarily truthful or valid. There are many examples of the way governments and other agencies publish data that are deliberately false, selective or distorted in order to support a particular policy or point of view (Bulmer, 1993a:4-5; da Corta and Venkateshwarlu, 1992:104). Pages of official and important-looking statistics can often disguise suspect data collection techniques and ill-informed analysis or deliberate tampering. We need to be just as careful with the use of secondary data - if not more so - as we are with the collection of our own primary data.

Sampling

Research is always constrained by a lack of time or resources. Whilst we would usually like to cast our net as widely as possible and gather as much data as we can to increase the confidence we have in our results, in nearly all cases it is simply not possible to gather data from a whole population (a national population census is a rare exception). Therefore we need to sample: to select a small group which is representative of the wider population (Bryman and Cramer, 1995:99-114; Bulmer, 1993b). If we can be confident that our sample is reasonably representative of the population, then we can extrapolate the results from our sample to the population. A polling survey of voter preferences prior to an election is a common example of sampling.

In order to make generalisations from the sample to the population, a sample needs to conform to certain rules. Firstly, it needs to be chosen in a representative way. It is possible to collect a non-representative (non-probability) sample that provides valuable information but cannot be used to generalise with any confidence about the entire population. While it is preferable to collect a representative sample (also referred to as probability sampling) this is not always possible. The most common reason for a non-representative sample is when you don't know who is included in the entire population. The entire population refers to all those with the same characteristic and with some natural boundary. For example, the population for a study of school children's access to vaccines could be all school children in the district or village you are concerned with, or, if it were a national study it would be all school children in the country. Conversely, if you were only concerned with lower primary school children in one village then these would make up your population. In the Third World the lack of recorded information or lack of access to information often means it is difficult to know the precise population (Zarkovich, 1993). When this is the case, it is possible to use one of four types of non-representative sampling:

1. **Convenience sample**: occurs when people are chosen because they are conveniently available. For example, interviewing circular migrants while back home in their village may be convenient but cannot be used to represent the entire population of circular migrants from the village.

2. **Snowball (or chain) sample**: this can be a useful technique for selecting respondents with particular characteristics where information on people with those characteristics is lacking (Nichols, 1991:71). It involves finding and selecting one person then asking is he/she knows others than suit your criteria (for example, farmers who have experimented with a new seed variety or women who attended a particular meeting). You can then find this next list of people and ask them for others, so your sample should keep expanding. It runs the risk of being very selective – some of your respondents may not know, or want to exclude, others – but it can be the most practical means of selection in some circumstances.

3. **Purposeful sample**: occurs when the researcher makes a judgement on whom to include in the sample. It requires a prior assessment of the typical characteristics of a target population. An example would be the selection of one or two villages with 'typical' health problems (Nichols, 1991:68). How representative the sample is depends largely on the judgement of the researcher but it cannot be said to be a probability sample because the choice of sample units is determined by subjective judgement (Peil, 1993:81).

4. **Quota sample**: occurs when people are chosen with characteristics representative of the total population. For example, a researcher interested in gender issues would select a sample that had the same proportion of males and females as the total population.

When we know the total membership of a population, usually from published data, or if the population is small enough, from our own numeration of the population, it becomes possible to select a representative sample. For the sample to be representative, each member of the population must be chosen at random and have the same probability of being selected. This process can be further refined by stratified sampling. This is done in order to capture certain sub-groups within the population. Using the previous example of the school children and vaccination, the school population could be stratified by parents' income. It is then possible to select a proportionately random number from each income group. That is, if 50 per cent of school children's families were low income then 50 per cent of the entire sample should come from this group. Another strategy for selecting a probability sample is the cluster or area sample (Frankfort-Nachmias and Nachmias, 1992: 180). The advantage of cluster sampling is it reduces the overall workload, especially in large studies. Clustering is done by dividing the population into large groupings and selecting probability samples from the groupings. Again, using the school children and vaccination example, if this was a national study, clustering could be used to divide the country into major provinces or states and from each state a school is randomly chosen for use in the sample. This technique would reduce the sample size but still provide the researcher with a probability sample.

In selecting a representative sample the researcher will be confronted with the problem of how many sampling units (or cases) are enough. This is an important consideration, as too few would undermine the validity of any generalisation the researcher makes from the sample. Equally, each interview/questionnaire 'not needed' is extra time in the field and creates additional costs. Therefore, it is important to know how many is enough. Where the population is small, it is not unreasonable to 'sample' the entire population, providing high level of accuracy and good data for later analysis. A rule of thumb is that usually 30 cases is the minimum required for any useful statistical analysis. However, statisticians often prefer 100 or more cases before doing any analysis. You should also consider the need for more cases if you intend to divide you sample into sub-populations. For example, if you divide the school children, from the previous example, into girls and boys to see if there are gender differences, then you will need a larger number of cases. Further, you should be aware you might reject certain cases later for various reasons and therefore you should make allowance for this when determining the sample size.

In any sample size there will be a sampling error or standard error. That is, the probability that the characteristics of your random sample does not reflect the characteristics of the total population. The smaller the sample and the more heterogeneous the population, the larger this standard error will be. Conversely, the larger the sample and the more homogeneous the population the smaller the standard error. Moreover, the total population has little bearing on the accuracy of your sample. You should also keep in mind that in a small sample a small increase in sample size reduces substantially the standard error. While the sample size you collect is partly determined by the statistical use you want to make of the data and the standard error you are willing to accept, in reality it is often determined by access to people and available time and money for fieldwork.

How can data be analysed?

Once the data has been collected there are several techniques for analysing and representing it. Using such techniques in conjunction with appropriate graphs provides a powerful means for representing information. From the raw data collected the first step is to create a data set. Such a data set is normally entered into a software package. With today's large range of sophisticated but simple to use software packages (such as Excel or SPSS), once the data has been entered, it is relatively simple for the computer to calculate the statistics and generate the graphs or tables. Such relative simplicity in generating statistical results and graphs has highlighted the importance for the researcher to understand how and why the data should be represented by particular statistical measures on graphs and tables. While the computer can generate endless statistical measures from data, the researcher must explain and justify them to the reader. Briefly, then, the following are some of the main statistical measurements for representing quantitative data:

Central tendency The three measures of central tendency are mean, mode and median. The mean is the arithmetic average, mode the most frequently occurring value and median the middle ranked observation. While central tendency analyses are very simple they offer a powerful tool for representing data. Data such as average age, income, weight or height for any given population provide an immediate image to the reader (see Box 3.1). These statistical measures are often used for introducing a population to the reader.

Frequency distribution is used to illustrate the distribution of a single variable across categories and allows us to appreciate diversity alongside the above measures of central tendency. It can be used for both discrete and continuous data. The number of times the variable occurs in each category is recorded (Nichols, 1991:84-6). Frequently that data is represented by graphs, including histograms and pie charts (see Box 3.1). Frequency distributions are also an excellent and simple way of introducing data. For example, to give an overview of a village, before entering into more specific issues, frequency distributions for income, age and education provide a 'snapshot' of the village and its diversity.

Dispersion Measurements of dispersion provide a picture of how the data is distributed around the central tendency: another important measure of diversity within a sample. For example, average income may be exactly the same for two villages closely located. However, one village may have a few very wealthy people with the rest being relatively poor, while the second village has everyone on roughly the same income. Such differences would not be revealed by the average income figure but would be by measurements of dispersion. It is possible to calculate the dispersion of data around the central tendency in several ways, however, the two most common are the use of the range which measures the difference between the highest and lowest values in the distribution; and the standard deviation, which calculates the difference in a population between every observation and the mean (see Box 3.1). The deviations are represented by one standardised figure that allows comparison to be made with standard deviations of other populations.

Box 3.1 Simple descriptive statistics for a single variable: measurements of average income, 2000

There are different ways we can depict data statistically. The following examples use World Bank data for mean income by country. A total of 170 countries for which data was available are analysed for the year 2000. Income data is given as $US.
(Source: www.devdata.worldbank.org/data-query/).

Central tendency

Mean income	$5,312	The numerical average (total Gross National Income divided by total population for the 170 countries)
Mode	$180	The most frequently occurring value (this is the mean income for four countries)
Median income:	$1,670	The middle value (85 values are greater and 85 are smaller)

Consider the worth of these three measurements. Which gives the best single picture of average incomes on a global scale and why?

Frequency distribution

The following diagram (Figure 3.1) presents a frequency histogram for different categories of income for the 170 countries. Note that the categories are not uniform (some cover a range of only $250 whilst others span $10,000). Why might we use such uneven categories? What conclusions might we draw about world income distribution from this figure?

Cross-tabulation is a simple means of examining the relationship between two variables and is a continuation of the use of a frequency distribution. For each observation two variables are measured and set out in a table. For example, if we wanted to measure gender income differences, we could construct a cross tabulation table with gender on the vertical axis and income groups along the horizontal axis. In each we would enter the frequency of that income group for males and females respectively. This would immediately allow a comparison between the variables gender and income. A variation of the cross tabulation is the use of a scattergram which plots the two variables on a graph (Nichols, 1991:87). However, the scattergram should only be used for representing variables that have a natural order. In the previous example gender does not have a natural order while income does

Figure 3.1 Frequency distribution of country mean income per capita, 2000

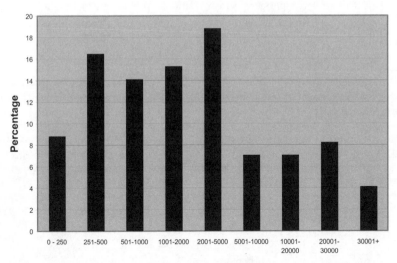

Income per capita ($US)

Dispersion

Range:	$100-$42,060	The lowest and highest values
Standard deviation:	$9,174	A statistical measurement to show average variation around the mean

Note that while the range gives a simple picture of variation, the standard deviation cannot be easily interpreted. Where we would see its use would be if we compared the standard deviation of two similar data sets (for example, the variation of income in countries of Asia compared with those in Africa and Europe.

and therefore it would not be appropriate to use this technique. On the other hand, the two variables of income and educational status would be suitable to represent on a scattergram (see Box 3.2)

Correlation coefficient is another means of measuring the relationship between two variables. In effect, the measurement of the correlation coefficient (using the Pearson r measurement) is the statistical equivalent of drawing a scattergram. The correlation coefficient is a single number in the range of -1 to 1 indicating the strength and direction of the relationship between two variables. When r = -1 there is a perfect negative relationship (as one variable increases, the other declines), when r = 1 there is a perfect positive relationship (as one increases, so does the other), while 0 indicates no relationship at all. An example of a positive relationship is between income and education, while there is usually a negative relationship between income size and infant mortality. The correlation coefficient can be illustrated and explained by drawing on its relationship with the scattergram. A scattergram could be constructed for a given population by graphing every observation as a dot on a scattergram for the variables income along the horizontal axis and education on the vertical axis (see Box 3.2). It is then possible to draw a line of best fit (the regression line). If there was a perfect positive relationship between income and education all observations (points) would fall on the straight line moving upwards to the right and the correlation coefficient would be 1. The more the points are scattered away from the regression line the weaker the relationship and the closer to number

Box 3.2 Measures of relationships between variables: average incomes and life expectancy, 2000

Beyond simple description of data sets, we can also begin to analyse relationships. Here we consider the same data set for average income as in Box 3.1 but also consider its relationship with data for average life expectancy at birth for the year 2000 (Source: http://devdata.worldbank.org/data-query/)

Cross tabulation

A scattergram (Figure 3.2) plots the data for each of the 170 countries with income on the horizontal axis and life expectancy on the vertical. We imply that income (GNI per capita) is an 'independent' variable and that life expectancy is to some extent 'dependent' on this - i.e. as income changes, there may be changes in life expectancy. The graph gives an interesting result from which we can infer some aspects of the relationship between income and life expectancy. We might expect that in wealthier countries people live longer and this seems to be the case. However, this is not a simple linear relation: there seems to be a marked improvement in life expectancy as income increases at the lower end (up to about $2000 per capita). Thereafter we seem to reach a threshold over about 70 years of age and further wealth is not as strongly translated into longer life spans.

Correlation coefficient

We can gain a better statistical measurement of the data in Figure 3.2 by employing the correlation coefficient. Applied to our data set, we get a correlation coefficient of 0.55. This indicates a positive and moderately strong relationship: as income increases so too does life expectancy. However, we have noted that the relationship changes around a per capita income of $2000. \if we calculate two correlation coefficients, one for the 93 countries with average incomes of $2000 per capita and below and one for the 77 countries above that mark, we get coefficients of 0.65 and 0.52 respectively. In other words, up to $2000 income per capita, there is a stronger relationship between income and life expectancy and this becomes weaker after the $2000 threshold.

If we were to draw a best fit (regression) line on the scattergram in Figure 3.2, we could find a weak straight line slope upwards from the left but a more accurate fit would come from a curved line moving upwards sharply from the left and then levelling out to the right.

Figure 3.2 Life expectancy and mean income per capita, 2000

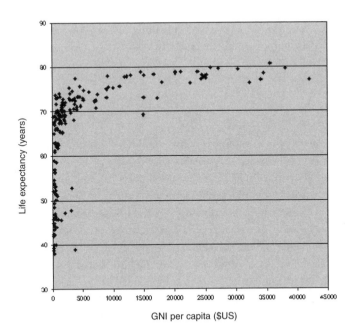

GNI per capita ($US)

will tend to zero. At zero the points are perfectly scattered across the graph and there is no relationship between the two variables. In more sophisticated analyses, multiple regression can be used to test the relative strength of different variables.

The above list is not exhaustive and there is a range of other statistical tests that are possible. The intention here is not to provide comprehensive and detailed explanations of how to do statistical analysis, but rather to introduce the fieldworker to some of the more common uses for quantitative data. Texts such as Babbie (2001), Bryman and Cramer (1995), De Vaus (1991) and Frankfort-Nachmias and Nachmias (1992) give more detail on these techniques and their application.

From the above discussion and examples it is clear that quantitative data collection offers several advantages in doing research in the Third World. If precise, objective and replicable answers are needed then quantitative data collection and research offers an appropriate methodology. For example, several research projects were conducted during the late 1990s on the impact of the 1997 Southeast Asia financial crisis (see the collection of papers in Manning and van Diermen, 2000). Impact studies by national and multi-lateral organisations included the impact of the crisis on calorie intake in rural villages; rural-urban migration patterns; inter-regional migration patterns; school retention rates; and employment and gender, as well as many others. Similar studies were undertaken in several different countries, and an important element of these studies has been to allow comparison of precise measurements in the magnitude of change that has occurred.

Limitations and pitfalls

We have seen that quantitative techniques can have much value in research in Development Studies. Used well, they can become a powerful set of tools in describing conditions, analysing problems and informing policy. However, it is easy to use them badly or inappropriately. The following issues are some of the most commonly encountered problems.

Representation

One of the most frequent criticisms of quantitative methods – and one of the greatest dangers in their use – is the issue of representation. We have seen above that some quantitative methods allow us to make conclusions about a large population based on our analysis of a smaller sample. Yet, unless we are scrupulous about the selection of our sample, we soon run into problems over the nature of that representation. Can men speak for women (or vice-versa)? can the rich speak for the poor? and who speaks for children, or the disabled or the elderly? Chambers (1983:13-25) reminds us that much research done in the rural Third World is subject to a range of biases that mean that many people are excluded from the researcher's work, typically women, those in remote areas, the poor, the elderly, the young and the disabled.[3] Similarly, feminist researchers (for example Falconer Al-Hindi, 2001) have criticised the way much research has been sexist because it has excluded or marginalised women in the selection of respondents, the formulation of questions asked, the interviewing practices and even the research design. If we do not ask the right people the right sort of questions in the right sort of way we will not be able to draw general conclusions no matter how good our data looks.

The collection and analysis of numbers is a powerful research tool and can allow us to draw conclusions and inferences from our data. This is particularly the case when we see strong relationships between data sets – correlation and regression analyses give us an indication of the nature and strength of such relationships. It is then tempting to suggest what the underlying processes might be. For example, it is common to see a close and negative relationship between rate of population growth and income: as income increases, population growth rates fall. So we might reasonably conclude that a good way of lowering the birth rate is to encourage economic growth. However, we could also see it the other way around (as many have done): a good way of encouraging economic growth is to limit population growth.

Whatever the answer might be, it should be apparent that our quantitative data do not give us a clear scientific indication of process, even though the evidence of a strong relationship is compelling. The leap from correlation to causation should be made with great caution (see Box 3.3).

Box 3.3 Relationships between variables: life expectancy and fertility, 2000

In our examples earlier with scattergrams, we saw how we might be able to infer relationships between income levels and life expectancy. We saw a reasonable positive correlation between the two and had cause to suggest that increased incomes could be associated with - maybe to help contribute to - longer life spans.

Here we consider two similar data sets for the year 2000: first, the same data for life expectancy; and second, data for fertility (the measurement of the average number of live births per woman in a country) (Source: http://devdata.worldbank.org/data-query/). These yield the following scattergram (Figure 3.3) and a correlation coefficient of -0.83.

First indications from the scattergram and correlation coefficient suggest to us that there is a strong negative relationship between the two: as the fertility rate increases, life expectancy falls. Note that the correlation coefficient of -0.83 is stronger than that relating life expectancy to income (0.55). We might be tempted to conclude that fertility (how many children women have) has a stronger impact on life expectancy than income. Yet this makes no intuitive sense and we are wrong to infer such causation from this relationship. In fact, both life expectancy and fertility rate are related to income - i.e. both perhaps have a similar underlying cause that is not apparent from our statistical analysis.

The meaning of data

Quantitative methods are attractive because there is an air of precision about the numbers we collect and analyse. We can say with an impression of authority that 34.7 per cent of respondents shared a particular characteristic - much more authoritative than a vague statement about the diversity in the life histories of ten people interviewed at length! Yet what do our numbers mean? One of the authors (John) worked on Kenyan colonial archives and used some statistics of livestock numbers in various districts in the first two decades of last century - estimates made by district officers (Overton, 1983). These looked very appealing for his analysis because they showed, variously, periods of slow increases followed by sudden declines. Located in official publications and reports they appeared to be systematically collected and reasonably accurate. However, this impression was soon dispelled when, in one district annual report, a district officer admitted truthfully that estimating livestock numbers was an impossibility and that most estimates were made using the previous year's figure and adding a slight growth factor, except in years when there was obvious hardship when the estimates would be slashed! The numbers were a fiction. Dan Brockington encountered similar problems when trying to quantify changes in bridewealth payments over time (Box 3.4).

Other difficulties arise when we ask people to give numbers for things they have little concept of in a numerical sense. In the West we are used to dealing with

Figure 3.3 Life expectancy and the family rate, 2000

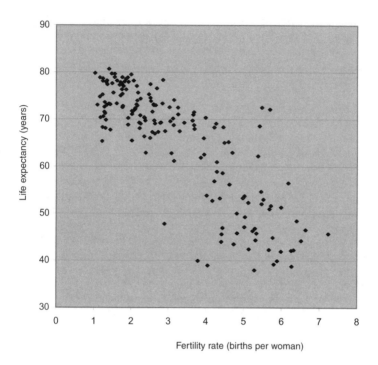

personal and household incomes: we know what our salaries are and we are used to making tax returns. Therefore, we seek and expect to find the same information from rural people in the Third World: we ask them their annual income. Faced with incomprehension – for regular salaries and wages are rare – we might resort to building up a picture of income sources over time ('how much do you usually get for selling your vegetables at the market?' followed by 'how many times a year do you sell your vegetables at the market?'). However, these are similarly problematic – people see money as something which comes and goes and the very idea of an annual (or weekly) income may be completely foreign. So our analyses of such data need to be treated with a great deal of caution (for example Overton, 1989: 71, 88-100)!

Even fairly obvious quantitative data might not be all it seems in a different cultural context (Bradburd, 1998:6-11). Researcher Margaret Chung recounts the story of her PhD research on women's fertility in Fiji (Chung, 1991:105) asking a simple question to women ('how many children have you given birth to?') surprisingly led to different responses from the same person at different times. She soon found that this was not so odd: a woman may have given birth to ten children, two of which may have died in infancy – are they still counted? Are stillbirths counted? Are children who are 'given' to close relatives to raise as their own counted? What

Box 3.4 The meaning of quantitative data: Impoverishment and bridewealth in pastoral societies

Dan Brockington's doctoral thesis (Brockington, 1998) concerns the impacts of eviction on pastoralists who were forcibly moved from the Mkomazi Game Reserve in Tanzania. There was a wealth of information to analyse including the performance of the livestock herds, the changes to livelihoods and reams of records collected in archives over the past 50 years. Most of the written records were by government officials but there were a few left by herders. Of these, one concerned the changes in bridewealth[a] that were needed given the recent impoverishment of herders following their eviction from the Reserve (instead of 15 cattle given previously, between 10 to 12 would suffice). How should this information be used? On one level the fact of the change is interesting evidence of local adaptation to new circumstances. But one of the examiners of the thesis objected that using this fact alone was 'thin description', using numbers without their context (c.f. Broch-Due and Anderson, 1999). What was needed was an investigation into the nature of the relationships between rich and poor herders. Stock distribution is inherently unequal in these societies, and the negotiation of bridewealth is fiercely contested by rich and poor, and among the poor themselves, some of whom cannot afford to provide animals for bridewealth payments, and others who have marriageable daughters and who desperately wish to gain more stock through bridewealth. Agreeing the number of cattle and delivering them is also an arena of contest and negotiation between men and women on both sides of the relationship. Bridewealth is never completely paid; it is the beginning of a long-term relationship between two families. In short, data on the number of cattle in bridewealth payments conceals highly complex social relationships whose dynamics and conflicts could have revealed much about the impact of eviction on pastoral societies, but which when reproduced as merely a number gave little hint of all that was going on.

[a] Bridewealth are the payments of money, goods and cattle which a groom

about children born out of wedlock who may have been raised by others since they were very young? Demography is as much an art as a science!

Given these problems with collecting and analysing much of the research data we use in Development Studies, it is worth remembering Lockwood's view that all data obtained by asking questions are 'qualitative' (1992:176).

Too much data

It is easy to be seduced by the attraction of quantitative data, especially when it appears easy to collect. It is tempting to add 'just another question' to a questionnaire survey and, in the field, it is common to adopt the vacuum cleaner method: gather every bit of data that is available and sort it out later. This can have advatages - it may allow you to collect data that originally you did not think were critical but which later turned out to have value – but it can easily lead to problems. Time in the field and in data analysis can extend beyond practical limits, questionnaires explode into large unwieldy exercises that alienate respondents, much data ends up being unused and, critically, the focus of research can become lost under the weight of data. In data collection it is always wise to keep in mind the central research question(s). If the data being sought does not contribute to answering that question, it should not be collected. Simply collecting more data does not mean better a research outcome: it may mean the opposite.[4]

Garbage-in-garbage-out

An old computer adage is 'garbage-in-garbage-out'. No matter how sophisticated one's methods of analysis or how complex one's statistical techniques, the results will be worthless if the raw data is flawed. Furthermore, sophisticated techniques are sometimes used to hide questionable data.

Therefore, researchers need to be wary of their data: a first priority is to ensure that the data to be collected will be authentic, valid and appropriate. It should have meaning – for those from whom it is collected as much as for the researcher. It should be inclusive – it should include all sectors of the target population, even those who appear less visible or 'important' than others. It should be truthful – fictions and half-facts as well as incomplete or incorrect observations easily creep in when working in different cultural contexts. And it should be accurate. Only when there is confidence in the quality of the data can attention turn to refining the methods of analysis.

Conclusion

In doing social science research in the Third World, quantitative data analysis is usually best used in conjunction with other qualitative techniques. Quantitative data analysis is strong at describing the 'what' but weak at explaining the 'why'. It is good at predicting what will happen, the magnitude of changes and the relationship between variables but not why things occur. For example, correlation analysis of data may show there is strong income disparity between males and females. However, it tells us nothing about why this exists. Therefore, when doing research in the Third World, quantitative methods are best used when integrated into a more holistic research design. Nevertheless, the degree to which quantitative data collection and analysis is used depends to a great extent on the nature of the research question and the preference of the researcher.

To conclude, several points should be borne in mind when using quantitative methods in a developing country context:

• Don't be intimidated! Statistics and statistical analysis, not to mention the particular problems faced in the collection and use of these in the Third World, may seem daunting especially to those without specialist training in statistics. Yet quantitative techniques need not be complex and they remain among the most important tools for researchers in Development Studies.

• Don't get too complicated. Often the most valuable and insightful use of quantitative data comes from fairly basic descriptive statistics.

• Let the questions determine the methods. Quantitative techniques, like any other, are merely means to conduct our research. Methods must be driven by the questions we wish to answer and the information we need to answer those questions (see Chapter 2). Avoid the temptation to apply a newly-learned and fashionable technique merely because you know it, rather than because it will enhance significantly what you are trying to find out.

• Don't outrun your competence. Quantitative techniques run the full gamut of tools from some of the simple descriptive methods described earlier to very sophisticated multi-factor analytical tools. As researchers we have to weigh up the costs and time of mastering such techniques against the benefit of what they bring to our work. Too often we can spend too long learning methods that will be of marginal use to our overall research task.

• Suspect the data. Especially in a developing country context, we have seen how the data we collect and analyse may be seriously flawed. Bad data, no matter how complex our methods of analysis, will produce bad results. Common-sense and healthy cynicism are good allies when questioning the data you collect (or the data collected by others) and their value for analysis.

Recommended reading

Babbie, E. (ed.) (2001) The Practice of Social Research Wadsworth, Belmont: CA.
A comprehensive general text with detailed chapters on a range of quantitative techniques and issues in quantitative research. An excellent guide.

Bryman, A. and Cramer, D. (1995) Quantitative Data Analysis for Social Scientists Routledge, London.
A good guide to a number of techniques of analysis with useful worked examples.

Bulmer, M. and Warwick, D.P. (eds) (1993) Social Research in Developing Countries UCL Press, London.
This edited book explores critical issues relating to conducting quantitative research in developing countries.

De Vaus, D.A. (ed.) (1991) Surveys in Social Research Allen and Unwin, London.
A general text with helpful chapters on surveys and questionnaires.

Nichols, P. (1991) Social Survey Methods: A Fieldguide for Development Workers Oxfam, Oxford.
A practical guide for development practitioners with a basic coverage of main techniques.

Notes

1.For an excellent critical essay on the use of quantitative techniques see Caws (1989).

2.See Adams and Megaw (1997:222-24) for tips on questionnaire design and administration.

3.See Chapter 9 for a discussion on appropriate ways of conducting research with marginalised groups.

4.See the discussion on leaving the field in Chapter 10.

4 Qualitative Research

Dan Brockington and Sian Sullivan

It is customary ... to say something about what is somewhat pretentiously called 'methodology'. My field method could be summed up as meeting people.
(Willis, 1981: xx)

Introduction

Qualitative research is characterised by three commitments (Bryman and Burgess, 1999). First it seeks to understand the world through interacting with, empathising with and interpreting the actions and perceptions of its actors. Qualitative methods are used to explore the meanings of people's worlds - the myriad personal impacts of impersonal social structures, and the nature and causes of individual behaviour. Second, qualitative research tends to collect data in natural settings, rather than artificial and constructed contexts (such as laboratories). Third, it tends to generate theory rather than test it. Qualitative methods work inductively, building up theory from observations, rather than deductively, testing theories by trying to refute their propositions.

Qualitative methods include a variety of techniques, from participant observation and the writing of ethnography, to semi-structured interviews, oral histories and group discussions (see Table 4.1). They can be considered as simply another set of ways of finding out about the world. But if we reflect on the reasons for asking questions which require qualitative methods, and the nature of the answers they provide, it becomes clear that qualitative approaches also embrace significant philosophical debates regarding the nature and implications of subjective experience, and the legitimacy or otherwise of reducing this to numerical and easily manipulated 'pieces' of data.

Qualitative methods have been used to find out about the world for as long as there has been language and speech. Their recognition as a formal category of methods is more recent but they are now flourishing deservedly with an important set of research tools.[1] Working with them can be exciting and revelatory, making for enjoyable and challenging fieldwork.

Table 4.1 Qualitative research techniques

Technique	Description	Potential problem
Interviewing	All sorts of forms are possible, from open conversations to semi-structured discussions around particular topics, to highly structured questionnaires (although it is hard for the latter to elicit good qualitative data).	Recoding the data is the difficulty here. Writing while people are speaking is off-putting. Tape recording then transcribing or summarising takes time. Be careful of exploitation. Interviews can result in a one-way traffic of information from which only the researcher benefits.
Focus Groups	A group discussion of a particular issue where it is instructive to learn from the way people discuss things as much as what they say.	Best undertaken when you know people well enough, or situations well enough that you can interpret the group dynamics. See criticisms of PRA below.
Conversation and Discourse Analysis	Intimate and detailed recording of conversation and talk where personal expressions, pauses and delivery are recorded and analysed.	A research tool that requires much effort. Conversation analysis is part of Discourse Analysis, a diffuse term which covers several disciplines. Make sure that the techniques of discourse analysis that you are using are appropriate for your questions.
Fieldwork Diaries	A day-to-day record of events, diet, work or observations kept by yourself or an informant.	Being a good diarist is not easy. Read published diaries to see what makes for good reading and consider whether they would also make good fieldwork notes. Have a look at Malinowski's (1967) private diary. Practice before you go into the field.
Life Histories and Oral Histories	Tape recorded histories of people, places and events. A detailed literature exists on how to do this properly. This technique provides unique insights into un-recorded situations and alternative views on written histories.	Be prepared to transcribe the tapes so that other people can have access to the raw data. These data have to be treated as any other – sceptically, looking for corroboration.
Photographs, Film and Video and Documents	Texts such as letters, archives and diaries make useful primary and secondary sources. So too are photographs, film and video (which are different sorts of text).	Detailed cataloguing of notes is required if the images and documents are voluminous or else it will be hard to trace which document provided what information.

cont.

Participant observation	This requires the researcher to immerse themselves in the place/ the societies they are studying. By living closely with the people you are studying it is possible to empathise with their way of looking at and interpreting their world. The note taking involved is rigorous and one is required to constantly test impressions and ideas	Some people's worlds are hard and unpleasant to experience. It requires great effort and determination to learn the language and to understand what people mean. All the techniques listed above can be used in participant observation. The skill is combining structured data collection with relaxing and letting things happen.

Qualitative methods have a reputation for being anecdotal, or associated with ideas that cannot be described with hard, secure facts. Sometimes it is implied that they are tools resorted to in situations where we cannot generate more precise and focused data. This is wrong. Qualitative methods can provide powerful insights into the world. They can be used effectively with people or places we think are familiar to us, as well as in situations somewhat removed, geographically and otherwise, from our own. Qualitative methods also are sometimes thought of as all that is not quantitative. Again, and as we discuss at the end of this chapter, this can be misleading. Qualitative methods can incorporate quantitative data and quantification. But they go beyond numbers to consider the meanings of quantitatively derived findings to the people they affect, and to problematise, rather than accept uncritically, the production of such data (see Box 3.4, Chapter 3).

When should we use qualitative methods? As with quantitative methods, discussed in the previous chapter, the answer is, when our questions require them. The importance of qualitative methods for the social sciences is best illustrated by considering the ideas that people have explored by using them. For example quantitative data will tell us about numbers of drug abusers, HIV infection rates, levels of street crime, the rates of urban decay and damage to housing stock and a host of other facts about problems among the urban poor. But how do we answer questions like why do people use drugs? What do drug users make of their use? Is drug use always a predicament for users? Or can entheogenic[2] substances engender positive and transformative experiences when used in settings conducive to this? What do drug dealers think of their trade? How do human relationships and social interactions function in these circumstances? For answers here we have to turn to qualitative methods.[3] To take another example, social scientists have talked about the production and reproduction of social classes and the perpetration of relationships of exploitation. But how and in what circumstances might the exploited reproduce their own exploitation? Do they perceive it as such? If they do not perceive their work as exploitation, then why not, and if they do, then do they resist their exploiters and how? Again for insights into these questions qualitative methods will be necessary.[4] In fact because of our subjective experiences of conducting research, it is nigh on impossible to *not* draw on qualitatively derived information in the process.

In the pages that follow we reflect on our experiences, and others', of practicing qualitative research. This chapter is not intended as a manual of techniques, nor is it an exhaustive theoretical discussion of how we can know anything. It is intended to stimulate thinking and discussion which can be followed up in the further reading offered at the end of the chapter. We reflect here on three key issues in qualitative research which reveal its strengths and weaknesses. First, we examine popular 'rapid' fieldwork methods and 'participatory' appraisal; second we discuss the challenge of postmodernism to ethnographic and anthropological fieldwork; third we look at phenomenological and embodiment approaches to research (which theorise and problematise the nature of subjective experience). Finally we consider what distinguishes qualitative methods from quantitative techniques. The common thread to our argument is that although Willis' statement (1981:xx, cited above) may sound naïve to some ears now, there is wisdom in it, which we ignore at our peril.

The popularity and perils of PRA

In the 1980s and 1990s research in developing countries was challenged and revived with a set of methods commonly known as Participatory Rural Appraisal (PRA). PRA includes a 'family of techniques' for ascertaining features of local groups and situations in ways that are meant to empower the people being researched, as well as being faster to carry out and to analyse than other techniques. PRA distinguished itself from earlier Rapid Rural Appraisal (RRA) practices – where the emphasis was on the rapidity of the techniques as opposed to the extent to which they were intended to empowering their participants. Later a new version came along in the form of Participatory Learning and Appraisal (PLA), which emphasised the junior, receiving role of the researchers involved.

In part, these techniques and approaches to research are offered as an alternative to the large-scale quantitative surveys which once characterised development research. They are also an attempt to challenge the dominance and power of the researcher and give more prominence to the voices of the researched peoples, to let them determine the content, direction and purpose of the research (e.g. Chambers, 1983; Guèye, 1999). Thus PRA, RRA and PLA are demand-driven fact-finding practices that emerged in a context of professional development work with a requirement for generating usable information as rapidly and accurately as possible, while satisfying the emerging mantra of 'participation' which has featured increasingly in development discourse since the early 1980s (Cooke and Kothari, 2001). As a suite of fieldwork tools, they are now being utilised in academic studies by social scientists across the globe, and some serious attention needs to be given to their validity as an academic research method.

PRA literature is heady stuff. There is a startling degree of concord and celebration in its tone. The emphasis is on spreading the good news of PRA: of the ways it offers of breaking free of the chains of conventional research practices and of the speed with which it offers information that can be useful and valuable to the people 'on the ground'. The techniques involved are numerous, comprising all sorts of group work, and mapping of time and space using charts and diagrams built on the spot using locally available materials (see Box 4.1). We do not wish to review the techniques here in detail, but they are worth looking at and are thoroughly documented in, for example, Cotton (1996) and Martin (1995). Relevant case-studies incorporating these methods can be found in Bishop and Scoones (1994), Hot Springs Working Group (1995), Keough (1998), Mazuchelli (1995) and Mitlin and Thompson (1995).

Box 4.1 Examples of PRA techniques

Wealth Ranking   Informants rank members of a group according to wealth and sort them into as many categories as they see fit. Needs to be accompanied by discussion about what makes people wealthy or poor.Categorisation can be done by having stones or other objects represent the families in question which are then put in different circles drawn on the ground. Useful for all sorts of things other than wealth.

Transects   Walk through the study site in various directions looking at resource use, and prominent features of the place, observing different practices taking place. Take several transects and vary their timing.

Mapping   A map drawn on the floor using stones, leaves, charcoal or other material to represent the locality, important resources in it, and social data (e.g. the number of people in each household).

Resource Evaluation   There are various ways of comparing the value, availability, cost and importance of various resources. Each resource can be allocated different numbers of stones for each variable. Or each resource can be compared against the other in a paired ranking thus:

		Ease of availability	
	Wood	Charcoal	Kerosene
Wood	x	c	w
Charcoal		x	c
Kerosene			x

This table shows that charcoal is more easily available than wood, wood than kerosene

Calendars   A table drawn on the floor and marked with symbols made from local materials which divides up the year into the appropriate seasons and illustrates what activities take place when. Can indicate times when people are particularly busy and under stress (e.g. facing food shortages).

Spider diagrams   For exploring connections and perceptions of connections between issues under investigation. Participants list the variables and elements which are involved in a particular issue and draw lines between them to illustrate how they are connected.

Timelines   Construct a history of a place or people with a table showing the important events in recent history. If possible try to establish the years and seasons when things happened. Also used to graphically illustrate a single issue (e.g. changes in cost of living over time).

NB. One of the virtues of PRA techniques is that they can use locally available materials - earth, leaves, twigs, seeds, stones - to construct the maps and diagrams which can be copied later onto paper. While this works for non-literate societies, in some places it is not appropriate and could be considered demeaning.

There are, however, some problems with the claims for research success made by practitioners of PRA. A tendency to respond to new ideas by changing the collective noun used for these methods in itself may imply a need for caution. More importantly, why be in such a hurry in the first place?[5] Is there any need at all to adopt such hasty techniques if more field time is possible? If we are to meet and talk to people, to be good conversationalists, is it wise to do so with one eye on the clock? Of course, the constraints of the 'real world' dictate that much development intervention is based on consultancies and research exercises with only a few days available for gathering information. But the outcome often is the production of inferior and partial data. Good information takes time and patience to gather and requires observation, checking, evaluating and cross-checking.

A second issue is that the application of PRA techniques frequently takes place in group-meetings which become public occasions generating information in the public domain. Even if groups are broken down by gender, age and class the issues discussed and debated in these meetings are still going to be contested and negotiated. Knowledge and information tend not to be revealed on these occasions by willing informants. Instead it is produced and created for an audience of researchers and among an audience of listening neighbours. One has to have an excellent conception of the relevant social, cultural and political contexts in order to access understanding of the knowledges produced and/or excluded on such occasions. As the cases in Boxes 4.2 and 4.3 indicate, it is wise to treat data gathered and bandied about in public with prudence and care. While such information can be immensely valuable in terms of reflecting on the circumstances within which it was produced (such as focus groups), its value will only become apparent by revisiting it, and the people who produced it, in different, less public, circumstances.

Because PRA techniques use group interviews and often are intended to benefit groups, a further problem is that they risk invoking an erroneous conception of 'community'. This term often has been used to describe the small-scale collections and agglomerations of people that so often are the focus of social science research and Development Studies. Hart offers a fitting admonition to the tendency to view small-scale rural societies through rose-tinted spectacles:

Box 4.2 Tactful public silence in Tanzania

My post-doctoral research involved 14 months work in the south of Tanzania investigating contests over natural resources. Integral to these conflicts was the performance of local government (Brockington, 2001), which was itself subject to scrutiny from regional government. Contests and conflicts were discussed each year in a large and unusual public meeting called by the Regional Commissioner who descended upon the village where I worked with a large body of his officials to hear complaints and enquire as to their resolution. These meetings began and ended my fieldwork. The first meeting introduced me to a string of issues which were important locally. It generated interesting information for that reason. The second meeting did the same but this time I knew more about who was speaking, the order in which they spoke, the agendas behind what they had to say, the politics of the party and recent elections about which local power struggles had hinged. I also suspected that there were a number of problems which were left unsaid. The meeting was much more than a list of problems. It was a performance, a game played before an audience of neighbours. Understanding what was said at the meeting required a year's work - it would have benefited much more from an additional year as well.

Source: Brockington, post-doctoral research in Tanzania, 1999-2000

Social life organised through kinship...is fundamentally disunited, and it is in response to this disunity that participants stress the opposite in their ideological pronouncements, emphasizing the idea of community and pretending that kinship ties express only solidarity. We, who retain in our language and sentiments the ideology without the substance of a society organised through kinship, project our own romantic nostalgia onto the faction-ridden and anxiety-prone family life of African villages. (1982: 40)

What makes people a 'community'? What holds people together, if anything at all, and what divides them? 'Community' politics frequently are ignored or their significance downplayed. In many cases rural communities in fact may just be geographical juxtapositions of people with little else in common apart from their local geography. The danger here is that PRA may imply that by listening to what may amount to a largely fictional community one can quickly understand what 'it' thinks, when there is no 'it' in the first place. How many divisions, how deep they run and which groups are discernable, may take a long and unpredictable time to fathom.

Finally, a popular variant of PRA is Participatory Action Research (PAR), in which the participants are actively engaged in researching their own condition in order to change it. This is often associated with disadvantaged or marginalised groups and has been known to result in exhilaratingly successful change. Its advocates point to the profoundly democratic nature of research by people into their own circumstances and the special authority and superior insights they can bring into their own lives.

But again there are questioning voices well summarised by Krimerman (2001). Popular participation can be incompetent. Research requires training and expertise, and the learning of valuable lessons from the literature regarding the prior experiences of other researchers. PAR tends to be evaluated according to the degree and nature of change which it brings about, not necessarily the knowledge which it creates or draws upon. Krimerman has argued that ignoring other knowledge can detract both from the research and the solutions attempted.

Krimerman notes further that depending on the circumstances it can be problematic to imbue people's knowledge about themselves with too much authority. Outsiders sometimes discern and understand better than they do an individual's or group's predicament. It is also true, however, that when we are dealing with marginalised or silenced voices researchers have a responsibility to

Box 4.3 Public meetings as data sources: wildlife, women and exclusion in Namibia

In 1994, I attended a meeting held by the Namibian Ministry of Environment and Tourism (MET) to discuss with a range of stakeholders possible new approaches to conservation in the north-west Namibian landscape. The focus of the meeting was to debate, with local people, the idea of establishing 'conservancies', i.e. new locally-run wildlife management institutions. Despite extensive knowledge and use of regional natural resources by women, all local women who attended the meeting were physically excluded from participating by being obliged to sit outside the shelter in which the meeting was held (Sullivan, 2000). This was justified by the MET convenors of the meeting on the strength that they were working within the constraints of the (male) traditional leadership. Notwithstanding the extent to which current forms of this traditional leadership are a construction of Namibia's colonial history, this is somewhat ironic given that the purpose of the meeting was to try and begin a process of new institution-building, enabling better representation and participation in the decentralisation of decision-making power.

From the perspective of conducting research, and as well as providing rather simple data regarding who may be able to speak at so-called public meetings, the structuring of such events perhaps can speak volumes about perceptions present among those initiating and leading public meetings. In this case, while strong leadership differentials exist between men and women among one ethnic division present at the meeting, these are by no means consistent for both the major ethnic 'groups' affected by the proposals discussed at the meeting. In interpretation, an issue, therefore, is whose traditional sensitivities the convenors of the meeting were trying to observe and why. The blatant exclusion of women at this meeting reveals further departures between rhetoric and practice when broader contexts are considered. Thus, although operating under a national programme with the inclusive title of 'Community Based Natural Resources Management' (CBNRM), a major component of 'the community' clearly was restricted from participating in discussion. Given conventional associations between men and animal wildlife (primarily), the exclusion of women perhaps further reflected the true focus of the meeting on a handful of species of high value in national and international arenas (i.e. large mammals of the endangered variety), as opposed to the broad base of species of local interest and use.

Source:Sullivan, doctoral research in Namibia, 1994

challenge this silencing, or at least to provide some sort of public space for alternative and/or occluded views to be aired (discussed further in Sullivan, 2000; 2002). As an African saying reminds us, until the hunted have their poets then songs of the hunt will always glorify the hunter, not the prey.

We hope that these issues will raise questions for anyone using PRA. We strongly encourage anyone who wishes to use PRA to examine the accounts of those who have tried it which are listed at the end of the chapter. But we do not want to write it off entirely. All methodologies have their flaws. Our task is not to come up with undisputable truths. Rather, as we shall see in the next section, we are required to evaluate and analyse flawed, messy and partial data based on flawed, messy and partial encounters. Spending more time in the field may help but it will not make these problems go away. If PRA techniques are used with awareness of their weaknesses, and if conclusions are qualified and contextualised accordingly, they can be useful.

Ethnography: participant observation, oral testimony and the production of texts

Ethnography implies both a particular suite of methods used to produce a range of qualitative data, and the end product or ethnographic text constructed from such interactions. The key methods are participant observation and oral testimony: the first emphasising the legitimacy of a researcher's interpretation of observed cultural phenomena from their participation and immersion in these phenomena (some recent ethnographies include Boddy, 1989; Bourgois, 1995; Hutchinson, 1996); the second emphasising a researcher's ability to allow people to 'speak for themselves' - to construct their own texts - via the recording and transcription of interview material (for examples, see Bollig and Mbunguha, 1997; Brinkman and Fleisch, 1999; Cross and Barker, 1992; Slim and Thompson, 1993; Sullivan, 2002). Overall, ethnographic approaches aim to be 'actor-oriented' in their attempts to convey reality from a subject's 'point of view', increasingly including those of the researcher as final author and editor of the ethnographic text (see below). Ethnography tends, therefore, to read as a conglomerate of interconnected 'facts', thoughts, perceptions and contextual material and, as such, frequently has been downplayed as less rigorous than analyses produced using quantitative approaches. Given poststructuralist critique of assumptions built into the 'harder' sciences, however (e.g. Kuhn, 1970; Latour, 1993; Lyotard, 1984; Nader, 1996), there seems to be no real reason why the 'social facts' generated by qualitative and interpretative approaches should not be considered as 'real' and accurate as those empowered with the confidence of numbers.

Recently all studies which involve methods associated with the production of ethnography have been reeling from a post-modern questioning of their premises, aims and circumstances. Clifford, for example, identifies:

> symptoms of a pervasive postcolonial crisis of ethnography authority. While the crisis has been felt most strongly by former hegemonic Western discourses, the questions it raises are of global significance. Who has the authority to speak for a group's identity or authenticity? What are the essential elements and boundary of culture? How do self and other clash and converse in the encounters of ethnography, travel, modern interethnic relations? What narratives of development, loss, and innovation can account for the present range of local oppositional movements? (Clifford, 1988: 8)

This crisis has several strands. As identified in Chapter 1, economic and other inequalities frequently implicit in relationships between researcher and researched, have contributed to a serious questioning of the legitimacy of fieldwork in Third World contexts, and, of course, of the notion of 'the Third World' itself. This, combined with the massively influential critique of the authority of authorship by thinkers such as Foucault, has conspired, with justification, to reduce confidence in the apparent authority of the academic 'expert' – who by definition is usually constructed within the particular intellectual morays of the academy and bolstered by the structural inequality that consolidates decision-making power among those already holding wealth and power. So, for example, the social sciences in the 1980s and 1990s increasingly have problematised the ways that structural relations of power and inequality act to confer spatial and temporal distance between ethnographer and subject. This distance then becomes essential to the ways in which social and economic differences are constructed: authorising dominant and domineering knowledges (or discourses) of 'the other' (e.g. Said, 1978), and making possible the transformation by which '[t]he Other's empirical presence [in fieldwork] turns into his [*sic*] theoretical absence [in ethnographic writing]' (Fabian, 1983: xi).

Thus there has been a questioning of the tendency in ethnography for ethnographers to adopt an authoritative viewpoint over 'a society' and then construct a portrait of 'its' norms and rules, often in an 'ethnographic present' tense. The depictions which resulted tended to be timeless 'still lives' which may well have accurately portrayed interactions and interdependencies but which did not give much insight into the dynamics and history of the people studied. This blindness to change seems strange in a discipline whose methods are meant to allow the researcher into such intimate contact with the lives of the people that they are working with. But the tendency has been surprisingly long-lived. Hutchinson's masterly and award-winning book about the Nuer, published in 1996, has the humble (though by no means simple) aim of not seeking a homogenised image of culture and society (Hutchinson, 1996: 28-9). Instead she wished to examine how conflicts of interest and power are worked out within and between diverse interests among the Nuer peoples. Such a purpose was necessary because of the generations of work which had gone into explaining the internal logic of a particular social system and how it works as it does, rather than the potential for change and contestation.

But the criticism is not just of an apparent lack of history, social process or sensitivity to the distribution of power in ethnography. It is also of the process of producing and creating ethnographic texts. The post-modern problematising of ethnography as first and foremost a writing practice (Clifford, 1986: 2) leaves us with the uncomfortable phenomenon whereby observation is reduced to 'the text' that describes it, and claims to empirical 'facts' are treated with varying degrees of suspicion (Clifford and Marcus, 1986). Ethnographies thus become prey to deconstruction as socially produced texts and as building blocks in the construction of accepted discourses (for approaches to textual analysis and deconstruction see, for example, Fowler, 1991; Spender, 1980). Extreme reflexivity regarding one's own subject position as a researcher (Hobart, 1996; Twyman et al. 1999), while important can also render the production of ethnography as something more akin to individual psycho-analysis than as a means of enabling alternative perspectives on the 'real world' to gain public space.

Thus the mandate of ethnographers to do ethnography is challenged. And it is a potentially paralysing attack. If there is no mandate then the only thing to do is to be quiet: to let other groups and individuals who can somehow claim more powerful or legitimate mandates take over the task. It leaves social scientists writing about ethnography itself, with ever-increasing reflexivity.

As one of us has argued elsewhere (Sullivan, 2002), perhaps the time is ripe for a revitalised, even realist, validation of the way(s) 'culture' filters and moulds the post-modern worlds that we engage in and create as both participants and observers. While ethnography, like other approaches to research, has had to shed old certainties, there are a range of exciting research foci in this new landscape. Our field 'sites' now comprise unrelenting interpenetrations of local and global; the actors of our research, not to mention ourselves, are 'permitted' to have changing and dynamic identities; and 'the Ethnographic Other' is as likely as ourselves to experience the dislocations and interconnections generated by recent decades of mass-communications technology. Given these circumstances, and in acknowledgement of the power and wealth differentials still afforded by access to education, citizenship, and so on, it is conceivable that an appropriate role for ethnography today might be the attempt to provide public space for views that otherwise are likely to go unheard. Undoubtedly, academic research will flavour these views with selection by the author, not to mention interpretation and context: it is for the reader to decide if these are justifiable or not, given the material presented. Following Gordon (2000), however, perhaps it is time to celebrate the subversive and advocacy potential of independent (as in not-institutionally-driven) ethnographic work - in consultation with a group, a people, a culture or counter-culture, who, due to some element of difference, lacks public voice. Such an approach has become increasingly important, for example, in attempts at a 'corrective and anti-colonial' African environmental history (Beinart, 2000: 270) that emphasises the role of particular environmental discourses in justifying and extending a colonial hegemony (Leach and Mearns, 1996).

The danger of reflexivity and of writing about writing is that it can ultimately only ignore the wider world about which these accounts were written in the first place. Philippe Bourgois, who spent thousands of hours recording the conversations and lives of crack dealers in Harlem, was dismayed at the elitism of postmodern critiques of ethnography. He writes that:

> Although postmodern ethnographers often claim to be subversive, their contestation of authority focuses on hyperliterate critiques of form through evocative vocabularies, playful syntaxes and polyphonous voices, rather than on engaging with tangible daily struggles. Postmodern debates titillate alienated, suburbanised intellectuals; they are completely out of touch with the urgent social crises of the inner city unemployed. (Bourgois, 1995: 14)

The critique is important because it has begun to cut short the pretensions and grander statements made by anthropologists and social theorists, and has encouraged an openness and co-operation in the task of writing about other people. Both Bourgois and Hutchinson shared their notes and ideas and early drafts of their written material with the people that they were working with (see also Chapter 11 on 'Writing and representing'). They debated and discussed them with their subjects. This cannot hide the fact that they retained final editorial control. But the processes leading up to these products were different, and we would argue much improved, from earlier work. Hutchinson became known as a good conversationalist, and people would seek her out in order to enjoy the pleasure of her company. Bourgois had dealers coming up to him and asking to have their lives recorded arguing that they were worth at least a chapter in his book. We have each had similar experiences in conducting ethnographic research in the context of illegal 'raves' and in 'squatted' premises in London (Sullivan, 2001), or being asked to visit and talk to herders and farmers in conflict in Tanzania (Brockington, 2001).

On subjectivity and experience: phenomenological and embodiment approaches

Subjective and experiential dimensions of research are receiving increasing emphasis in the social sciences. Felt aspects, bodily and psychologically, of what people do increasingly are the concern of the researcher. Another aspect of this relates to the bearing of the experiences of the researcher on the process of fieldwork, the interpretations of research 'findings' and, as discussed above, the writing-up - the metaphorical 'setting in stone' - of the work. Willis, for example, who, as noted above, summarised his methodology as 'meeting people', also provides a detailed description of the psychological and 'almost bodily' tensions produced within him as he wrote down and categorised descriptions of his encounters (1981: xxi). In other words, the experience of research does not end with one's exit from the field: it overflows as the sensations produced by memories of place, people and events conjured up in the process of constructing a written story from the fieldnotes and data brought home (see Chapter 11 for a discussion on returning home).

A highlighting of the role/s of subjective experience in research can be considered in part as a response to the sense that felt experience has tended to be written out of the views of reality legitimised by the European Enlightenment project that took-off in the 1600s and 1700s. Building on classification and categorisation as its conceptual cornerstone, Enlightenment thinking left behind a legacy of conventional dualisms between mind and body, culture and nature, reason and emotion, male and female, science and art, and so on (e.g. Merchant, 1980). Knowledge and research built on these essential dichotomies, however, undermines the seamlessness existing between these categories as often perceived by those framed as 'Other'. This has been highlighted in feminist and post-structuralist writings (e.g. Belenky et al., 1986; Fabian, 1983), building on ideas expressed in the theoretical expositions of key thinkers in the critique of a Hegelian search for a philosophy of

Box 4.4 Phenomenology and embodiment: implications for fieldwork

We all have a body, and we all have subjective experiences of ourselves. Our bodies make possible and constrain the experiences of the world that we have. The experiences that we have are integrated bodily - embodied - as well as psychologically in our subjective and variously conscious constructions of 'the self'. Given these underlying strata of being it should be possible to draw on body- and self-knowledge as research tools. This should enhance understanding of people's actions and body language, their perceptions of their actions, what they may verbalise regarding these perceptions, and the impacts on body and self of the actions of others and of significant contexts - particularly the role/s of culture, power and ideology in 'inscribing' the body, and the ways in which people may subvert such inscriptions. A challenge implicit in such an approach to research, however, is the tension generated between the sharing of experiences as part of the fieldwork process - in a sense 'upfronting' the participation component of 'participant observation' - and the ability to reflect on these experiences and on their implications in relation to research aims. As Crouch, (2001: 63) describes, the process involves both othering ourselves as researchers, and being othered to varying extents by those whose practices, perceptions and worlds we are researching.

Crouch is a cultural geographer who is concerned explicitly with a rethinking of 'how people live and feel' (2001: 61). In a recent paper he draws on ethnographic work with recreational caravanners in the UK to 'explore people's accounts of what they do, their tactics, imaginations and movements' in relation to broader contexts that people may draw on in these personal narratives and actions. Importantly, by highlighting the 'existential immediacy' of the body, as well as people's 'felt multi-dimensional relationship with the world' (Crouch, 2001: 62), such work renders peoples - their bodily-selves - as agentive in relation to the spaces they inhabit. Although he and his fellow researchers drew in this project on interviewing as a field technique, they also considered their own felt sensations, bodily and psychologically, as data in the processes of both 'doing' the research and of reflecting on their encounters with caravanners and their own caravanning process. The field thereby 'emerges as a site of constant renegotiation, of the self, others, researcher and researched, ... through a process of uneven counter' (Crouch, 2001: 72) - an acknowledgement that is extremely significant given the structural inequalities frequently encountered (and making possible) fieldwork in 'Third World' contexts.

As Crouch argues, such an approach to fieldwork, thinking and writing makes possible great acceptance of the nuanced complexity of what people do, and of how they explain and express these 'doings'. Given a world where differences between people have been, and remain, used as justifications for persecution in many contexts, such an approach to the richly varied fora of human action might be considered relevant indeed.

ultimate reason and rationality. In Jean-Paul Sartre's existentialism, for example, attention is drawn to the ways that people experience their existence and thereby make choices based on their experiences (e.g. Sartre, 1969). For Heidegger, emphasis is placed on human subjects as 'Beings-in-the-world' (or Dasein), thus breaking down the distinctions between individual and context or place (e.g. Heidegger, 1962). Here we have the seeds of a phenomenology of being – a philosophical genre centred on the phenomena of the perceived world as known only through one's subjective experience of 'it'.

More recently such thinking has been extended by the extraordinarily influential social theorist Michel Foucault, in his multiple theses illustrating the ways in which subjective experience and 'the body' also are politically and historically situated (Foucault, 1977; 1990). By highlighting the nexus of power relationships that legitimate particular knowledges in particular situations and times in history, Foucault paves the way for an elucidation of the myriad and experientially-based knowledges of the multiple peoples excluded from power. This clearly is relevant for research in Third World contexts, as expounded by the Columbian author Arturo Escobar (1995; 1996).

Merleau-Ponty (1962) has extended a thinking through of the bodily grounds and constraints of experienced phenomena. Thus 'Being-in-the-world' is further 'concretised' as embodied experience – such that 'embodiment is an existential condition in which the body is the subjective source or intersubjective ground of experience' (Csordas, 1999: 143). Given that we all have bodies and we all experience felt, bodily sensations as well as mental reflections regarding these, 'the body' and 'its' sensations thus can become effective means for communication and interpretation in research. Phenomenological and embodiment approaches to field-based research and writing thus have much to offer in terms of validating ways of knowing and experiencing the world that are not easily shoehorned into interview surveys and quantitative analyses. As such they are becoming increasingly important in the human sciences (e.g. Bender, 1998; Crouch, 2001; Ingold, 2000; Sullivan, 2001; Tilley, 1994; Weiss and Haber, 1999). Box 4.4 considers some methodological implications of pursuing a phenomenological approach to research.

Qualitative not quantitative?

There is a tendency to treat qualitative and quantitative methods as not really compatible. Smith for example writes that qualitative methods are concerned with subjective understanding rather than statistical description and analysis (1994: 491). But statistical descriptions cover all manner of things. As Hammersley points out, it is hard to get away from statistics (Hammersley, 1992). Any form of words meaning 'more than', 'less than', 'frequently' or 'regularly' and the like are quantitative claims. Many could be put into numerical form. The difference, Hammersley argues, is in the high degree of precision which statistical approaches use, not in the fact of dealing with quantities. Conversely, however, statistical descriptions alone rarely take on the systems of meaning which qualitative methodologies seek to uncover. Qualitative methods could be seen to embrace quantitative techniques and use them for different, and perhaps more nuanced purposes.

Box 4.5 Combining qualitative and quantitative data: plants, people and practice in north-west Namibia

My doctoral thesis (Sullivan, 1998) had two primary aims. First, to analyse patterns and determinants of natural resource use and management by Khoe-speaking Damara farmers in arid north-west Namibia. And second, to assess the ecological implications of this resource-use in the context of the unpredictable variations in primary productivity characteristic of dry-land environments. Given these objectives, a combination of quantitative and qualitative anthropological and ecological techniques were employed. For example, the use of gathered non-timber products for food and medicine was monitored in 7 repeat-surveys over an 18 month period for a sample of 45 households comprising 2017 individual 'diet-days'. Qualitative data derived from the experience of collecting resources with people on collecting trips within the broader landscape and from informal discussions and interactions with local people. With regard to the second research objective, woody and herbaceous vegetation datasets were also compiled, the former comprising 2760 plant individuals in a stratified sample of 75 transects and the latter consisting of 48 qradrats, half fenced to exclude livestock, in which herbaceous vegetation was monitored over two growing seasons. A number of standard ecological variables, including patterns in community floristics, diversity, cover and population structure, were used to explore the prediction that concentrations of people and live-stock cause measurable impacts on vegetation around settlements. More recently, recorded oral testimony material focusing on the perceptions of individuals of landscape change and environmental management practices have been collated (Sullivan, 2000; 2002).

In other words, an attempt was made in my thesis to explore the multifaceted relationships between people and environment with a similarly multifarious set of research methods - combining social anthropology, human ecology and natural science tools, concepts and field techniques. While this enabled a complex analysis of complex relationships, a number of problems also were generated by the attempt to try and integrate such broadly different approaches to research. Although my thesis was passed with no changes, as one of the examiners noted in their report '[t]he result is a thesis in two halves...rather schizophrenic in that each part is conceptually, methodologically and stylistically distinct'.

Source: Sullivan, doctoral research in Namibia, 1994

From the quantitative side, an error is a tendency to treat qualitative data as somehow inferior or less 'real' than 'hard' statistical information. For example, we have heard well-qualified seminar speakers apologise for offering 'anecdotes not data', as if stories from the field were somehow less rigorous than other forms of information. All stories have a context and we need carefully to interpret and record them, as we will see below. But treated properly they are as strong, relevant and interesting as data that are numerical or otherwise easily categorised.

Qualitative and quantitative methods are not mutually exclusive approaches to learning. Both can be necessary depending on the question that is being asked. We have both combined complex statistical analyses of data with detailed qualitative interviews to learn more about the places and people we were studying. The latter make for richer and 'thicker' descriptions of observed phenomena (Geertz, 1973). Importantly, we need to choose the types of methods that are appropriate for collecting data on the research questions we might be interested in and to know how to combine different types of data into powerful and relevant analyses (Box 4.5).

Though it is important to combine these tools, it is rarely easy. Perhaps the hardest thing when doing fieldwork is how to manage one's time. Collecting, cataloguing and entering qualitative data is exhausting work. Tape-recorded interviews need to be transcribed (preferably) or summarised shortly after they are taken. Transcriptions need to be annotated with the detail of body language and other impressions significant for the interview. Historical records need to be interrogated, and written records of meetings need to be discussed with those who were there. Each encounter generates a string of leads to be followed up and checked. Collecting rigorous qualitative data is hard work. Equally, collecting quantitative data of household surveys or vegetation formations is also demanding. It can be repetitive and boring. It is often pressured and rushed, especially if there is a large sample to be completed in a set time, as with repeat-round surveys. The fixed agenda of collecting given samples can make it hard to follow up leads and new developments as they arise. In short, combining the two approaches is difficult. Qualitative data collection does not offer a break to quantitative data collection; instead it offers new demands. At the same time, rigorous quantitative work on meaningful samples is not to be taken lightly. Added to these difficulties are the everyday problems of working in a second language, and in tropical climes where, as both of us have experienced, a researcher may have to contend with a host of aggressive diseases – most inconvenient for fieldwork schedules.[6]

Conclusion

We have argued that qualitative research is essential if we are to understand what makes our world meaningful for people. It offers powerful techniques which can reveal a great deal, and they can also be combined effectively with quantitative data. As new techniques evolve, those conducting fieldwork are being presented with new ways of doing research. We have also argued that the claims of publicly conducted research, and the authority of ethnography need to be carefully considered. In writing up we need to be suitably but pragmatically wary of transforming and transmuting rich multi-textured field experiences into the written word (see Chapter 11).

Qualitative research requires cognizance of the position and powers of the researcher and the politics of doing research. Critical consideration of this process is an important element of any successful project, particularly given the inequalities built into the process of field research in Third World contexts. The in-depth nature of engagement that characterises qualitative research clearly thus is only as good as the degree of critical reflexivity pursued by the researcher. This inevitably means treading a fine line between this and self-indulgent naval-gazing. If this line is trod healthily however, it is both instructive and rewarding.

Methodology may just mean a series of meetings with people, but if researchers are appropriately self-aware, and meetings are characterised by good listening, and conversation, we will have much to learn about the world in which we live. The basic requirement for good research, qualitative or quantitative, is that one is friendly and engaging with people, and open to learning from what they tell you and from what you observe and experience.

Recommended Reading

General
Bryman, A. and Burgess, R. G. (1999) *Qualitative Research* Sage Publications, London.
Exhaustive and comprehensive. The definitive guide.

Barley, N. (1983) *The Innocent Anthropologist. Notes from a Mud Hut* Penguin, London.
A hilarious book, compulsory reading.

PRA
Chambers, R. (1991) Shortcut and participatory methods for gaining social information for projects.
In M. Cernea (ed.) *Putting People First. Sociological Variables in Rural Development* World Bank, Washington DC, pp. 515-37.
Robert Chambers is the guru of PRA. Compulsory reading on its advantages.

Mosse, D. (1994) Authority, gender and knowledge: theoretical reflections on the practice of participatory rural appraisal. *Development and Change* 25: 497-526.

Bevan, P. (2000) Who's a goody? Demythologising the PRA agenda. *Journal of International Development* 12: 751-59.
Both of the above articles provide useful critiques of the claims and practices of PRA.

Ethnography and oral testimonies
Bourgois, P. (1995) In Search of Respect. Selling crack in El Barrio Cambridge University Press, Cambridge.
An extraordinary tour-de-force on the insights ethnography can offer when done well.

Ellen, R. F. (1984) *Ethnographic Research: A Guide to General Conduct* Academic Press, London.
An often-cited text which is a classic in its field.

Clifford, J. and Marcus, G. E. (eds) (1986). *Writing Culture. The Poetics and Politics of Ethnography* University of California Press, Berkeley.

Fabian, J. (1983) *Time and the Other: How Anthropology Makes Its Object* Columbia University Press, New York.
Both of the above are vital readings to explore the problems of ethnography's claims.

Phenomenology

Crouch, D. (2001) Spatialities and the feeling of doing. *Social and Cultural Geography* 2(1): 61-75. Crouch's paper has been discussed in some detail in Box 4.4. His work is particularly useful in elucidating the ways in which phenomenological and embodiment ideas can inform fieldwork practice, highlighting for example the interpretative significance of the subjective experiences of the fieldworker.

Weiss, G. and Haber, H.F. (eds) (1999) *Perspectives on Embodiment: The Intersections of Nature and Culture* Routledge, London.
This edited collection of essays emphasises both the theoretical and empirical significance of conceptualising and experiencing 'the body' as subject as well as object of research, and provides an extremely timely introduction to the value of embodiment approaches for thoughtful and reflexive field research.

Notes

1. Though not nearly as recent as Smith suggests when she states that they are 'a product of the advent of humanistic geography' (1994: 491). Participant observation is much older than that. Anthropologists, following the somewhat hypocritical urgings of Malinowski (Kuper, 1983), were among the first to set about formal (though often ill-defined) fieldwork using a variety of qualitative and quantitative techniques but doing so while all the time 'immersed' in the language and norms of their study site. This established, in the British school at least, participant observation as a central method in any attempt to find out about the wider world. The Chicago School of Sociology is also widely, though perhaps erroneously, perceived to have been responsible for promoting qualitative methods in the United States (Bulmer, 1984).

2. The term 'entheogen' - literally 'becoming divine within' - has been coined by entheobotanist Jonathan Ott (e.g. Ott, 1996) and others to refer to substances, normally derived from plant material, that when consumed stimulate subjective mystical and religious experiences.

3. An extraordinary illustration of this is Bourgois' book In Search of Respect (1995), an award-winning and powerful but disturbing insight into poverty and drug dealing in New York.

4. For some fascinating answers see Willis' book Learning to Labour (1977), about how young school leavers accept the lowest low-prospect jobs, or Scott's Weapons of the Weak (1985), about how peasants in Malaysia resist exploitation by land owners and wealthier farmers.

5. Robert Chambers, PRA's arch-protagonist, once told one of us (Dan) of a PRA activity undertaken among pastoral communities in East Africa which had involved a mapping exercise. He spoke with praise of an excellent map produced by one youth in only four hours, after which the research party had had to leave. But how legitimate can this single and rapidly produced representation of the lie of the land possibly be? It is good, if 'results' are needed, that such material can be so quickly available, but a bigger question is why were only four hours available for the research in the first place? Problems here relate to whose view is represented in such PRA 'products', the danger of fixing fluid categories in two-dimensional representations of landscapes, and the ways in which land marked as claimed or unused in one mapping exercise with one group of people might be contested by others whose views might be occluded in the process (e.g. Hodgson and Schroeder, 2002; Peluso, 1995; Sullivan, 2002).

6. Practical difficulties associated with data collection are discussed further in Chapters 5 and 7.

PART II

PREPARATION FOR THE FIELD

5 Practical issues

Helen Leslie and Donovan Storey

Introduction

Fieldwork is one of those undertakings that you simply cannot be too prepared for. Aside from the methodological and academic matters that you will need to consider, there are an enormous amount of practical issues to carefully work through as you plan to embark on what may turn out to be the experience of a lifetime. Being adequately and appropriately prepared for fieldwork will not only facilitate a positive dimension to this experience, but also ultimately influence the success of your research project (Nash, 2000a; Robson et al., 1997).

This chapter, in drawing from our own and on others' first hand experiences of the field, discusses a number of practical issues and suggests ways in which you can approach or begin to deal with some of them – from information on how to secure research funding to advice on what to pack and where to stay once in the field. That is not to say that you should read this as a blueprint for planning fieldwork. Ultimately planning will be determined by your own choice of research project and by your personal attributes and qualities (see Chapter 6).

Funding

While personal and realistic accounts of development fieldwork are very useful in pre-empting many practical issues that may occur in the field, funding, one of the most important issues that arises when planning development fieldwork, is rarely mentioned in such accounts. It is almost as if there is some sort of unspoken taboo about discussing money, or that fieldworkers feel that it is insensitive to broadcast any relative affluence in today's tight funding environment. In reality, however, it may be funding even more than methodological or topical interests that will determine the nature of your fieldwork. After all, until you can find the money to secure a flight to your chosen field site, it will be very difficult to even begin your fieldwork!

Early considerations

To increase your chances of securing funding, it is best to begin applying for grants as early into your research as possible (Nash, 2000b). Raising money can often be a lengthy process and many funding bodies only offer their grants once a year. Some donor agencies also require detailed and complex proposals that inevitably take several weeks to prepare. As novice researchers with little or no track record in grant applications, post-graduate students often find the process much more difficult than anticipated (Devereux and Hoddinott, 1992:5). Soliciting the help of supervisors and peers is, therefore, a useful first step to take in preparing grant applications.

An additional early consideration is the political affiliation/s of the funding body you may be targeting. While one of the authors (Helen) heard it said by an activist friend that 'all money is dirty money' there are some funding bodies that are more explicitly tied to the very governments, military juntas and economic agencies that may have historically oppressed the people who will become your research participants, than others. Conflicts of interest can thus arise (see Box 8.3, Chapter 8). Sluka (1995:282), for example, outlines the case of an American sociologist who only discovered on return from the field that his research on student groups in Chile was sponsored by a funding organisation tied to the American military. As Sluka (1995:283) stresses, alongside the ethical issues such funding sources raise, 'it can be dangerous to accept funding from agencies that one's research participants find objectionable'. Investigating the sources of your funding and considering how your research participants view these sources may resolve such ethical dilemmas.

Funding sources

Devereux and Hoddinott (1992:5) have divided the main sources of funding commonly targeted for development fieldwork into two main categories – major (external) institutional donors and miscellaneous donors. Major institutional donors are governmental and non-governmental organisations such as NZAID in New Zealand, AusAID in Australia, the Economic and Social Committee for Overseas Research in the UK and the Ford Foundation in the United States. Some of these major donors give large grants but have very strict and complex application procedures. Additionally, such organisations have their own agendas or research priorities and can be notably pro-economist or anti-anthropologist (Devereux and Hoddinott, 1992:5). You should also be aware that being successful with one application does not necessarily mean that your research will be bankrolled. For example, while NZAID supports a wide range of research projects, it offers only $NZ3000 as a maximum grant thus effectively limiting the amount of time that can be spent in the field.

Miscellaneous donors, on the other hand, are organisations such as charities and university grants committees. As smaller organisations they usually offer more modest sums of money but often without the demands and complications of major donor agencies.[1] Lists of such donors can be found in libraries and from university grants and scholarships offices (also see Nash, 2000b). If these donors do not have a set date in which to submit your application, it is worth sending off a number of letters (with a brief research proposal and budget attached) to agencies that you may have identified as sympathetic to your research question (Devereux and Hoddinott, 1992:5). Note too that many funding agencies have websites on which they list funding criteria, application forms and titles of projects supported in the past, thus this avenue is also worth exploring.

Postgraduate scholarships may also offer additional funds for research. These are often the chief resource for international students. However, scholarship holders should carefully note what support exists for conducting home-based research when they apply for various scholarships. Students on AusAID scholarships, for example, have funding for fieldwork build into their scholarships and can use their yearly stipend and money for air-travel home to fund their fieldwork requirements. Additional funds for research are sometimes advertised through your university postgraduate office or through the university's office for research. It is worth bookmarking these sites on your PC and keeping a regular check on any information posted.

Often, however, and despite your best efforts at applying for funding, you may not be able to secure enough financial support to complete the kind of research project you had envisaged. In this case, it may be necessary to revise your proposal to perhaps spend less time in the field, or to delay your fieldwork until you have secured adequate support.

A final and perhaps last-ditch option to finance your fieldwork is to take out a loan. In many countries, government-driven student loans have often been utilised for such a purpose. Whether it is a student loan or a regular bank loan that finances your fieldwork, this option is not particularly idyllic. Because the money is coming directly from your own purse you are likely to ask for less than is probably needed and you will be burdened with the pressure of finding ways to pay back the loan during the most important writing-up stage of your research (Devereux and Hoddinott, 1992:6). Nevertheless, while not ideal, funding research through borrowing may well be an appropriate means when no other avenues exist.

Establishing contacts

As with applying for funding for your research, it is best to begin the process of establishing contacts in the field as early as possible. This is important not only for the obvious reason of facilitating access to the field site, but also because you may need to know someone very early on in the piece who can send you the documentation necessary to fulfill the requirements of your university human ethics committee or visa application. Generally this documentation will take the form of a letter of approval from a local official or village elder and can be crucial in ultimately determining whether your application for research permission is granted. In Malaysia, the government previously required that researchers named Malay citizens who would serve as financial and political guarantors of you and your research project (see Box 8.6, Chapter 8).

How to establish contact

While global communication has become infinitely easier, establishing contacts with Third World peoples through email and the World Wide Web can still be problematic. Internet servers are notoriously unreliable in many places and emails can easily be ignored, or lost, meaning that your best efforts to contact individuals can go unnoticed. Not all government officials, NGOs or key contacts have access to email. Although some researchers seem to manage quite well with email communication to the field, it may be a better bet to send letters, fax messages, or phone – at least during the important initial contact stage. In the case that your communications receive no response, try an intermediary. You could, for example, write to your consulate or high commission in the country concerned to see if they can put you in contact with someone relevant or use emails to 'snowball' to other relevant contacts.

What kind of letters should you write to establish contact with people in the field? Often there is a temptation to 'cut and paste' sections of your research proposal into an introductory letter thus avoiding the need to explain your research goals and question in more simple terms. In discussing the problems she encountered with gaining access to her field site, Lareau (1996:203) advises against sending long letters which obscure or bury the most important part of the letter – outlining what it is that you want the organisation/individual to do. Lareau also advises against sending different introductory letters. In the case of a long and academic letter that she sent to a district official through which she hoped to gain access to her field site – a school – Lareau wrote different, less detailed letters to teachers and the principal. Her strategy backfired however, when the district official passed on her letter to these same individuals. In hindsight Lareau believes that introductory letters should be short, direct and focus more on the needs of the researcher and the proposed role of the organisation/individual contacted, than on the academic or intellectual goals of the project itself. A summary of your research proposal can always be attached if you think the individual or organization may want more details.

A final way of establishing contact with the research community is to spend time with people of the same nationality before you enter the field. Many different ethnic groups have associations in universities that organise social and cultural events and your participation in such events can often lead to helpful contacts and advice. A New Zealand Master's student planning to conduct her research in the Cook Islands spent many a Sunday attending church services frequented by Cook Islanders who had migrated to New Zealand. This action proved invaluable for not only developing cultural awareness, but also for establishing contacts and social networks to aid her fieldwork in the Cook Islands. Another possibility is to offer to do proof-reading for a student from the country you are going to in exchange for language lessons.

Finally, a warning. Do not expect a flood of responses to your emails, letters or faxes. Generally, the people whom you will most likely want to contact will be very busy, and probably will not even directly read your requests. If you get a response, then great, but do not lose heart or take it as a portent of things to come if you do not hear back from someone. In fact, your attempt at contact may well be remembered once you have arrived and contacted the person directly. Keep in mind that in many non-Western cultures personal contact is still much more preferable than other forms of communication. Indeed, even experienced researchers find that the most successful way to gain interviews and material is to simply turn up at someone's office to make an appointment in person – or even to sit and wait for a meeting.

Who to contact

Having decided upon the mode of contact to pursue, the next question becomes 'who to contact'? Do you, for example, contact the head of the organisation you plan to study or should you send a letter directly to the coordinator of the project in which you are most interested? There are unfortunately no hard and fast rules that can guide you in your decision making on this issue. As a general rule, however, it is advisable that you send as many letters to as many people in the organisation/community as possible. Make sure that one of these letters reaches someone of importance or standing such as an NGO head, government official or village elder as these people are more likely to have the power to both facilitate your access to the field and legitimise your presence once you are there.

Along with members of the intended research community, it is also a good idea to contact other researchers currently in the field or recently returned. From these individuals you can gain valuable information about such practicalities as the cost of living and the extension of research visas. These early contacts can also lay the foundations for friendships and social support once in the field. Helen's contact with an American PhD student living in San Salvador, for example, enabled her to feel more relaxed about whether or not she would be kicked out of the country after her month long visa had expired (Helen intended to be in El Salvador for at least seven months). In response to her obvious angst over the matter, Kelley assured Helen that she knew of many New Zealanders and Australians who renewed their visas on a regular basis by popping across the boarder into Guatemala.

Research 'permission': documentation and gatekeepers

There are at least two levels of permission that you will need to negotiate in order to conduct fieldwork. The first is at the official level and involves, in most cases, a research permit or visa. Gaining official permission and the appropriate documentation to do your fieldwork may be as straightforward as filling in a research visa application and waiting a few weeks – or it may be a much more serious impediment requiring months of attempted communication between yourself and the relevant authorities. Initially, you need to consider the implications of your research and the site you have chosen. Explicitly, getting official permission to conduct research on China's one child policy or Israel's nuclear capabilities would be difficult to say the least. Be realistic and do some homework on your (potential) topic and possible field sites. Doing research on population policy elsewhere in Asia, or defence issues facing states not in a constant atmosphere of conflict would be more realistic possibilities. Otherwise a flat refusal or, perhaps worse, a protracted non-reply resulting in eternal limbo, will be the likely outcome.

A further issue may also arise for students going back 'home' to do their field-work. While 'locals' may have several advantages over foreign researchers, such as being conversant in political procedures, culture and having contacts, there may also be some disadvantages. These researchers collecting data may be seen as more of a threat, for example, as they have a greater opportunity to distribute their findings locally. The bottom line for all is then: plan ahead and be realistic in where you go to do certain research.

Researchers also need to be aware that, in some cases, gaining official approval at more than one level is necessary. That impressive looking visa gained from an embassy in one's home country may prove frustratingly inadequate once in the field. Indeed, permission may need to be further granted from regional or local authorities. In most cases a 'higher level' authorization helps ease or overcome more local resistance, but this may not always be the case.

Visas and government approval do not necessarily represent the end of the road regarding consent. Indeed, in some fieldwork contexts official approval is only the first step of many towards gaining legitimacy (see Chapter 8, 'Gatekeepers'). Having a research visa issued in Bangkok to study indigenous peoples in Northern Thailand may mean very little to the communities themselves once you arrive. Likewise, approval from the Philippine government to do research on Muslim sep-aratist groups in the southern Philippines would in no way imply that it was possi-ble, or safe, to do so. In fact, in some instances 'official' documentation may create a deal of suspicion when such groups are in dispute with national authorities. Box 5.1 debates the importance, or otherwise, of gaining official visas.

In many instances it will be local 'gatekeepers' who will need to be satisfied before an adequate level of fieldwork can be undertaken. In some cases this will be informal 'permission' – people's consent will be indicated by their degree of par-ticipation and enthusiasm for you and your work. This is perhaps the most impor-tant and relevant permission you will be granted and will continue to strive for and negotiate even on a daily basis. In other communities this may be more rigorous, involving a further set of ethical guidelines and commitments. Examples of this may be found in Polynesian cultures, where chiefs or local *Kaumatua* (Maori elders) need to be satisfied regarding the merits, ethical issues and future implications of your research. The requirements of such gatekeepers, coupled with the formal require-ments of governments, may necessitate considerable foresight, awareness and plan-ning on the part of the researcher, especially at the Masters level where time can be very precious.

Box 5.1: The visa

Over 1986-88 a brief (and somewhat light-hearted) debate in *Area* took place on the merits or otherwise of obtaining official research visas. It began with two notes, one by Peter Knight and another by J Douglas Porteous (1986), a Canadian geographer, lamenting the lack of foreign-based fieldwork in favour of home-based technical research and the absence of geographers living dangerously, and getting their 'boots muddy'. In particular Porteous differentiated between remote sensing ('clean, cold, detached, easy') and 'intimate sensing' (which, in the Third World, is 'complex, difficult and often filthy').

A reply to this challenge came the following year from Belinda Dodson, a research student at Cambridge. While Dodson agreed 'wholeheartedly with their sentiments' the problem lay with 'the obstacles placed in the paths of would-be researchers of the Third World by Third World governments': 'No longer can one don one's pith helmet and head for Darkest Africa laden with rum and Bibles, funded with a grant from the Royal Geographical Society. Not only may the RGS not supply the funds, but the embassy or high commission may not grant the research visa'. Dodson singled out Indian bureaucracy 'a foe more formidable than any Bengal tiger or tropical disease', as the reason for abandoning a research project in Northern Bihar for Bangladesh. Finally, she warned of the dangers of attempting to get by with a tourist visa.

In Porteous' reply (1988), entitled 'No excuses, Belinda' (and the final instalment of this debate), he challenged those dependent on official sanction for research. Several research trips to Chile in the 1970s were based on tourist entry, Porteous noted, under all sorts of regimes which probably wouldn't have okayed his work. He concluded: 'I believe that geographers who wish to research or experience Third World landscapes should, in certain circumstances, judiciously ignore, avoid or circumvent the rules. If the geographer is dealing with a repressive regime, as in Chile, this violation of sovereignty is not unethical. I gained a richer appreciation of South Africa recently by breaking a law or two'.

Health and safety

When preparing for development fieldwork, health and safety concerns should be paramount. As Devereux and Hoddinott (1992:14) stress, 'fieldwork can be an unhealthy occupation' and virtually every person who has conducted development fieldwork will have had some experience of illness and/or danger before returning home. While the vast differences between home and fieldwork environments (climate, lifestyle, food) makes it difficult to avoid such experiences, being well prepared before entering the field can help ward off some of the more serious illnesses/dangers, particularly those that have the potential to ruin your fieldwork altogether.

That is not to suggest, however, that fieldwork is necessarily dangerous. It would be unwise to wrap yourself in cotton wool on arrival and then expect to build rapport with locals who may well interpret your reluctance to try local food, venture beyond your neighbourhood or leave home without your first aid kit, as a scathing indictment on their culture and way of life. The obvious approach to take is one of balance and flexibility. Experience as much as you can of the lifestyles of the people with whom you will be working but, at the same time, make sure that you have taken the precautions that will mitigate against some of the more serious illnesses/issues that you may be faced with in the field.

Health preparations

One of the first things you can do in preparing for a healthy fieldwork experience is to contact, or get your General Practitioner (GP) to contact, your local tropical health centre.[2] These organisations have the most up-to-date information on country-specific vaccinations and health conditions and can advise you on the kinds of immunisations/precautions that you will need to take before entering the field. These centres also perform immunisations, although often at premium prices. It might be more advisable to receive immunisations from your GP where subsidies on certain vaccinations apply.

Whatever your views or beliefs in conspiracy theories on immunisation, it is strongly advisable that you receive what is deemed necessary by medical authorities before entering the field. New and much more effective vaccines have replaced many that were less than satisfactory in the past (such as the vaccine for Hepatitis A), and there is no joy to be found in suffering Typhoid or Hepatitis A in what may be a strange and hostile environment, particularly when such diseases could have been prevented. Among travellers and researchers in the Third World alike, there seems to be some rivalry over who can lay claim to the most nasty illnesses; please remember that some diseases are life-threatening and others can cause permanent damage to an individual's health.

Healthy preparations for fieldwork also include obtaining travel insurance (preferably the kind which will airlift you to your country of origin in the case of serious illness and will pre-pay costs rather than reimburse), noting your blood group, and packing a comprehensive first aid kit (Devereux and Hoddinott, 1992:14; Box 5.2). While not necessarily advocating self-diagnoses and treatment, a guide such as Dirk G. Schroeder's Staying Healthy in Asia, Africa and Latin America (Schroeder, 1993) may prove an invaluable asset in the field.

Box 5.2: First aid materials

In this kit you will need such items as basic dressing material (a few medium size airstrip dressings are a better bet than sterile pads that need to be affixed with tape), a crepe bandage (to use for ankle and knee strains),

---

a thermometer (to keep an eye on levels of fever and to diagnose infection) medications such as paracetamol, rubber gloves, an antifungal cream (tea-tree oil is a cheap and effective option here) and a broad spectrum antibiotic, several small syringes and needles for intramuscular injections (particularly if you are going to a country where HIV/AIDs is endemic) and lastly some iodine or other antiseptic lotion. Many of these items can be purchased straight from a pharmacy, but others, such as antibiotics will need to be prescribed to you by your GP. You should note that some of these resources may be in demand in many communities – though there are issues in researchers acting as dispensers of medical equipment (See Box 7.2, Chapter 7).

If you are planning to conduct your fieldwork in a country prone to malaria, it is important that you thoroughly investigate the different kinds of malaria prevention tablets and insect repellents that can be used in your chosen field site. There are a number of brands on the market, some of which can be quite toxic when taken over long periods, so it is best to be an informed consumer and to choose the most appropriate and effective brand. As malaria tablets can be exorbitantly expensive when purchased over the counter, check to see if you can purchase the tablets more cheaply through your GP (see also the section on packing below for advice on protective clothing and mosquito nets). Nevertheless, the old axiom 'prevention is always better than the cure' applies here. Getting comprehensive immunisations, preventing mosquito bites, having a good first aid kit, drinking clean water, keeping clear of old or unprotected food, and staying clean (especially one's hands) are all basic forms of prevention that can go a very long way toward a healthy fieldwork experience. Finally, although you may not be planning to initiate or establish sexual relations while in the field, it is essential that you make preparations to protect your own and other's sexual health. Condoms may well be readily available in the country in which you intend to conduct fieldwork, but if you are planning to spend a period of time in a remote location, availability may turn out to be an issue. It is best then, to take a supply of condoms with you.

Along with these practical preparations for healthy fieldwork, it is also important that you prepare yourself mentally for what you may face in the field (see Chapter 6, 'preparing for discomfort and depression'). Think about how you might cope with feeling sick and try to envisage what kinds of help/support you will seek if you are struck down with dysentery or some other problem. Devereux and Hoddinott (1992:14) advocate building a sickness 'allowance' into your work schedule planning and stress that fieldworkers must be prepared to give themselves plenty of rest periods. In this way you are less likely to get run down and in turn, make yourself vulnerable to contracting something debilitating.

Safety preparations

Very much related to the above preparation for healthy fieldwork, is the thought that you will need to put into preparing for safe fieldwork. Obviously these considerations are paramount if you intend to conduct your fieldwork in a conflict or post-conflict zone or in a city known for violence such as Port Moresby, Johannesburg or San Salvador. If this indeed is the case, Sluka (1995:282) suggests two considerations that need to be made when planning for fieldwork in dangerous or violent social contexts.

Firstly, it is important to realistically evaluate the 'degree of danger' that you may be exposed to in the field and its potential sources. Here you might consider what level of risk you are prepared to take and the kinds of individual actions that would potentially lessen or increase such risk. Assuming that the majority of researchers would draw the line at a 'direct threat to life or limb', Sluka (1995:282) stresses both the need for a plan of escape from the situation and recognition that you may have to terminate your fieldwork if the risks become too great (see Chapter 8, 'Safety of the researcher and responsibilities to self').

Secondly, before entering the field, discuss the potential safety risks of your proposed research with your colleagues and supervisors. A check of your own country's travel advisories is a useful initial call. Remember however, that you are the one who is more likely to be cognisant with the current situation in the field, so try to trust your own judgement if the advice that ensues is alarmist or inappropriate. Sluka suggests contacting experts in your field and conducting a pre-fieldwork visit before you make any final decisions about your fieldwork. While Helen was unable to visit El Salvador prior to her fieldwork, a detailed email reply from Noam Chomsky enabled her to frame more realistically the kinds of risks she would be exposed to when living in post-conflict San Salvador.

When preparing for safe fieldwork it is also important to have some idea of what to expect in terms of everyday life. Many accounts of fieldwork in violent settings speak for example of the fear engendered by the visibility of weapons (see for example, Lee, 1995:28). This was certainly the case during Helen's fieldwork in El Salvador where semi-automatic touting security personnel even guarded stalls of car batteries! In such situations, Lee believes the researcher becomes a 'routine coward', or someone to whom recognising and avoiding potentially dangerous situations is second nature. Building rapport and learning from research participants enables the researcher to put into practice these safety mechanisms, although as some researchers have stressed, local judgement often varies on potentially risky situations (Lee, 1995:28-29).

Travel guidebooks (such as the *Lonely Planet* or *Rough Guide* series) and information from your high commission, embassy or consulate can, in addition, be useful in building a mental picture of potential dangers/risks in the field.[3] Howell (1990) also provides a fairly comprehensive range of dangers faced by researchers, from physical violence to accidents. Women researchers should take note of the guidelines for women travellers routinely discussed in travel guidebooks and academic literature and wherever possible plan to avoid those areas/situations where sexual assault is commonplace. As horrible as it may be to contemplate, women researchers are no more immune to sexual assault than any other women and should be mindful of the increased risk of sexual violence that follows or accompanies violent social conflict in general. Once in the field, women researchers should also be aware of the advice of local people who have current knowledge of the dangers that exist in their own communities. During Helen's fieldwork in El Salvador, for example, she decided to abandon her plan to visit women participants in their homes in an isolated rural area upon hearing of the recent rape of a development worker in the vicinity. While all fieldwork is potentially dangerous, the psychological stress placed upon the researcher is heightened in situations of violence. Here there is a temptation to use the stress of researching violent social conflict to legitimise under-involvement in the research process. Witnessing traumatic situations can also affect the researcher's capacity to collect relevant and appropriate data and may even cause the researcher to 'omit or distort relevant data' (Lee, 1995:14).

As is discussed in Chapters 6 and 7, anxiety and depression are common reactions to these stresses of fieldwork and should not be viewed as extraordinary or shameful. Recognising that these health concerns may arise, however, will aid the researcher in more comprehensively preparing for the health and safety issues that will impact on a successful fieldwork experience.

Places to stay, or not to stay

After travel, the most pressing logistical consideration will most likely be accommodation. Your choice of where to stay though should reflect more than purely cost and level of comfort[4] – it also involves issues of community acceptance or marginalisation, safety, security and well being, and access to information. The researcher should then seriously consider several personal and professional implications about where they stay.

Cost

Assuming that most researchers are not able to access unlimited funds, cost is likely to be a primary concern during fieldwork. As any well-travelled backpacker on a limited budget will attest, what you spend on a bed for the night is directly proportional to what you eat and do the next day, and so the temptation is to cut accommodation costs. This is also true for fieldwork, though the pressures are greater as not only food but published and unpublished documents, transportation, gifts, communication and essential shopping also consume limited budgets. It would be tempting then to advise, or encourage, frequenting the cheapest form of accommodation possible, but this too has its drawbacks. Staying in 20-bed backpacker dormitory may be great socially, but it is hardly conducive to late night reading or planning the next day's interview questions. Living in a 'tourist ghetto', in the case of urban research, is also likely to be distracting and will restrict productive work time to daylight hours (minus travel time). In some instances such areas are not particularly safe at night, and security for your gear may also be an issue. Finding a balance between cost and functionality then is important, but it is not likely to just be financial reasons that prove the deciding factor: researchers will also, in most cases, want to be close to the community or activity they are studying, if not within it.

Where to stay – and why

For those doing rural fieldwork or work in marginal communities it is access to the research site(s) which will be the most pressing concern. While living close to your place of research may be possible, commercial accommodation is limited in proximity to marginal or marginalised communities even in the case of large cities. So surely the best remaining option then is to live within your study area, even in the house of your key respondents? For some, while this would help offset logistical problems, open the door to late night research, and help build strong relationships and greater understanding, living within one's fieldwork site for 24/7 can be emotionally overwhelming, physically draining and, in conflict situations, outright life threatening!

Without a doubt, living within one's research site is potentially thrilling (at the personal level) and productive (with regards to data). It may also be an expectation, say, with regards to anthropological research. For most though it is likely to be a matter of choice, and opportunity, and so there are several personal and epistemological issues to consider here that can either work for or against you. First and foremost, living within a community can potentially bring rewards of acceptance and trust, both of which are invaluable for research. Especially in poorer or powerless communities nothing perhaps conveys a message of commitment or acceptance more than living as part of a community. It may also have the consequence of disarming community suspicion, resistance or hostility – though this will not always be the case. Finally, by literally 'being there' a much greater appreciation of issues and a context for data will eventuate – even if one's methodological tools are survey-based.

Against this, however, must be considered some potential problems, which may or may not outweigh the aforementioned benefits. Living in remote and/or poor communities is a serious commitment and needs as much forethought and preparation as possible. Access to food, telecommunications, outside news and the comforts of a hot bath or personal space may initially, and from home, seem like relatively minor inconveniences (much the same as going on holiday perhaps?), but after weeks then months may take on momentous proportions! Eating a bland repetitive diet that one is unaccustomed to can lead to serious health problems. Sleeping on unwashed bedding in tropical overnight temperatures within airless rooms (the windows shut for safety in squatter settlements) can lead to feelings of being perpetually filthy. Being disconnected from relatives and friends and from any news beyond the neighbour's latest movements may also be somewhat tedious

Being unable to find any space or time to read, reflect or plan might be seriously frustrating. Finally, living within one's research site may also involve continuous forms of reciprocity, in the form of financial contributions, and/or in forms such as baby sitting, going along on shopping errands, or even taking an active part in karaoke (against your best judgement perhaps). Again, while these are potentially satisfying and productive encounters, they do need to be factored into your every-day existence outside of just being a researcher. Even for the most ardent advocate of total immersion then one must be realistic, and find opportunities to get away, even if for only a few hours. For those in rural contexts this may prove to be particularly difficult.

Even living within a community will involve some degree of choice and preference. Doing research on subversive political activities while living with community political leaders would be an obvious problem, but there are less clear-cut variations of this. Likewise you may find yourself 'pigeon-holed' – female researchers may find themselves only with women, male researchers only with men, and so on. Despite your best intentions of living 'on site', unwittingly through your choice of accommodation, you may well find yourself to be an 'outsider' to a number of people in the community, such as those who are of a different class, caste or ethnic group from the people you are living with.

Choosing accommodation then is far from been a purely straightforward issue but involves resource and logistical pressures, and issues of personal or professional choice and commitment. While choosing to live within a community can bring enormous benefits, there are also potential problems and unintended repercussions that need to be considered (at least as much as can be forethought). Above all perhaps, be flexible and realistic. Your principal aim while in the field is to carry out your research aims to the best of your abilities so choose a place to stay which allows you to do this the most effectively, and accept limitations.

Where to go and when to go

Discussing where to go may at first appear rather superfluous, given that some research is highly specific with regards to topic and location, or is 'home' for many international students. Yet for most first-time thesis students why such a decision (i.e. the fieldwork site) is taken is often not so coherent. Are students driven by place or topic, and in how many cases are some research sites essential? It may be that many students are not conscious of the implications of certain choices they make regarding their intended destination and the timing of their work. Thinking through why you are going, where and when may seem like obvious points, though students still opt for remote or difficult locations for reasons which are unclear to them. In many cases 'easier' choices can be made for environments where students might not feel so isolated (they may have visited previously), have access to telecommunications, are working in contexts in which language is not a serious barrier and which they feel comfortable. This is not to make the case for fieldwork that precludes difficult or distant 'exotic' sites, but rather to encourage a coherent decision-making process linked to the requirements of research-based thesis work and minimising the risk of 'fieldwork failure'. This is less of a concern for doctoral researchers, due to greater resources of time, but some of these issues may still be relevant.

There are good reasons to choose certain places to go. Obviously, the primary concern should still be academic! But this still leaves considerable choice. There is much to be said for starting from a position of some strength, and such advantages of similar diet, language, educational systems and a location where your family or friends can more easily visit are not trite considerations. A Masters student based in Australasia may find the implications of ageing on developing countries as relevant in the Cook Islands as China. This is not to suggest at all that some places are in any way 'softer' than others. In many cases familiarity breeds complacency and culture shock can be just as great (see Chapter 7, 'Culture shock').

In some cases, where historical relations have brought countries together, much advantage can be generated through making contact with expatriate populations at home before you leave for fieldwork. Such contact may also help in post-fieldwork writing and in keeping in touch later. In a situation of only having 12–16 weeks for field research these choices may prove safer bets than traveling across the globe to be confronted with a whole host of challenges with very little support or reference points. Above all, due consideration to where you are going and why, may go a long way to offset some of the challenges you will inevitably face (see Chapter 6, 'Motivation and selection of research topic').

Once you have more clearly thought through where you are going and why, the final issue is when? Again, there will be constraints on choice. Family and friends, finances and feeling prepared enough to go are some likely factors. Some disciplines, departments or your supervisor may also have preferences or stipulations regarding when in the research process fieldwork should be conducted. These are some of the 'home' factors and they will vary with each individual situation. If there is any universal advice here is should be this: never go feeling unprepared (with the caveat that some claim never to be 'ready'!).

There are also several 'away' or destination factors you should consider. Obviously, these are context specific and you must do the necessary background reading on where you are going. Issues include climate (especially the impact of rainy seasons on rural research or periods of extreme heat, see Raybeck, 1996); religious or other national festivals (which may last weeks); Ramadan (see Box 5.3); and election time (and any foreseeable context for political conflict). Unless your research is particularly associated with such events, it may prove wise to avoid them.[5] Research is still possible during such periods however and, in the case of Masters research, you may have little flexibility with timing. It becomes important then to plan ahead, to develop effective research strategies, and integrate these into your methodologies.

Box 5.3: Doing research during Ramadan

Donna Loveridge, a Masters student studying urban governance in Dhaka, conducted fieldwork in Bangladesh during Ramadan in 2001. While time constraints meant this was unavoidable and provided challenges, fieldwork was still possible. In particular, it meant conducting interviews very early in the morning before people became tired, and eating discretely in her hotel room during the day. Most offices closed at 3 p.m. which meant that the latest possible interview time was 1 or 2 p.m. Because of traffic congestion (which worsened during Ramadan), it was rarely possible to conduct more than two interviews per day. While this provided obvious limitations, it also gave the researcher a greater appreciation of the difficulties of conducting business and government during the Muslim month of fasting than would have been the case had she avoided it.

Source: Loveridge (2001: 8)

Packing

Because development fieldwork takes place in many and varied Third World contexts, what you will need to take to the field will depend on the kind of environment you will be exposed to and the resources available in those environments. It may, therefore, be a waste of time to load your backpack or suitcase with toilet paper when toilet paper is readily available in most countries of the world. Other goods, however, are more difficult to come by and your possession of them may become the difference between a comfortable and successful fieldwork experience and one that is fraught with problems and difficulties. Like all preparations for development fieldwork then, packing for the field requires considerable thought and planning.

While the clothing that you will need to take will obviously depend on the specific social and cultural context in which you will be working (males and females should solicit advice on appropriate dress in their destination area and take this advice seriously),[6] several general suggestions apply. Clothing that is light and dries easily is preferable to items that may take hours to dry in damp/cold climates. While cotton is breathable and a good choice of fabric to wear close to the skin in tropical environments, there are many forms of clothing manufactured with light new synthetic fabrics (such as polartech and other microfibres) that are ideal for fieldwork. These can be purchased from any mountain equipment/camping type store and are well worth the investment.

Another essential item to pack and also well worth the investment is a good pair of waterproof sandals or boots. Wherever you plan to conduct your fieldwork you will most probably be doing a great deal of walking. It is therefore essential that you have comfortable and hardwearing footwear. Helen had purchased a pair of leather sandals (at great expense) for this specific purpose prior to her arrival in San Salvador but found that they were hopeless in the tropical storms that descended upon the city every afternoon. Not only were her feet constantly wet and uncomfortable from the damp leather, but they also developed a nasty fungal infection which took months to clear. Waterproof footwear made of synthetic products (such as gortex) is then more useful to pack in these instances.

Along with ensuring any medicinal items such as anti-malarial tablets will last the entire period of your fieldwork, in countries where malaria is endemic it is also important to pack additional malaria prevention equipment/clothing. A mosquito net and full strength Deet (N,N-diethylmetatoluamide) insect repellent are necessary preventative items as are items of clothing that can be worn out at night to completely cover your arms and legs (i.e. long sleeve tops and long pants). It may indeed be possible to purchase a mosquito net and other preventative items in the field, but there is no harm in packing extra supplies such as bottles of repellent. Often these items can be expensive to buy in the field and may not always be available. Finally, light coloured clothing is also preferable to dark clothing if you want to avoid mosquitoes.

As you will be seen as a researcher from an overseas or Western university, assumptions will be made in the field about your relative wealth/status whether you are a researcher returning home to do research or not. It is best, therefore, to avoid packing too many valuable items as these symbols of wealth (such as expensive wristwatches) may be stolen or at least act to place you in a more vulnerable position. Keeping a small change purse containing a small amount of money on your person is a good idea in many contexts as it can be easily given away if need be and appears less flashy and 'Western' than the money belts or 'bumbags' that you see travellers/tourists wear. It is important, however, to pack spares of other valuable items such as glasses or contact lenses so that you have extra on hand in the event of loss or breakage.

Although they may appear showy and may at times draw unwanted attention, it is important also to consider which kinds of research tools will be necessary for you to conduct successful fieldwork. You will need to decide whether to pack such electrical items as a laptop computer, a video camera or a dictaphone, and to consider which items and models may work best in your chosen fieldwork setting. Adams and Megaw are quite sceptical, for example, about the value of laptops in the field:

> It is curious that the wonders of microcomputers should have been accompanied by a waning of confidence in such highly quantified approaches, but it is so. Most research students find it difficult to imagine life in the field without a computer. In practice many find it useless (because of poor power supplies), a burden (for fear of theft), or an embarrassment (yet another impossible luxury stashed deep in that purple rucksack). Occasionally, of course, it can be invaluable, and can allow in-field data analysis that is important if the fieldwork programme is multi-stage and demands decisions halfway through. (1997:222)

The availability of electricity will obviously be an issue that will need to be assessed if you are planning to pack a laptop and if you are intent on using a video camera. Cultural ramifications will need to be ascertained. In some Mayan communities in Mexico and other parts of Central America, for example, taking photos or using a video camera is believed to steal the soul of the subject concerned and is thus forbidden. Additional factors such as the effect of tropical environments on electronics; fears of theft; and the relevance of technology to your research approach are all important considerations as you pack your bags.[7]

Finally, there are many miscellaneous items that you can pack that may not be essential to fieldwork but may, nevertheless, facilitate a more successful fieldwork experience. Hahn (1990:72), for example, found that family photos enabled her to make friends with the Tongan women working in her guesthouse when other friendship overtures had failed. Souvenirs and other gift items are similarly useful in making friends and providing reciprocity for information given and kindness bestowed (see Chapter 8, 'Reciprocity').

Above, we have simply outlined certain items that we feel would be invaluable for fieldwork. You may come up with others, especially if you consult a guidebook specific to your region of study, or decide that many of the items we have suggested are superfluous to your requirements. Again, and as in all cases with fieldwork planning, the choice is ultimately yours.

Conclusion

As you will have gathered from reading this chapter, planning for fieldwork is no simple exercise. There are many decisions to be made about such issues as when to go to the field, which funding organisations to target, and who to contact in regards to research permission and clearance. In this chapter we have attempted to make your decision making a little easier by outlining the options available and by drawing on our experiences and those of other researchers as to what has worked/not worked in the past and why.

The key points we have made on the practical issues associated with preparation for the field can be summarised by the following statements: begin preparing for fieldwork as early as possible (particularly in regards to obtaining funding); permission for research may need to be sought at several official and unofficial levels; fieldwork can be an unhealthy occupation which requires careful physical and psychological preparation (an issue which will be explored in depth in Chapter 6); do some homework on personal security in choosing field sites – and seek a wide range of opinions on this and; be flexible and realistic when it comes to thinking about where you will stay in the field and what you need to pack. Above all, this chapter has argued that preparing for the field is an integral part of fieldwork itself.

Development Fieldwork

Recommended readings

Howell, N. (1990) *Surviving Fieldwork: a report of the Advisory Panel on Health and Safety in Fieldwork* American Anthropological Association, Washington, DC.
This text provides a comprehensive overview of the dangers faced by fieldworkers.

Nash, D.J. (2000) Doing independent overseas fieldwork 1: practicalities and pitfalls. *Journal of Geography in Higher Education* 24 (1):139-49.

Robson, E. and Willis, K. with Elmhirst, R.E. (1997) Practical tips. In E. Robson and K. Willis (eds) *Postgraduate fieldwork in developing countries* Monograph No.9, Developing Areas Research Group (RGS-IBG), London.
Both the above provide good introductions to preparation for fieldwork.

Schroeder, D.G. (1993) *Staying Healthy in Asia, Africa and Latin America* Moon Publications, Chico, CA.
An excellent resource on health for those in the field.

Useful websites

Two introductory websites for planning and packing for Third World travel are:

www.ease.com/~randyj/rjfootls.htm

www.d2.dir.scd.yahoo.com/recreation/travel/travel_tips_and_tools/

Further resources

Lonely Planet Travel Guide Country Series

The Rough Guide Country Series

Notes

1. Note however, that university grants are typically subject to gaining ethical approval, an often-arduous process in itself (see Chapter 8).

2. An excellent online source of health information is the US Department of Health and Human Services 'Health Information for International Travel 2001-2002' www.cdc.gov/travel/yellowbook.pdf

3. In any case, you should inform your High Commission or Embassy of your intended research and the period you will spend in the country concerned.

4. Some may not even make it from the airport on arrival. Donna McSherry has been publishing an online report on airports around the world, including comfort ratings for sleeping at airports! As of August 2002 it had nearly 1600 listings (www.sleepinginair-ports.net/airports.htm).

5. This is not, however, a promotion of 'development tourism'. Chambers (1997) offers an excellent critique of the shortcomings of research which 'sticks to the tarmac', avoids rainy seasons, and stays within the comfort zone, etc. of researchers, thus avoiding the realities of life for many in the Third World.

6. In many cases it may be disrespectful for males to wear shorts to an interview with a government official and in some Pacific Island countries it is absolutely unacceptable for women to go swimming unless fully clothed.

7. In some cases though, for example in geological research, equipment may be essential. A good reference on issues arising from being 'equipment-dependent' is Endfield and O'Connor (1997).

6 Personal Issues

Henry Scheyvens and Barbara Nowak

Swarms of mosquitoes, a torrential downpour, the temperature and humidity uncomfortably high – it is the subtropics after all. Sitting on a wooden plank under a shelter, struggling to keep the pages dry and the ink flowing, all the while trying to write a coherent piece of work.

Introduction

Is this fieldwork in the Third World? Far from it! Actually, a friend and I (Henry) are presently sailing along the Queensland coast of Australia, camping on whatever beaches we find ourselves at as we go. I am writing for the book you are presently reading. However, there are similarities to my present predicament and those of my fieldwork experience in Bangladesh and the Philippines that was part of my recently completed doctoral research program. These similarities are worth teasing out as they make a good starting point for considering preparation for first time fieldwork in the Third World.

Six weeks ago I really knew nothing about sailing. Like the researcher undertaking fieldwork in the Third World for the first time, I was anxious. Like most postgraduate students I was on a very tight budget. And, ultimately, I knew at times that I would find myself in positions of physical and perhaps psychological hardship. The craft my friend and I had purchased to embark on our present adventure is only 14 feet in length and, at a cost of A$700, could not be described as a luxury vessel. To the contrary, it has no cabin and we are usually wet most of the day and totally exposed to the elements. Yet, despite our lack of experience and small finances we are slowly making our way up the Queensland coast. Recognising the general novelty of our approach, we have been befriended by some of the interesting characters who live in remote locations along the coastline.

Just as a small budget and an absence of experience have not posed insurmountable obstacles to the challenge we have set ourselves, they seldom impede the strongly motivated researcher from embarking on their first period of fieldwork.

Rather, what at first appears a reason for anxiety may well be an advantage to the researcher. A person undertaking fieldwork for the first time will lack experience but brings with them a fresh perspective. A small budget can also contribute to our learning. We may not be able to afford the air-conditioned rooms nor the continental menu of the best hotels. Instead, we may have to live with a local family, eat at roadside stalls and ride the crowded and cramped city buses. How could such things possibly contribute to our fieldwork experience? In the process of being carried back and forth with the ebb and flow of everyday living in a foreign environment, we gain a feeling for what life is like in our host country or community. Although at times it will be difficult for us, our understanding and appreciation of life in the Third World will surely be so much sharper than someone who is only comfortable in their hotel room away from the noise, bustle and attention. This is also true for Third World students conducting 'home-based' research in unfamiliar territory (Box 6.1).

Box 6.1 A peaceful sleep in the village

In October 2001, I returned to my home country of Nepal to conduct research for my PhD on gender issues associated with alternative energy programmes in rural areas. Although I was born in a remote rural village in Nepal, as an adult I had been based in Kathmandu and I had become used to the modern comforts of city life.

Nevertheless after being away from Nepal for two years in distant New Zealand, it was such a fresh feeling to travel the basic roads of my home country in an old public bus seeing the beautiful paddy and wheat fields, rivers, waterfalls, and the natural forest. Even the crowds of people and frequent checks of the bus by the army did not bother me. Walking uphill and down for two to four hours to get from the bus station to the villages was not as exhausting as it sounds because my research colleagues were fond of making jokes along the way.

I felt safe staying with a Tamang family in one village. It was a pleasure to sleep above the livestock shed where the grains were stored, and eat the local food every morning and evening. An old man in the family cherished us as his children without expecting us to treat him as a father in return: he is unforgettable. Also a treasure was the woman of the house who, burdened with many chores, was only free to talk to me in the evenings. While my research colleagues snored away in the background, she would often talk to me until late at night, sharing her feelings both personal and social.

Source: Ishara Mahat, PhD candidate, Massey University

Our main point in this introductory section is to help quell some of the anxieties that researchers might have about their first fieldwork experience in the Third World. Yes, you may face many constraints; yes, you may have no experience in the communities/countries where you will conduct fieldwork; and yes, you may have no idea of how others you require information or assistance from will respond. If we let our imaginations run loose, the fears we can dream up are endless. Walcott (1995:94) advises us to 'Rest easy'. Almost all researchers whose interests take them to the Third World return with invaluable experiences and more than sufficient data to complete their inquiries.

Venturing into the unknown brings unique experiences for each individual. Thinking in advance about the kinds of issues we might face, and how me might deal with these, helps us to develop response mechanisms to cope with difficulties. Issues that might be considered personal not only affect us. Through our behaviour and attitude they also affect those we interact with; hence, our planning must include the well being of others and not just ourselves. This chapter discusses the following personal issues that may be of concern to researchers prior to leaving for the field and once in their field environment: motivation and selection of research topic; the importance of creating a good impression; desirable personal traits; an open-mind and willingness to learn; the 'human element' in making judgements; preparing for discomfort and depression; and taking families or partners into the field.

Motivation and selection of research topic

Why are you intending to undertake research in the Third World? What do you hope to achieve? Why have you chosen the topic of your research? Postgraduate students and other researchers need to have very clear answers to these questions. During the course of your studies you will face many unforeseen hurdles. Are you sufficiently motivated to dedicate the time and energy required to complete your postgraduate qualifications or research inquiries?

Occasionally during the course of their research degrees some students will lament over why they chose a particular topic, or whether it has any value. Perhaps this is not surprising. Walcott (1995:134) complains that so much of postgraduate research is but the 'churning out of uninteresting and unimportant studies in fulfil-ment of a research "ritual"'. As mentioned in Chapter 2, whatever your motivation for enlisting in a particular research program, you should search for a research topic that excites you. The course of your research program may last for several years. During that period you can expect to face difficulties in conceptualisation, in remaining focused and in making sense of the literature. During fieldwork you will face many other challenges. If this is to last several months, or over a year, what topic will sustain you through the difficult times? It will help if it is a topic that you are passionate about.

You should also give serious consideration to the question of which is the best country/countries in which to undertake your proposed research. It is preferable that you select a country that you have a strong interest in. During fieldwork your interest in the country will be apparent to your informants and others, and they can be expected to respond positively to this. Moreover, if you are able to take time off from data gathering it can be invaluable to your learning to visit places of interest, attend local events or to merely experience the many manifestations of day-to-day life.

While undertaking fieldwork in Bangladesh, Henry took time off to attend a One-Day international cricket match. He enjoyed the competition and became familiar with a topic useful for starting conversations. Soon after, Bangladesh gained status as a 'test playing' nation. By following the national side, he was showing interest in something outside the poverty and natural calamities that more commonly draw the attention of the international media. He was taking interest in something that Bangladeshis might be proud of, not ashamed of. But this type of interest must be genuine. Tokenism of any sort is easily seen through.

Creating a good impression

Creating a good impression is indispensable to the successful completion of many research programs. Permission will be needed for most research (see Chapter 5) and, in any case, more information is likely to be provided if good relations are established from the outset. So, how can we create a good impression? Firstly, you should be able to show that you are knowledgeable about issues in the country/localities you are studying. Those you are seeking information or assistance from are more likely to be favourably disposed towards your requests if you can show you are well-informed. Prior to commencing fieldwork most people engage in a lengthy review of the literature on their subject area. This should stand you in good stead, but you should include in your reading literature on a broad range of issues including customs, social structure and political economy of your host country. Information on recent events can also be garnered from on-line newspapers.

Secondly, you must be able to impress upon others that your research questions are worthy of investigation. Are they? There are topics that have little value, either academic or practical. Others may have academic merit, but are hard to justify in the eyes of development professionals in the country concerned (see Box 6.2), or those living in the communities you are studying. Reading research reports from the country you intend conducting fieldwork in should help you gain an appreciation of what topics might be relevant to the lives of the people you will be working with.

> **Box 6.2 Assessing the merit of research topics**
>
> A researcher wished to examine a housing loan scheme for poor villagers in Bangladesh. The particular interest of the researcher was how space in the newly constructed houses is used. The Bangladeshi manager of the implementing institution, with about 20 years of village-level development experience behind her, could not see the relevance of this topic to the livelihood of poor households whose members have so few possessions

that space allocation is not a critical issue for them. Issues such as the social and economic benefits of the new houses, and whether borrowers were able to meet the repayment obligations of their housing loans, seemed more important to the manager.

Researchers should realise that they may have to justify topics – however carefully planned in their far away institutions – to a range of different stakeholders in the country concerned, and that there may be merit in embracing both academic and practical issues in their topics. Consulting widely with local people can lead to many useful suggestions.

If you consider your topic as having practical value, you need to be able to explain this value in a succinct fashion. If your topic has mainly academic value, then it may be harder, though not impossible, to convince 'practically-minded' institutions of its merits. For example, Henry's doctoral research included a case study of Shapla Neer, a Japanese NGO operating in Bangladesh. The study had a strong practical dimension as Henry focused on the impact of Shapla Neer's development programs and sought to make recommendations for how these might be improved. Nevertheless, staff of Shapla Neer would have most likely supported the study if its objective was solely to gain a better understanding of Japanese NGOs. Such a study could be promoted on the basis that outside Japan very little literature exists on Japanese NGOs, yet their number is rapidly expanding and their relationship with the state is undergoing important changes.

Thirdly, you should be able to present yourself as a professional. Making an effort to be knowledgeable is central to having a professional approach. Dress and manner are also indispensable to creating a professional image. Before travelling abroad you should educate yourself on the subject of appropriate behaviour, dress and cultural norms of the country you are visiting. Travel guidebooks may provide useful guidelines and speaking with nationals or expatriates will help. In Third World countries even poor people generally attempt to take pride in their appearance. While it may be appropriate for students at Western universities to dress casually on their home campuses, you should consider dressing neatly when approaching outside institutions. There is a personal dimension to this issue because we may have to surrender much-cherished images we attempt to create through our choice of clothing. It is doubtful, for example, that we would be received favourably if we arrived at a country office of the World Bank dressed in 'gothic' or 'grunge' style.

Mannerisms are similarly important. Polite behaviour is something we should have already cultivated, but it is also important that we are able to show we can listen carefully. We won't create a good impression if someone must provide us with the same information more than once, or, if in our hurry or excitement, we misinterpret what they say. We can arrive at interviews or first meetings so full of energy and ideas, or with a set agenda in mind, that we cannot respond to circumstances as they develop. In some instances it may be appropriate to engage in small talk before turning to our research needs; in other instances, for example, when meeting an overworked official, we may have to dispense with the preliminary niceties of conversation. Creating a good impression requires a flexible approach to first meetings and the willingness to adjust according to the needs of others.

Our academic training can encourage us to argue or contest what others say. In order to create a good first impression, however, we may have to practice patience and discretion. Without being dishonest, it may be judicious to initially play down some of our concerns and wait for a later opportunity before raising them. Alternatively, we may be able to present our concerns in a constructive, non-threatening fashion. Overall, having the patience to develop good rapport with communities and institutions, and to build their trust in us during initial meetings, will serve our fieldwork interests well. This is a topic discussed further in Chapter 7.

Desirable personal traits

Certain personal traits make good fieldwork possible. They will enhance the fieldwork experience for our informants and us, and could even improve the quality of our data. The issue of our personality is seldom a topic of discussion in university courses: we study others rather than ourselves. While desirable personal traits cannot be taught, perhaps those who are willing can make the effort to cultivate them. Walcott (1995:87) observes that the 'human relations aspect of fieldwork is enhanced for those to whom such qualities as empathy, sympathy, or at least everyday courtesy and patience come naturally'. 'Empathy', 'sympathy', 'courtesy' and 'patience'; all these terms describe being considerate of others. Showing consideration is aided by efforts to understand the worldviews of others and the experiences these are based on. Weaver (1998) instructs travellers to the Third World to 'travel in a spirit of humility and with a genuine desire to learn more about the people of your host country. Be sensitively aware of the feelings of other people, thus preventing what might be offensive behavior on your part'.

Researchers should be tolerant. The values and views of those we study may be very different to our own and may be an ongoing source of frustration, and even anger. You might be troubled by the seclusion of women or what appears a relaxed attitude to solid waste disposal. You should consider that for locals your views or behaviour might be equally perplexing. Your informants may wonder how your partner or husband could allow you to travel abroad alone, or why you don't have any children. Another potential source of frustration is that public services may be far less than what you are used to. Expect to practice tolerance and patience if you are dealing with bureaucracy. It may be common practice, for example, to give extra money to post office workers to have your parcels sent. We may see this as bribery; locals may view this in the same way Americans view tipping – money provided for service rendered. Remember also that people of our host countries have to live all their lives with what for us are only very short-term frustrations. If they can be tolerant, so can we.

During periods of frustration tact will serve the researcher well. Tact lubricates the process of conducting fieldwork. It is important to take care with issues such as when to speak out, when to hold one's tongue and how to phrase what you wish to say. When you can do nothing about those things that frustrate you, finding something funny about your experiences or observations may make life more bear-

---

Box 6.3 Humour on a Dhaka bus

A passenger told the following self-depreciating yet humorous story to Henry as they shared a seat on an overcrowded Dhaka bus:

'Bangladesh is a poor country as you know. But, we cannot move forward. You see, us Bangladeshis we simply love to break the law. If the light is red, we go. Can you believe it! If the light is green, we stop. What kind of thinking is that! When we approach a round-about, do we all go the same way? No. We each try and take the shortest route. No wonder our country can make no progress!

Now I live in London where I deliver pizzas for Pizza Hut. But, my wife gets very angry with me. Each week I come home with a 30 pound fine. I am delivering a pizza. I come to a red light. What do I do? I am a Bangladeshi. When I get home my wife says "You stupid man!"'

Source: Henry Scheyvens, doctoral research in Bangladesh, 1998-1999

---

able (Box 6.3).

Researchers also need to be determined. Our frustrations may be many. Our research may fall far behind schedule, the mosquitoes may seem to be our personal tormentors, we may suffer illness, and we may have much less privacy than what we are used to. It is not enough to be excited by our research: to see it through, we must be determined. Determination is also needed to overcome periods of self-doubt. We may at times lose faith in ourselves, in our methodology, in the value of our fieldwork and in our competency (see Box 6.4). As Walcott (1995:94) writes: 'Self-doubt must be held in check so that you can go about your business of conducting research, even when you may not always be sure what that entails'. Being determined must be counterbalanced with a preparedness to pull out of fieldwork that is not worth persisting with, or if personal troubles are too great to cope with.

Box 6.4 An overriding feeling of bothering people

When I was in the field I would intermittently feel depressed or lonely. These feelings would get mixed with feelings of incompetence. Why was I there? What was I doing? Why in the world would these people want to talk with me, someone who constantly bothered them asking them dumb questions? I would think to myself: 'Here I am, a rich American woman,

---

hassling very poor people who work very hard to try to ensure their families' health and well-being. People who go off to work at 6 in the morning and sometimes earlier, and come home late in the afternoon, don't want to be bothered by someone asking them dumb questions! All these people want to do is relax and be left alone. The last thing they wanted was to see me coming to bother them!'

When I felt like this I learned to relax and not stress myself. I would stay close to my house and read. I read voraciously when in the field. All the classics I should have read at university! After a few days of time out, I would start to regain my confidence and would slowly return to visiting with people, just talking; I would ask questions later – and I did.

Source: Barbara Nowak, doctoral research in Malaysia, 1980-1982

Researchers need to be emotionally prepared for rejection. A few villagers refused to answer Lockwood's surveys, some arguing that they were pointless (Lockwood, 1992:171). Hoddinott (1992:77) found that one household head advised other villagers to have nothing to do with his survey. Unbeknown to the student preparing enthusiastically for research in a foreign setting, their intended fieldwork site may be 'over-researched' from the perspective of locals, with competition for community consultation time coming from consultants and government officials as well as other research students (Box 6.5). Negative responses may do little for your self-esteem, especially if you already have doubts about the merits of your research.

Box 6.5 The problem of over-researched projects or communities

So many consultants, not enough action, say Niueans

'Niueans say they are being "over consulted". Researchers working on the Niue 'Sustainable Living Community' project report that people are overloaded by the many consultants that call for meeting after meeting. The researchers say the common complaint from the local people is that they are tired of review after review where not much happens after recommendations are submitted.

Most of the year a steady stream of consultants pass through the big raised coral atoll with a small population (1,700). They come from government, regional and international agencies delving into every imaginable aspect of life on the island'.

Source: Niue Economic Review/PINA Nius Online 21 April, 2002

An open mind and willingness to learn

Good research requires an open mind. This does not mean you cannot hold strong opinions about your subject matter. Rather, a willingness to learn depends upon preparedness to surrender long held views and beliefs, or to expect the unexpected. Lewis (1991:57), recalling his fieldwork in Bangladesh for his doctoral research, wrote that 'no one ever answered my questions the way I expected them to, but, if they had there would have been little point in asking them'. For Walcott a willingness to learn is being receptive to new information: 'A fieldworker must rely on his or her ability to surrender to what the field observations actually reveal rather than prematurely to superimpose structure on them' (Walcott, 1995:191).

Having an open mind is likewise important when reflecting on the people and their culture that we are in contact with during the course of fieldwork. Two dangers present themselves: we may idolise a foreign people and their culture or, conversely, we may consider them in some way inferior. This applies both to foreign researchers and those conducting home-based research in an unfamiliar setting, for example, a Javanese person who goes to explore land tenure in Kalimantan.

We might romanticise about a foreign culture for a number of reasons. Firstly, our prior reading may have posited indigenous peoples as 'environmental saviours' of tropical rainforests, or we may have been motivated by activist literature on the plight of oppressed minorities. Secondly, when in a foreign environment we may, and most probably will, stand out. Caucasian students/researchers especially may be complimented and even fawned upon by those seeking to curry favour with them. In some countries there may be a certain status associated with having a Western 'friend'. We do not receive such adulation in our home countries and may feel that in this foreign setting we are in some way special. On return to our home countries we become again but 'one of the crowd' and may miss the attention we had during our fieldwork. If we are affected in this manner, in our seminars and writings we are likely to have only good things to say about the country we visited: our judgement has become clouded by the special treatment we received.

Conversely, our observations can be distorted if we are poorly disposed to the foreign environment in which we conduct fieldwork. We may consider our own cultural beliefs and practices as superior. We find a custom we dislike, and, failing to consider it as part of another worldview, we label it inferior, or worse, uncivilised. Some Western researchers may see the sense in why people of another country prefer to wash themselves with water after using the toilet, rather than use pieces of tissue. Others may not be so open-minded. Unwittingly, reactions to local customs, which at first sight may appear far removed from our formal data gathering activities, could begin to affect our analysis.

Our best protection from these dangers is to regularly reflect on what we observe and experience, to monitor our emotional responses and to examine whether these are warranted or not. Keeping a field diary, a personal account of experiences and emotions, should assist with this reflection process (see Chapter 7). We should be prudent in examining practices in their cultural contexts before rushing to remonstrate with others.

The 'human element' in making judgements

In some types of research judgements must be made as to whether something is good, bad or somewhere in-between. Judgements in the social sciences are never value free. It is now quite common for researchers involved in cross-cultural studies to describe their subjectivity; more so in ethnographic research than in survey-based studies. Even the most apparently 'scientific' of paradigms are based on one worldview or another (Hoksbergen, 1986:285; see also Chapter 2).

In research that involves evaluation, the researcher should firstly identify and make explicit the values behind the judgements that are being made. These values are reflected in our political positions as well as our theoretical frameworks. A humanist, for example, might evaluate a development intervention using a basic needs framework that reflects her/his concern for poverty. A feminist, on the other hand, might evaluate the intervention using an empowerment framework that highlights the power dimension of intra-household gender relations. Neither should forget that their judgements will be based on certain values and worldviews. If your research is motivated by a concern for poverty, the position of women, the repression of minority groups or other social injustices in the Third World, then don't be afraid to state so in your written work.

There are other aspects of our humanness that must be recognised in evaluation-based research. Chambers (1983) has pointed out that in Western universities we seem to be praised more for criticism than for writing about success. Our Western education may also leave us feeling that that nothing but a perfect solution to a particular problem will do. We study one development approach/theory after another expecting to find something that is foolproof. The combined result of these two phenomena is that researchers involved in evaluation may tend to highlight shortcomings and fail to recognise the achievements of the projects, programs or policies that they are investigating, and the obstacles that have been overcome in reaching these achievements. See Box 6.6 for an example of different ways in which micro-credit programmes in Bangladesh have been viewed.

As outside researchers we are generally in the 'field' for a relatively short period of time. The commitment of the institutions and individuals we study may span decades. We return to our world of relative luxury to write our reports or dissertations: these institutions and individuals (assuming they are well-meaning) continue to struggle to improve standards of living or for whatever cause they promote. Separated by large distances from them, it becomes easy for us to criticise. We need only be accountable to our peers who may have little understanding of the institutions, programs and countries we are researching.

On the other side of the coin, we must be equally wary of glorifying the institutions and individuals we study. If they provide us with a degree of insulation from the difficulties of living in the Third World, we could unwittingly view them through rose-tinted lenses. The local NGO, government agency or research body might provide us with an air-conditioned office, computer facilities, comfortable transportation, lodgings and entertainment, or bias could arise because of the positive relationships we develop with staff who share with us similar interests, language and educational backgrounds. Regular reflection on the nature of our relationships with individuals and institutions we are in contact with during the course of fieldwork is necessary in order that these relationships do not bias our research findings.

Box 6.6 Micro-credit in Bangladesh: success or failure?

In Bangladesh a debate has been raging for some time regarding the control of micro-credit by women. One institution Henry examined has a policy of preferring to extend small loans to women. A number of studies have shown that in some instances women hand the loans they receive over to their male relatives. How should this be viewed? Some commentators highlight this as a shortcoming of the micro-credit program and their reports are generally very unfavourable (Rahman, 1999; Teare, 1996). Others argue that, because Bangladesh is a country in which women have traditionally had no access to credit, even if only half of the women borrowers retain control over loan use then this is a considerable achievement (Todd, 1996).

In the debate on women's control over loans some are seeing the glass as half full, others as half empty. If our Western education encourages criticism, and if the field of Development Studies encourages us to seek perfect solutions, then we may be more likely to see the glass as half empty. But, is this fair? Perhaps we need to temper our idealism with a greater appreciation of the social reality and extremely difficult circumstances in which development organisations sometimes operate.

Preparing for discomfort and depression

Walsh (1995:5) describes research as an 'act of creation'. 'Like so many creators before you', he continues, 'you will feel isolated and lonely; you will doubt your ability and the worth of your work; and you will experience discouragement and even depression'. During the course of fieldwork you can expect at times to feel homesick, to miss the company of your friends and family, and to miss the pastimes you would normally enjoy. Yet another source of 'fieldwork blues', as these moments of depression are sometimes referred to, is stress: the stress of introducing yourself to strangers and strange organisations, the stress of forever being careful with how you behave and what you say so as not to offend, and stress resulting from culture shock (see Chapter 7 for a detailed discussion of culture shock).

It would seem normal to want to avoid hardship or discomfort during fieldwork. However, often those experiences that are the most difficult for us provide important opportunities for learning. We should take advantage of opportunities to learn that fall outside our structured data gathering activities, even when these involve a degree of discomfort (see Box 6.7).

> **Box 6.7 Living in the 'old city'**
>
> *During my six months of fieldwork in Bangladesh I purposefully chose to live in the old part of Dhaka, the capital. The relatively low cost of accommodation certainly suited my budget, but life was a lot harder than what it would have been had I chosen to stay in one of the more modern suburbs. Outside the very down-market Hotel Sugandha where I stayed was the busy Nawabpur Road. Often jammed tight with rickshaws, human-drawn carts and foot traffic, and with open sewers on either side, it was more than challenging to walk along. During the hartals, or nation-wide strikes, it was a scene of running conflict between supporters of the then main opposition party, the BNP, and the incumbent regime, the Awami League. Small home-made bombs would be thrown, the occasional gunshot could be heard, rickshaw wallahs attempting to ply their trade would be beaten and their rickshaws set alight. At times it was not a comfortable place to be, but it was educational. No reading of literature could ever provide the same sense of feeling for how politics is expressed at street level.*
>
> *Source: Henry Scheyvens, doctoral research in Bangladesh, 1998-1999*

Some will rightly argue that it is not necessary to place oneself in uncomfortable situations to understand them. Certainly, you do not have to ride the public buses in Dhaka to be aware of their overcrowding, nor the seriousness of the city's air pollution. But for someone investigating poverty, as Henry was, perhaps this kind of exposure gave him a deeper appreciation for the human struggle that is taking place in this overpopulated, under-serviced city. However, we should not associate the discomfort we might sometimes endure during our research with some kind of glory. There are some researchers who, on return from their fieldwork, seem to enjoy providing painfully long descriptions of nothing but the frustrations they experienced. Goward (1984:94) suggests that some researchers attempt to play up their hardships 'as if the feel they need to impress upon themselves and the reader that what they were doing was legitimate work and not just a glorified vacation abroad'.

To collect information, especially to undertake interviews, requires considerable energy. It would not do to place ourselves in so many trying situations that we end up jaded to the point that our data gathering was adversely affected. It is thus worth considering in advance how you might re-energise yourself during periods of research if this becomes necessary: in most cases it probably will. The possibilities are many and will depend upon your individual needs. A periodic visit to the capital city might provide those working in remote localities with a break from their informants, a change in diet and access to modern facilities. Occasionally 'treating' oneself to a movie or finding a place that makes good coffee, may be enough to re-energise others. Those involved in long periods of research may wish to return home for a short while or have their loved ones visit them. Planning for re-energising activities can and should take place prior to departure for fieldwork (see also Chapter 5).

Families and partners in the field

The above discussion assumes that researchers are undertaking fieldwork as individuals, but this is not always the case. We now turn to the subject of researchers who are in close relationships and/or who are raising families.[1] Deciding whether to take one's partner and/or children into the field is not always an easy task but it helps that this issue has been debated more openly in the literature since the mid 1980s (Butler and Turner, 1987; Cassell, 1987a; Flinn et al., 1998). There are advantages of having one's family present during fieldwork, but there are also drawbacks. The logistics of organising for a large group make taking families difficult. Problems involve financing the travels of family members, possible loss of income for the partner of the researcher, consideration of health and safety and comfort needs of all family members especially the children, children's education and general household maintenance.

The length of fieldwork might be a factor in determining whether or not the researcher's family joins him/her. For relatively long periods of fieldwork the researcher's partner may have to resign from their employment. When a family accompanies a researcher, more often than not they will need to find accommodation separate from other households. This can potentially interfere with data collection for those involved in participant-observation who would otherwise have lived with a local family. One possible solution may be for the partner or family to join the researcher near the field site for a brief holiday in the middle or at the end of their fieldwork. This way, the family can see the environment the researcher worked in thus gaining an appreciation of their loved one's experiences.

While some of the complications of having family present can be difficult to resolve, there are also some real benefits of having family members accompany researchers into the field. Although having family present means that researchers must dedicate time to them, the family can enable researchers to be more productive by eliminating 'down time' associated with loneliness. The presence of family members might also provide an entrée into parts of the community that might otherwise have been off limits to the researcher.

Below, separate sections are devoted to discussing the merits of bringing partners to the field and children to the field.

Partners in the field

Whether a partner should accompany the researcher into the field is a question that needs to be treated very carefully. There will be drawbacks and advantages for both the research and non-research partner regardless of what decision is made. Whether one's partner is male or female you should discuss with them what their role will be during the period of fieldwork. They may be able to assist you with everyday living, with your research and also emotionally. However, they too must be prepared for the difficulties of living in a very different setting to that which they are accustomed. Undertaking tasks such as laundry, cooking and shopping are often more time consuming in the field yet critical for maintenance of good health. Tasks which modern appliances make easy can take on several orders of difficulty when a partner has to adopt new skills to complete them. Doing laundry, for example, may entail hauling water or carrying the laundry to the water source and then hand washing with a bar of soap. Such tasks are repetitive, time-consuming and require a lot of energy. Is your partner prepared to take on these responsibilities?

Other activities partners might become involved in include acting as a research assistant by typing field notes, cataloguing photographs or scientific samples such as soil or cultural artefacts, and maintaining research equipment such as cameras, generators or computers. Partners can also become a second set of ears to hear things that the researcher might not understand or is restricted from hearing. They might find themselves talking with local villagers and doing supplemental research. For example, in a Muslim country a wife might assist her husband by talking with local village women who would be off-limits to a male.

The emotional support a partner provides can also be very important. Fieldwork can be a very isolating experience, especially if the researcher is unfamiliar with the vernacular. A partner is someone you can talk to about what it is you think you heard or understood. S/he is someone to converse with about the frustrations of the day.

While having a partner present can certainly be rewarding, the researcher must be prepared to spend time and energy meeting the needs of their partner. The partner may not be so enthralled by the researcher's fieldwork and they may find life in a strange setting very trying. The researcher must be willing to 'put down their notepad' in order to spend time with their partner – something that should be considered in the planning stage of fieldwork.

The question of whether to take one's partner is further complicated for homosexual researchers. Disclosure of one's homosexuality is more likely if the partner accompanies the researcher into the field. In a community that is not accepting of homosexuality, being open about one's sexual orientation could threaten the research program. Nevertheless, a researcher is asking the community to be open and honest about their lives, thus ethically shouldn't the researcher do the same? Blackwood (1995) pondered this issue during her stay in Sumatra. Her solution was to tell community members she was engaged to be married and that her fiancé was back home, without disclosing her homosexuality. However, Blackwood found playing the 'deceptive' role of a heterosexual woman a strain.

> Everyday I played the nice, polite, naïve, heterosexual American woman and was thereby unable to share with anyone the part of my life that was about my lesbian identity and family … the denial of a significant part of my life was a tremendous blow to my self-esteem. (1995:59)

In hindsight, Blackwood concluded that her deception 'established my superiority over the people in the village because it implied they should not, or did not need to, know such things about "their" anthropologist' (1995:57). Nevertheless,

Blackwood mentions she still is not sure she would choose to openly go into a field situation as a gay person (1995:73, footnote 3). After a lengthy period in the field, Blackwood (1995) did confide in her 'field mother', describing her field mother's response as guarded acceptance that came with the warning not to divulge her homosexuality to other villagers.

Gay and lesbian researchers need to consider whether they can temporarily deny their 'self' and live with a false identity as a straight researcher. If they do not believe they can, finding a research project or a research location which will be accepting or provide concealment could be a solution. If a homosexual researcher wishes to hide the identity of his/her partner, establishing a household outside the community might be a solution. Choosing a location where there is a degree of anonymity such as some urban locations is possibly one option.

Regardless of sexual orientation, field research can place a relationship under stress. To the question of whether or not fieldwork put stress on their marriage one anthropologist replied, 'Only until we got a divorce' (Howell, 1990: 168). The non-research partner might feel 'left out' by both their partner who is focused on research and by the local community who might not be welcoming. The partner is now in a foreign place with possibly few modern day conveniences and little knowledge of what is expected. Yet, it is taken for granted that they will remain in full control of their emotions as well as provide for their partner's emotional and physical needs. The rewards for the researcher may be in the form of financial assistance and a furthering of their career interests. Their non-research partner may wonder at times what is in it for them.

While trouble may be brewing for couples who go into the field together, trouble may also lie in wait for those who decide that the non-research partner should remain at home. There are always difficulties in separation. Stress might develop for the partner who remains at home if they are left to do all the parenting and home keeping, especially if their career is placed on hold in order for them to take on these roles. Whereas upon returning home the researcher might feel the need to talk about their field experiences, their partner might feel the researcher should think more about home life. The close bond between couples is often temporarily disrupted due to long periods of fieldwork, and despite their enthusiasm for being reunited, on their return they may have to allow each other time to re-adjust to being part of a relationship.

Children in the field

Deciding whether or not to take children into the field is another difficult decision to make. No one wants to be separated from their children for an extended period of time, but no one wants to place their children in a vulnerable, even life threatening situation. When making the decision as to whether she and her children would accompany their anthropologist husband/father on a two-year field trip, Patricia Hitchcock felt that:

> We all had very real needs that could be met only if we stayed together. The children needed a father. Two years apart would bring John home a stranger; none of us would be able to understand what he had been through or what he was thinking or writing about. To me, this would not be a marriage. (1987:175)

Most researchers who have written about taking children remark that they believe it humanises them to the community (Cassell, 1987a; Flinn et al., 1998; Howell, 1990). With children present the researcher is seen as someone similar to others in their research area, with families and family obligations. For a woman, in particular, going into a fieldwork situation and leaving her family at home is something incomprehensible to people from many cultures. It makes the researcher look quite strange. A researcher accompanied by family implies the researcher recognises the importance of family and maintains their ties and responsibilities (Cassell, 1987b:259).

Nevertheless, having children present poses serious challenges that should not be treated lightly. While infrequent, there are cases when children of researchers in the field have died (see for example, Hitchcock, 1987 who writes about the death of her son in Nepal). Anyone contemplating taking children in the field must include consideration of their health and sanitation (Lanigan and Wheeler, 2002). Time is another critical issue. Children, by their very nature, are demanding of attention. They have needs that parents must fulfil and this may include home schooling if they are in the field with you over an extended period of time. Having families in the field will also typically mean that you need to prepare nutritious, substantial meals. It is much easier for a fieldworker when on their own to find a local household willing to provide a place at their 'table'. Having a family in the field usually means time must be spent on domestic chores including shopping, cooking and cleaning. The exception is societies in which hiring domestic help is the norm for many people. Thus, for example, Cupples (2002) found that it was much easier to get assistance with childcare for her two children during fieldwork in Nicaragua than when at home in New Zealand.

Prior knowledge of the field situation will aid in considering whether to bring your children with you. Speaking with other researchers who have been in the region or local residents can help in your deliberations. Bringing children into a situation that is not only physically but also emotionally challenging will be stressful to all. Hugh-Jones (1987:29) suggests that it might be best for the field researcher to go ahead and set up the field site before bringing their children over. Established friendships between researcher and some community members may well help in the children's transition (Hugh-Jones, 1987). However, for single parents, who are more likely than not women, there may be no choice but to either take their children with them or simply not do fieldwork.

You must not only consider how having children present might impact on your research but also how the overseas experience might impact on them. Although researchers might be reluctant to take children with them, especially if they are very young, the experience can be very positive for the children

(Whiteford and Whiteford, 1987:118). Barbara found that, despite a number of challenges, her son grew from his experiences in the field (Box 6.8). He now often speaks about the time in Malaysia and expresses a desire to return to visit his friends. He regularly asks when the family are going back. He tells his friends or anyone willing to listen the stories of the macaques that chased him, the crabs that bit him and the snails he helped collect and cook. His experiences have sparked an interest in geography and in other cultures. He wants to travel to other places and learn about other people.

Box 6.8 The pros and cons of having my son present during fieldwork in Malaysia

It is my belief that having my son David in the field with me gave Btsisi' villagers new insight into who I was. I had lived in the village previously for 18 months as a single woman. I returned for a visit years later as a woman about to marry and then again with a husband and two year old son, and again in 1998 when he was seven. I must have taken on a new dimension to them. Previously it had been just me; I was some very strange woman who was quite old to be unmarried by their standards. Returning later with a family, or part of one, gave me a bit more humanity.

When David joined me for the short visit in 1998, I had adopted family and friends thus David was automatically integrated into the community kin network. He had a grandfather, aunts and uncles, and lots of siblings (cousins) to play with and watch out for him. People were loving, accepting and tolerant of him. He has light red hair and grey eyes; something quite unique to the villagers. He made friends very quickly with young children of my adopted family. They played all the time, but could not understand each other's speech. Regardless, they chattered away as if language was no barrier. The villagers laughingly would say 'the children are like ducks and chicken: one speaks chicken, the other duck '.

I purposely chose not to actually stay overnight in the village with David in 1998, however, as the village had no running water, nor any sanitation facilities. My adopted sister lived only a few minutes from the village in a large commercial plantation housing settlement. This housing had a reasonably secure water supply, thus the water was of an acceptable quality, and there were sufficient amounts for bathing. As it wasn't very far from the village and many villagers came near the house to buy their daily supplies, I thought this was an excellent compromise.

David was dependent upon me for many things he would not normally be dependent on me for. Being unaccustomed to bathing the local way, he needed me to assist him. He also found that he even needed help in the toilet being unaccustomed to pit latrines and the many bugs, particularly fire ants, inhabiting the walls of the toilet. He was somewhat insecure. Oftentimes he clung to me which was very unlike local children. It was annoying and became disruptive to my work. I would get upset with him and tell him so. It was a part of me I didn't like the Btsisi' people seeing.

> *In 2002, I went again to visit Btsisi'. This time, my whole family went with me. My husband who is an anthropologist and who previously lived in Malaysia was able to speak with Btsisi'. David felt as if we had gone home. He had developed a friendship with my 'younger brother' and his wife and family in 1998. He remembered them with fondness and fell right back into their warm embrace. My daughter who was six, felt shy and was clingy, not letting me go for the first 24 hours. But the same couple who so enamoured David also made Lena feel comfortable and in no time she was going off with them and fully enjoying the attention they lavished on her.*
>
> *But research was not easy with my children. They were sometimes bored and wanted to go to the sea to swim. When people wanted to talk with us, I couldn't say, 'Excuse me, not now, my children want to go to the beach.' That would be impolite and something Btsisi' could not understand since their children remain quiet and in the background when around adults.*
>
> *As a consequence of taking my family into the field the work I wanted to accomplish was not as successful as I would have liked but my children gained enormously from the experience. They saw how privileged they are; that there are people in this world with so very little in terms of material possessions. My children are better for the experiences and it is something they will always remember with great fondness.*
>
> *Source: Barbara Nowak, post-doctorate research in Malaysia 1998, 2002*

Conclusion

Fieldwork is an adventure. Like any adventure, before we begin we will have many anxieties. We cannot foresee all the challenges we will face, nor the outcome of our endeavours – the best we can do is to prepare for the adventure as thoroughly as conceivably possible. Our preparation must include consideration for a wide array of personal issues and should start with the selection of a topic that we are passionate about. Passion is needed because in the field we can expect to confront physical difficulties, frustrations and doubt. If we are not truly excited by our research, it may be impossible to see it through these testing moments. We will also have to convince those we seek assistance from of the merits of our research program. Creating a good impression will likewise be aided by efforts to build rapport, a broad knowledge of our host country/countries, and a genuine interest in the people we meet. Even if at times we doubt our capabilities, we must view and present ourselves as professionals.

A variety of desirable personal traits that make good fieldwork possible have been raised and should be pondered before departing for fieldwork. We have discussed the importance of having an open mind and continually reflecting upon our reactions to local customs and the people we meet. Finally, we have considered the pros and cons of taking families and partners into the field. By thinking in advance about these personal issues we can make the research experience more rewarding for our participants, our friends and family and ourselves.

Recommended reading

Francis, E. (1992) Qualitative research: collecting life histories. In S.Devereux and J. Hoddinott (eds) *Fieldwork in Developing Countries* Lynne Rienner, Boulder, Colorado. pp. 86-101.

Razavi, S. (1992) Fieldwork in a familiar setting: the role of politics at the national, community and household levels. In S.Devereux and J. Hoddinott (eds) *Fieldwork in Developing Countries* Lynne Rienner, Boulder, Colorado. pp. 152-63.
Chapters 6 and 10 of Devereux and Hoddinott's volume provide interesting reflections on personal issues faced by both a Western researcher and a student returning to her home country to conduct fieldwork.

Flinn, J., Marshall, L. and Armstrong J. (eds) (1998) *Fieldwork and Families: Constructing New Models for Ethnographic Research* University of Hawaii Press, Honolulu.
An edited text with a range of good examples of the benefits but also potential difficulties of bringing families to the field.

Walcott, H.F. (1995) *The Art of Fieldwork* AltaMira Press, Walnut Creek.
Walcott offers a self-critical assessment of his three decades of anthropological fieldwork providing encouragement and much material for contemplation for researchers of the Third World.

Note

1. Note that this section discussed the researcher's existing close relationships – those established before fieldwork commences. Chapter 8 has a section on 'Sex and sexuality' which is devoted more to the possibility of intimate relationships between researchers and local people.

PART III

IN THE FIELD

7 Entering the Field

Helen Leslie and Donovan Storey

Fieldwork involves an examination of one's intellectual abilities and emotional control. To some extent experience can be an advantage in coping with the demands of research as 'fieldwork is a cumulative and synthetic affair in which the best work of any scholar builds on past experiences, good organization and careful preparation' (Veeck, 2001: 34-5). The difficulty is that, for many, this is their first taste of research, or even their first overseas experience (OE). While preparation can help, you will still have to confront your initiation into the field largely alone. On the one hand, you may be full of excitement and anticipation at the prospect of finally doing the research that you have been meticulously visualising and planning for months or even years. Or, you may be paralysed with the kind of fear, self-doubt and uncertainty that is commonplace for, particularly, first-time researchers. Feelings of going mad, panic in the field and constant high anxiety (which may even lead some to abandon or avoid fieldwork entirely), are all normal predicaments faced by most researchers (Clarke, 1975).

For those researchers who will be conducting fieldwork across gender, ethnic, class and national divides, visions of the 'exotic other' may shape beliefs and expectations of the field. For those researchers who are going home to conduct their research, anxieties may be related to one's returning role as a researcher, member of an extended family, absent friend, newly crowned 'expert' and so on. This readjustment may be quite difficult for some. For Ifi Amadiume, returning home to conduct research in her native Nigeria was not so much about studying her people as 'decolonising her mind' from the racist and essentialist experiences that had characterised both her life in London and her formal study of social anthropology (Amadiume, 1993:182).

Whatever you may anticipate when embarking on development fieldwork, surviving your field experience on a personal level will always be a challenge. We believe much can be achieved by the researcher through thorough logistical preparation (avoid arriving at night, knowing something about the place you are going to, etc.) but also an awareness of the magnitude of emotional and physical challenges involved. These latter issues will be unpredictable, but may be offset if the researcher has at least rudimentary language skills, initial contacts, and does not arrive with unrealistic expectations of what can be achieved – especially in those early days/weeks.

The first day

> I had not imagined that I would be alone. I had envisaged something a little more bureaucratic, given the red tape surrounding my research visa. The people would be expecting me; perhaps a councillor would accompany me. But there I was alone and aware that I had to present myself and my plans to my startled hosts – who had just mistaken me for a clinic sister on patrol.(Macintrye,1993:44)

Although you will have to constantly manage personal and emotional issues as they arise, getting through the first day for many is an achievement in itself. Although few find time to write of their experiences of arrival (Macintyre 1993:44), fewer still forget it. Dumont (1978: 48) has argued that 'entering the field is probably the most dramatic and shocking event' while Schwartz (cited in Wax, 1971: 18) has concurred that his initial period was 'one of disorientation, shock, and disequilibrium'. Helen's experience of travelling to her field site went like this:

> The bus from Guatemala to the city of San Salvador was slow and excruciatingly stuffy. We passed the body of a dead man lying unnoticed on the side of the road. The person who was supposed to meet me at the bus station had not turned up. I sat on my luggage in the crowded and dirty station and fought hard to quell the rising panic.

Donovan's first journal entry, after arriving from the airport into a Manila squatter settlement, read:

> Arrival at house a real shock. The access road consisted of rail tracks dotted with small fires. Terrifying. Trains pass regularly! They toot all the way through to clear lines of people, they give the house a real shake and the dog howls.

He had a feeling of 'this is it' and a desire to get the very next plane home.[1]

Stories abound among researchers of failed meetings, shattered expectations and all consuming panic on their first day in the field. Whether it is being simply dropped off without any form of welcome[2] such as Martha Macintyre landing on Tubetube Island, Papua New Guinea, or the 'invasion of the senses' that accompanies arrival in Third World cities, and often airports, your initial experience is likely to be one full of emotions – of excitement, fear, self-consciousness, anxiety and, hopefully still, unbridled enthusiasm. Getting through your first day will not only give you a sense of well-earned achievement, but will also begin to equip you with the tools that you will need in what will be your new home and workplace for the foreseeable future. It may be reassuring to note that most of the 'shocking' incidents of fieldwork occur soon after arrival (DeVita, 1990) – but that they needn't act as a portent for what is to come.

Expectations and well thought-out plans often go awry in development field-work precisely because everyday life in the Third World is characterised by uncertainty. Airports and public transportation terminals can be notoriously confusing, overwhelming and a good place to get ripped off. Buses and other forms of public transport often arrive late or not at all, faxes and emails signaling your arrival are sometimes not received and, despite the fact that your research is the most important thing in the world to you at the time, your plans are often a low priority for other people. Don't lose your cool – or confidence. Entering into a screaming match at immigration over a three month visa which should have been six, or getting agitated at the late arrival of someone to meet you will not get you far, nor will moaning about these problems when you finally arrive at your destination. Creating a poor first impression may be difficult to undo even after an extended period of fieldwork. Dumont feels that 'entrance is a time of maximum sensitivity on the part of the [researcher] and the people he/she studies' (Dumont, 1978: 48) but perhaps the stakes are not quite so high as he suggests: 'I knew damn well the stakes of the game: one goof and I was out of anthropology and the remote glimmering of an academic career' (Dumont, 1978: 44).

Even when plans and expectations end in disarray on your first day it is important to 'ride-out' this period. This is the start of the process that Kleinmann et al. (1992) describe as researchers gaining control of their projects 'by first allowing themselves to lose it'. For some this loss of control or vulnerability, from day one, will be more difficult to cope with than others.

A useful starting point in this quest to remain calm is to sit back and take stock for a few moments. It is just your first day in the field. It does not matter that you do not have the necessary visa, or that the concrete jungle that you see before you has shattered your image of a city of 'only' 500,000. You will probably be in the field for at least couple of months and there will be plenty of time to get official permission and to re-orientate yourself to your surroundings. You may even find you grow to appreciate, if not love, your new environment, though you might not believe it initially.

If, as was the case with Helen's first day in El Salvador, you are not met at the village, train, bus station, or airport by the pre-arranged person, it is foremostly important to get yourself settled into safe and secure accommodation so that you can begin to adjust to your new surroundings. Living arrangements have traditionally been of great ideological and methodological importance in fieldwork. Living among respondents, discussed in Chapter 5, has both advantages and disadvantages. Nevertheless, if you do find yourself alone upon arriving in the field and have not pre-arranged accommodation with a family or a guesthouse/hotel, a backpacker's guide book such as the *Lonely Planet* or *Rough Guide* will enable you to find reasonable accommodation until you finalise your living arrangements. Even here, if negotiating public transport fills you with fear, take a 'courtesy bus' to the most affordable hotel. The important thing is to find a place to unwind, take stock and get oriented.

The morning after

Once safely ensconced within a research community or in your guesthouse/hotel, it is a good idea to jot down some brief notes detailing your initial impressions of the field and the ways in which these impressions met or do not meet your expectations. This form of reflection will be useful later in the research process not only as evidence of how you have adapted (even after a few days or weeks), but also to relate your experiences of fieldwork on paper to others as well as provide an outlet for any frustrations you feel. It may be hard to believe, but you will often forget even the most harrowing details of your first day in the field by the time you come to write up your thesis. Such reflection will help in seeing how your thinking on the people and places you study has changed. For example, Macintyre (1993:44) found that her dairy revealed little about her first day in the field and that her memory of it now has been reduced to 'a jumble of curious faces, conversations mediated by the school teacher, and ... boxes in disarray'.

While the above strategies may assist you in surviving your first day in the field, Devereux and Hoddinott (1992:10-11) argue that a preliminary visit to the field can reduce some of the anxiety and uncertainty that you will experience. If you have the funding to make it possible, a preliminary visit to the field has both practical and methodological advantages. A preliminary trip will assist in formulating academic and bureaucratic networks, making fieldwork logistics such as research permission more streamlined. A preliminary visit also allows the researcher to 'hit the ground running' as many of the obstacles to beginning fieldwork will have already been cleared. For researchers who are returning home to conduct fieldwork, a preliminary visit may be unnecessary although it could pay to check on the availability of services and equipment (such as email facilities, transport schedules, etc.) if the returnee has not been home for a while.

No matter how well you cope with the first day in the field, whether it is through a preliminary visit or through the various coping mechanisms you may wish to employ, your ability to be flexible will be of paramount importance both on your first day in the field and for the many weeks to come. Writing on his experiences of fieldwork among the indigenous people of Guatemala in the 1930s, Wagley (1983) recounts that one of the most telling traits of fieldwork that he discovered was its dependency on unpredictable accidents and human variations. Flexibility, or the evaluating, challenging and discarding of research activities (Grills, 1998:13), is necessary to get the most out of your fieldwork in the Third World. Having survived your first day in the field, you will already be well on your way to mastering it. But that is not to imply that you will have wholly handled all the challenges that come your way during fieldwork.

Culture shock

Culture shock has long been recognised and discussed, particularly in the context of anthropological fieldwork. Culture shock can be understood as an 'individual or group response to exposure to a new environment, whether it is a result of migration, invasion, colonisation, or some other social or political upheaval' (Seymour-Smith, 1986:69). Culture shock is common among groups such as immigrants, refugees, tourists, expatriate students and business people, and occurs during between-society and within-society intercultural contacts and exchanges (Ward et.al., 2001:5). Culture shock conjures up images of wild eyed and desperate researchers, researchers who are wandering aimlessly or researchers to whom fieldwork, and the people who constitute the field, have become a source of anger and frustration. For many, however, the experience of culture shock is more subtle than these examples would suggest.

Agar (cited in Wolcott) summarises the impact of culture shock:

> The shock comes from the sudden immersion in the lifeways of a group different from yourself. Suddenly you do not know the rules anymore. You do not know how to interpret the stream of motions and noises that surround you. You have no idea what is expected of you. Many of the assumptions that form the bedrock of your existence are mercilessly ripped out from under you. (1995: 94)

Likewise, Bradburd, (1998:18) likened it to 'the discomfort of not quite knowing what was going on and what we were supposed to do'.

Culture shock has traditionally been seen as something that is experienced by outsiders entering an alien environment. More recently, as researchers from the Third World chose to conduct studies their studies abroad, culture shock is beginning to be recognised by those researchers who conduct home-based research in the Third World.

What causes culture shock?

Various theories exist as to why culture shock occurs. One theory argues that individuals are more likely to seek out, have fun with, feel comfortable with and even vote for those other individuals with whom they share common characteristics such as values and physical attributes. Another theory stresses that some societies have more sociocultural features in common than other societies. Hence, a New Zealand researcher is more likely to experience culture shock in Japan rather than Australia, a country with which New Zealand arguably shares key structural and value elements (Ward et al., 2001:10). Care must be taken here though, as at times this feeling of familiarity can lead to delayed shock. Roces and Roces note:

> Most Westerners who come to the Philippines are pleasantly surprised to find that English is spoken everywhere, and that young people are dressed in jeans. ... All the trappings of the American lifestyle are visible – Hollywood films, discos, an English-speaking media with a press fond of American journalistic expressions, fastfood chains, supermarkets, five-star hotels, Christian churches, credit cards. It's all familiar. (1985: 1)

However they go on to warn that:

> A delayed shock follows soon after; for while the Westernised trapping are much too visible, there is an elusive difference. The Western visitor finds he [sic] is talking the same language, but not communicating at all. With a sinking feeling he realised he is...in an entirely different world.

Culture shock is also dependent on the social practice of stereotyping, in that it the ways in which we perceive others, and the influence of cultural syndromes. Here, cultures are contrasted according to patterns of beliefs, behaviour, attitudes and norms. It is argued, for example, that there are large cultural differences between individualism versus collectivism. Cognitive styles differ as do actions and the expressions of emotions. Thus, when individualists and collectivists meet there are likely to be clashes leading to ineffectual communication and other social and psychological barriers (Ward et al., 2001:14-15).

Despite the rather essentialistic flavour to the above theories, there is no denying that stressful situations do often arise during intercultural interactions whether or not they are between individuals who have prior knowledge of the cultural context. In fact, it may be even more difficult for the researcher 'going home' because they are less likely to expect it. They are also likely to have to confront quite different social contexts than they are used to. For Rossana Couto, a Brazilian returning 'home' to do research on fair trade organisations in favelas and the Amazon, feelings of being an 'outsider' were very strong. Indeed, Amazonian Indians referred to her as an American, given her fair complexion, dependence on a 'foreign' language (Portuguese!) and her use of a backpack (Couto, 2002). Seemingly the distinction between 'outsiders' and 'insiders' can be a subjective one.

For researchers who are conducting fieldwork in the Third World, these situations are further compounded by a dawning awareness that the task in hand (data collection) is much more difficult than previously thought. As Harry Wolcott (1995:94) colourfully illustrates:

> The complexity of your task grows before your eyes, with more and more you want to understand you realise that you understand less and less. At such times you cannot help wondering if any fieldworker before you has confronted anything quite like this!

For Elizabeth Hahn, conducting fieldwork in Tonga became a daily battle when feelings of cultural isolation prevented even the most simple of fieldwork tasks from being achieved. Reflecting on her latest humiliation, Hahn confessed that she was,

> tempted to succumb to...cultural isolation and accept it instead of continuing to try and transcend the cultural barrier. I became discouraged as the difficulties of setting up residence continued and the intricacy of Tongan culture grew with closer scrutiny. In short, the complexities of fieldwork were multiplying daily, discernable patterns were not. (1990:72)

Having to achieve what seems like the insurmountable in an environment that is intrinsically alien or ambiguous, is enough to place stress on even the most laid back of researchers. By learning how to detect the onset of culture shock and putting in place strategies to deal with it, however, culture shock can be managed.

Detecting and dealing with culture shock

A fellow researcher once described culture shock as a feeling of helplessness. Others have described it as a sense of drowning or a feeling of being totally out of control (Goopy, pers. comm., 2002). In fact culture shock is a label that can be applied to a whole range of responses to the forms of stress discussed above. These responses include irrational or inappropriate behaviour, apathy, disorientation and depression (Seymour-Smith, 1986:69).

Depression, a common manifestation of culture shock, is an almost inescapable consequence of development fieldwork, particularly if a researcher is unaccompanied and planning to be in the field for some time. Depression or 'fieldwork blues' may occur as a result of feelings of loneliness which are in turn generated by feelings of cultural alienation and isolation. Depression may also be brought about through the numerous physical health problems that often befall fieldworkers: 'few experiences are more depressing than sweating out a fever on a bed thousands of miles away from home' (Devereux and Hoddinott, 1992:15).

If you do begin to feel depressed during your fieldwork, or if you are beginning to feel as though you are losing command of your thoughts and feelings, it is important that you acknowledge that you may be experiencing culture shock. Remind yourself then that culture shock is not a mental illness, that you are not in fact 'going crazy'. Rather, you are having a normal reaction to a situation or series of events over which you have very little control. Once acknowledged, you can then go about the business of fieldwork remembering at the same time that culture shock may often reoccur and you may thus need to revisit coping mechanisms several times rather than once.

A good place to start is to give yourself some 'time out'. While dependent of course on where you are conducting your fieldwork, finding things familiar can often help dilute feelings of cultural alienation. After listening to harrowing stories of war trauma suffered by El Salvadoran women over the course of a week or so, Helen would often need to give herself a break from the intense emotional investment that came with conducting such interviews. As shallow as it seemed to her at the time, she found relaxation and solace at the swanky air-conditioned mall, only a bus ride away from her tiny apartment. Here, she would catch the latest B grade action thriller starring the likes of Arnold Schwarzenegger or Jean Claude Van Damme, or sit in the food court and eat some manner or another of highly processed and fatty food! Music, newspapers, and even the internet may also alleviate homesickness.

You may even find yourself with a unique withdrawal – that of isolation from former academic support structures, such as fellow students – and even your supervisor! Quite often, particularly for researchers lacking language capacity and living in remote communities, a lack of stimulation outside of their work can cause a feeling of repetition or boredom to set in. Similarly, you may yearn for an opportunity in which to critically discuss what you are doing with others (assuming that sharing of such information is not possible within the community). Ways of offsetting this may be to spend some time exchanging ideas with your supervisor via email, making some contacts at local educational institutions, or even with NGOs based in the region. While it is important to maintain ethical principles in discussing your research, some time out to discuss the context of your work may be helpful in releasing some mental energy and generating some ideas. Similarly, diaries may also serve this purpose (see Box 7.1).

Box 7.1 Keeping in touch

With others
There was a time, not that long ago (which may shock younger researchers!), when supervisor and student parted ways for the duration of fieldwork. This was almost always the case with rural or remote research. Even in urban research, often the only affordable and reliable form of communication with supervisors, friends and family was through a local [it]*poste restante[it]*. Months could pass between a letter sent and some feedback – which was often irrelevant when it finally came. Things have obviously changed a great deal, for better or worse. Now almost constant contact can be achieved – except for those who work in very remote regions. Email, texting or satellite phones can deliver instant or 'same-day' replies to our questions. However, while it is possible, and even tempting, to keep communicating with supervisors and friends at home this may not necessarily benefit your research at all times. There is a place for feedback, but a degree of self-reliance and working through issues yourself remains an essential part of good fieldwork.

With your own research: diaries
Keeping personal and research diaries can be a very effective way of developing your ideas, recording experiences and letting off some emotional steam. Donovan used both a personal (the 'green book') and a reflective research diary while doing his PhD fieldwork in the Philippines. The latter was dubbed the 'blue book' (because of its colour – not how it made him feel!) which he kept separate from his personal diary. The blue book was particularly helpful as an evolving think pad for research design, methodology, listing (changing) goals, linking ideas and information, and included a running checklist of questions that needed to be answered. Thus, the blue book helped to think through ideas and have them recorded and was particularly helpful in the initial period of research (re)design (see Chapter 2) and methodological orientation. Subsequently, the research evolved through the pages and gave him a written record of changing directions, ideas and propositions. At the time he thought this record would be especially useful when he returned to write up the research, but in fact it was most valuable while still in the field. Some of the ideas became important, others not, but the real value lay in the writing of them at the time.

Source: Storey (1997)

There are very few researchers, Wolcott (1995) argues, who can ever really know what they will discover during their fieldwork, or what use they will make out of the interviews and other descriptive material that they have been painstakingly recording. Hence when feelings of anxiety and insecurity related to uncompleted questionnaires or failed methodologies rear their ugly head step back, review your initial expectations, look at the data that you have already collected and know that, at the end of the day, 'most fieldworkers return home with far more data than they can ever analyse' (Devereux and Hoddinott, 1992:16). Just 'being there' for many is an achievement in itself – and remember, all fieldworkers express doubts at some stage. As one example, Wikan's feelings of despair when deciding whether or not to leave an urban poor community in Cairo, which she was researching, illustrates this, as well as the importance of also having confidants in the field:

> Beyond the world of the poor, there was also a vital source of support.... But for her I might have given up. I remember one moment in particular when she saved me. I had appeared on her doorstep after a long absence, looking wretched. I felt an utter failure as an anthropologist and as a human being because I could not bear my physical and mental surroundings: the filth, the stench, the misery. And now my last vestige of hope, my willpower, was also failing me. Laila lectured me on the senselessness of thinking I could do it! She chided my teachers for instilling in me such a vain hope. No foreigner could possibly cope, when not even an Egyptian could ....That did it. From then on I felt a sense of accomplishment rather than doom. And so I kept at it. (1996: 329)

Wikan ended up moving out of the urban poor settlement where she had tried to live and into an apartment, but her research objectives were accomplished nonetheless.

Finally, as most fieldwork is characterised by uncertainty and this uncertainty can lead to culture shock, it may be useful to adopt what Wolcott (1995:92) has termed a 'tolerance for ambiguity'. To be certain and in control of our lives is a central cultural tenant of many Western societies. Thus, when a research participant answers 'six maybe five' to your question 'how many children do you have', it is only natural if you have been socialised in certainty, to feel confused and maybe a little annoyed! To the Ndebele informant Wolcott (1995:93) is describing, however, this ambiguity is a calculated one. While his six children were all present and accounted for when he last saw them, something catastrophic may have happened to them in the interim. In the Third World many things can never be taken for granted. A tolerance for ambiguity will enable you to develop a more relaxed demeanour during fieldwork and may also in the final analysis, enable you to more effectively combat culture shock.

Behaviour during fieldwork

Very much related to the issue of culture shock, and dealing with it, is the mine-field that is maintaining appropriate behaviour whilst conducting development fieldwork (these issues are also addressed in Chapter 6). The whole notion of 'appropriate behaviour' is complex because it is tied up and intertwined with cultural constructions of morality, gender, class, ethnicity, socialisation processes and individual personalities (Ellen, 1984:100–104). Thus, what may be considered appropriate behaviour for a researcher may be seen as down-right rude or offensive to the individuals or society with whom he/she is interacting (see DeVita, 1990; 2000). As development fieldwork necessarily involves forming relationships with others (Devereux and Hoddinott, 1992:16), and contemporary fieldwork processes pay overt attention to the subjective (de Laine, 2000:2), there is just no avoiding the need to critically examine, or at least give some thought to the ways that we behave during fieldwork. This also includes an awareness of the politics of everyday life. As Hershfield et.al. (1983: 241) state with regards to rural fieldwork, 'interviewers should know a great deal about village life – forms of social organization, leadership, mores, behavioural patterns – before undertaking data collection'. Similarly, community politics must also be considered a critical part of everyday life in urban settings.

How to get on with others

It would be a mistake to suggest, or believe, that successful adaptation to culture shock is about accepting what you previously thought unacceptable. As Smith-Bowen has forewarned 'it is an error to assume that to know is to understand and that to understand is to like' (cited in Clarke, 1975: 114). Getting along with others in a mutually pleasing fashion is a skill that cannot, unfortunately, be easily learnt. Factors include sex, age, wealth, ethnicity, religious, and political philosophies (Gaskell and Eichler, 2001) as well as the 'tag' that communities will ascribe to you and your research, despite or in spite of your explanations (Ellen, 1984:103). There are some factors then, such as your 'demographics' and people's positioning of you, that even the most experienced researchers cannot fully control. 'Insiders' as well as 'outsiders' are affected by this (see Ite, 1997: 79). However, it is important not to try to be someone you are not – you will most likely be found out (see Chapter 8, 'Truth and deception').

Being a person to whom qualities such as sympathy, empathy, kindness and even courtesy and patience come easily, will certainly facilitate a smoother field-work experience (Wolcott, 1995:87), as will the researcher's ability to negotiate the roles which link the researcher with others (de Laine, 2000:94; Crick, 1989; see also Chapter 6, 'Desirable personal traits'). For example, even basic forms of reciprocity can go a long way. In interviewing farmers in China, Veeck (2001: 37) took news-paper clippings of US crop prices for respondents to share and discuss (see Chapter 8, 'Reciprocity'). However, even in reciprocity problems can arise. The following examples (Box 7.2) may help illustrate dilemmas that face researchers in the field more often than not.

For those researchers who find interpersonal skills difficult to master, it will be a relief to know that, in the words of one anthropologist 'foot in the mouth is not fatal' (Flinn, 1990). The generosity and goodwill with which many fieldwork participants greet awkwardness and even downright blunders is a constant source of amazement to researchers (see for example, Counts, 1990; Ellen, 1984:102). You should be aware that there are significant differences in the way different cultures respond to predicaments: in the event of a mishap laughter may be the most appropriate response (DeVita, 1990; 2000). Personal 'weaknesses' may also prove to be strengths in some cultural contexts. Successful fieldwork for Flinn (1990), a self-proclaimed shy person, was facilitated not by her innate confidence or ability to be flexible, but rather by her qualities of modesty and quietness. Finally, while 'one of the mysteries of entering a new culture is figuring out how to accomplish life's simple, ordinary tasks: providing ourselves with food and water, learning how and where to go to the bathroom when there is no bathroom, and keeping clean' (Bradburd, 1998: 59), you will adapt to local variants: 'Culture is a powerful thing, especially at three o'clock in the morning' (Bradburd, 1998: 61).

Box 7.2: Helping others: some dilemmas

Researchers may refuse to offer assistance in order not to significantly change their environment or to favour individuals or groups over others. Robson refused to teach illiterate villagers basic literacy – despite many self doubts over this decision (Robson, 1997: 60-61). In another case, Dumont refused to share his antibiotics to treat a scratch,[3] and shortly after also denied a child's request for some more fishing hooks. Dumont consequently confronted community anger: 'Not only was I "ignorant", but I was a "miser". How come I did not want to give or to cure? [Dumont was from a medical background.] Why could I not go to Caracas to bring more supplies? Why was I such a bad guy? Why was I so ugly too? How come my wives were not here with me? Why did I not go back home? And in purporting to helping the sick beforehand, "how come I was such a liar"'? Dumont managed to ride out these complaints, but it was nonetheless a very depressing experience.

He was relieved to find, the next morning, that his relationships had virtually returned to normal, and perhaps there is a lesson in this for researchers (Dumont, 1978: 51). Wolcott (1995: 92) notes the need for the 'art of diplomacy' when avoiding demands which are excessive or based on fiction but decisions regarding intervention are clearly not easy ones to deal with. Considerations will most likely include the nature of your relationship to different people or groups in the community and how accepting or refusing requests would change this; creating unrealistic expectations of the researcher and/or dependence; and moving into areas beyond your competence.

Often your ability to behave appropriately in the field will depend on the ways in which people perceive you. Helen has argued elsewhere that research participants will respond to the researcher in relation to their situated social constructions of the researcher's social world (Leslie and McAllister, 2002). Thus, Flinn (1990) found that the women in the remote Micronesian Island in which she conducted her field-work were more inclined to speak openly to her knowing that she was a mother. Likewise, Helen found that her research participants in El Salvador were more relaxed and keen to discuss issues knowing that she was a nurse as well as a researcher.

Cultural sensitivity

Along with the personal qualities of the researcher and the perceptions of the researcher held by people in the field, the ability of the researcher to be culturally sensitive, or otherwise, will also impact on successful fieldwork experiences. While it is impossible to learn everything there is to know about another culture or indeed to keep abreast of subtle cultural changes that may have occurred in a researcher's absence, it is useful to be constantly mindful in fieldwork of the ethnocentrism or cultural baggage that all individuals carry with them wherever they go (Hammond, 1990).

If ethnocentrism can be understood as an individual's cultural biases, then cultural sensitivity is the individual's ability to acknowledge biases and to be non-judgmental when interacting with or studying other cultures (Scaglion, 1990). Putting aside your cultural biases in an attempt to enter the field unencumbered, however, is an unrealistic expectation for any researcher. Even the most experienced and sensitive individual will occasionally make cultural faux pas. Despite the imme-diate embarrassment and perhaps even offence that they may cause, mistakes are unlikely to seriously undermine the research or researcher however.

Helen's experience of riding buses in El Salvador, is one case in point. After months of having to clamber over passengers who would stubbornly position themselves in the aisle seat of the bus, she had jumped to the erroneous conclusion that since the war had ended, Salvadoran people had become individualistic and self-preserving. One day when she was chatting with her Spanish teacher, she dis-covered that Salvadorans purposefully position themselves in the aisle seat in the hope of avoiding an unwanted, gun wielding companion (robber or kidnapper) tak-ing advantage of the space available next to them. Thus, to her embarrassment she learnt a valuable lesson not only about her own ethnocentrism, but also about the ways in which Salvadoran people daily negotiate the culture of violence in their society.

Such sensitivities are also an important part of actual data collection. For exam-ple, there are important cultural factors which need to be taken into consideration when asking questions. So, while Wuelker (1993: 165) has argued that non-Asians interviewing Asians are 'fiascos' others, such as Jones noted that cross-cultural interviewing is possible given certain understandings. Namely, it is wise to:

Keep the atmosphere agreeable and the topic pleasant, avoid affronting or humiliating another, don't disagree with one of higher status, make compliments where possible, delay the main subject with small talk, and never fail to offer hospitality. (1983: 254)

Finally, 'getting on with others' also involves understanding that, as much as you need your personal space and time out from being the center of attention, or, 'being in the thick of the heard all the time' (Mead, quoted in Ellen, 1984:105), your research respondents may also feel this way at times. Developing an awareness of when people are jaded from your questions, or would like some privacy from your presence is an important tool.[4] You should have some appreciation how others see you and when to make yourself scarce. Hopefully then you won't be on the end of the following:

Stay outta my life, Van Maanen. I don't have nothing to say to you and you don't have nothing to say to me ... I don't know what you want and I wouldn't give a shit even if I did. You mind your business and I'll mind mine. (Van Maanen, 1991: 36)

Working with others: research assistants

Depending on factors such as the size and scope of your research and the amount of funding you have available, you might find it necessary and indeed useful to hire a Research Assistant (RA). RAs can be an enormous asset during fieldwork. Not only can they provide help with the nuts and bolts of data collection (surveys, interviews, etc.) but also with the more intangible aspects of fieldwork such as gaining access to research participants and facilitating your acceptance into the research community (Ellen, 1984:118). The right research assistant can thus be seen as an 'ambassador at large', guiding and screening the research process so that the researcher is able to make the most of their fieldwork experience (Devereux and Hoddinott, 1992:27).

Devereux and Hoddinott argue that if you were to draw up a job description for an ideal RA it would probably include:

communication skills, good knowledge of English (or French, or Spanish) as well as the local language(s), a perceptive intelligence, inexhaustible patience, unfailing dependability, and an ability to get along with all elements of the local population. (1992:27)

While it may seem impossible to find someone who fits such a bill, there will always be individuals who, despite a lack of one or two of the above qualities, will make excellent RAs. It all depends, of course, on the kind of assistance you will be requiring. If you need your RA to act as a translator, then you will obviously need someone with fluency in both your first language and the local language in which you will be working. Likewise, if entry into the research community is your primary concern, then a RA who is well known and trusted by the community will be a valuable asset.

RAs can be drawn from a variety of sources, each of which will have their own advantages and disadvantages. Some researchers will seek an educated individual such as a teacher, student or public servant to act as their RA. This way you can be assured that the RA will understand the nature of your research and will not lead participants into areas of questioning which have no relevance. Educated assistants may be difficult to find, however, and may have more constraints on their time than less educated individuals (Devereux and Hoddinott, 1992:27). For some balance between education and accessibility, many researchers seek RAs from high schools (during school holidays of course!). Veeck (2001: 36) concurs, suggesting visiting the local high school for the most cost effective and loyal translator you could imagine. Finally, students are perhaps less likely to attempt to interpret for you – and more likely to give straight verbatim translations.

Often a researcher will opt for an individual from the local community to act as their RA. Local knowledge can help prevent the embarrassing and sometimes costly faux pas, mentioned in previous sections of this chapter (and Chapter 6) and can be invaluable when identifying possible research participants. On the other hand, a local RA has the potential to dominate the form of data collected by directing the researcher to their own friends and family. The more involved the researcher becomes with his/her RA the more likely he/she is to be identified as a member of the RA's social group. This can be problematic, particularly if the researcher wants to access an alternative group and collect broad rather than specific data on the research community (Ellen, 1984:118).

Ethnicity, age, status and sex are all important considerations when selecting an RA. In Fiji, Walsh (1996) found that the ethnicity and gender of surveyors had at least some influence on respondents and the data which was collected. Choosing an assistant of the opposite sex can have its advantages as Heyer (1992:206) discovered during her fieldwork in Kenya and India. Heyer found that male RAs offered her more protection in awkward situations and often counterbalanced the fact that she was a woman conducting fieldwork. Conversely, male RAs may not be granted access to the private worlds of women participants as easily as women RAs. When Shahrashoub Razavi (1992:158) was conducting her fieldwork in rural Iran, for example, she found that the reservations of her women participants 'disappeared immediately' once she had dispensed with the male RA she had employed.

Whether you decide to employ an educated outsider or a RA from the local community, one of the most important factors to successful fieldwork will be the personal relationship you develop with your RA. While the researcher obviously has much to gain both professionally and personally from the relationship, RAs too can be enriched by the experience. This was certainly the case with the relationship that was forged between Helen's RA, Natalia, and Helen during fieldwork in El Salvador. Reflecting on the experience of working as Helen's RA, Natalia (pers. comm., 1998) wrote that she felt, 'so good to have collaborated in what you are creating...I feel proud...Thanks for the 'ego-boost'. Collaborative research may prove more than an 'ego-boost' however, and give local researchers an opportunity to gain experience and develop research skills. It is important that this assistance is subsequently recognised in the thesis (on collaboration see Gaskell and Eichler, 2001).

As was the case with Helen's fieldwork in El Salvador, many researchers who do not have sufficient command of the vernacular in which to conduct research, employ a RA to act as their interpreter. Having an interpreter on hand gives the researcher the flexibility of being able to take notes during interviews but has the disadvantage of them receiving information second-hand. This can be very problematic as the interpreter may take it upon her/himself to omit or change elements of the interview to prevent potential embarrassment or because they believe the information is irrelevant or of little use to the research topic (Devereux and Hoddinott, 1992:25) Thus, there is an important distinction to be made here between translating and interpreting.

It is important therefore to spend time with your interpreter before you launch into interviews or observations and develop some kind of professional relationship early on. While it may be beneficial for RAs to become friends, it is more important that they can effectively help you with your research. During your initial meetings discuss in detail both the nature of the research project and the role of your interpreter in facilitating your chosen methodology. Here you need to clearly state whether you require your interpreter to translate literally (i.e. exactly what the participant is saying), or whether you would prefer a more concise translation. It is important also to consider who will direct the interview, particularly if you have chosen a semi-structured interview format. Some knowledge of the vernacular will enable you to recognise when research participants are straying from the questions and will also give you the confidence to be able to detect possible misinterpretations or adaptations of the participants' responses (Heyer, 1992:204). Spend some time thinking about what you want from you RA and what you are prepared to offer them. Problems of setting wages, conditions and expectations are common (Robson, 1997: 70-72), even among researchers going home. For example, a Namibian PhD student found that recruiting research assistants in Windhoek and Oshakati was one of the most challenging tasks he had to grapple with during fieldwork (Box 7.3).

Box 7.3 Recruitment of research assistants: dilemmas facing an indigenous researcher

Like many indigenous researchers, I initially assumed that hiring research assistants was going to be the easiest task but it turned out to be one of the most difficult. Unlike an overseas researcher, an indigenous researcher may at least be aware of some cultural, social and political factors that do not appear in the literature but which are very important to the recruitment of research assistants. But normally, indigenous researchers tend to approach research from an indigenous perspective, which is more social than economic. I found myself in trouble because my research assistants expected me to pay them like an overseas researcher or large organisation. This was far beyond my budget and it cost me time to negotiate a local rate.

The University of Namibia assisted me by providing a list of experienced enumerators from which 6 were selected. This selection was based on CVs that reflected my area of research. But our first meeting sparked difficulties over the amount they were to be paid per questionnaire. They wanted to be paid the average amount that the National Planning Commission, the University and UN agencies paid. I argued that I was an individual/indigenous Namibian and it was unfair for them to ask what they would of the UN. As part of my defence, I also raised the issue of cultural obligation, which forced some compromise because as a Namibian I should not have been expected to pay at all. Nevertheless, they rightfully countered because we were in Windhoek everything depended on money.

Negotiations centred not only on money but also transportation, meal allowances, and where assistants wanted to work. At one stage I had offered to reduce the rate of payment by offering transport from the suburb Katutura to the former white suburb, Windhoek South. It was only at the last minute of the negotiations when I was alerted by one of the females that what we had agreed on was the amount per questionnaire without their lunch. The lunch amount raised the bill beyond my expectations. Negotiations on this issue lasted for a further week and a half. Finally, because particular tribes and languages dominate some Windhoek suburbs, each participant had to be assigned to a suburb where he/she was culturally comfortable.

The approach I used in Windhoek differed slightly with that which I used in Oshakati. In Windhoek I completed the negotiations with the assistants. In Oshakati we needed a mediator to serve as a witness. Because Oshakati was 'foreign' to me (outside of my tribal area), I was treated with suspicion, especially as I did not speak the local vernacular. Because I could not identify myself with any reputable organisation, except my New Zealand institution, my research assistants felt that I was probably a liar who was planning to run away without paying them. They wanted our meeting to be attended by the senior traditional headman of the city. But he was a busy person and our attempts to contact him failed. Finally, I made an offer to pay them half of the amount per questionnaire each day. This softened their position but they still needed the Acting Town Clerk to serve as a witness on what we had agreed upon. Initially, they wanted me to reveal what I had paid my research assistants in Windhoek so that we could use that as the basis for our negotiations. They also expected that I would pay for all transport. But they finally accepted my point that even the government does not pay transport for its employees. Apart from that, the design of the city suburbs fell within a walkable distance and did not require transport. But I had to pay for their lunch each day. Oshakati negotiations took nearly two weeks.

Finally, negotiating my position vis-à-vis research assistants was also difficult. What was my relationship to them, and to the outside world? Being an indigenous researcher, who was regarded as naturally poor, it

> *was difficult to convince my research assistants that I was going to foot the bill with success. Also, an indigenous researcher may find some difficulties because his/her fellow indigenous people see him/her as somebody who is trying to practice a different culture called 'research' in the wrong place. Sometimes I felt they wanted to punish me under the assumption that I was pretending to be 'upper class', when I deserved to be in the lower one.*
>
> *Source: Frederick Sikabongo, PhD Candidate, Massey University*

Finally, if you decide to audiotape your interviews, rather than have your RA translate on the spot, it is worth considering asking your RA to transcribe the interviews for you. This will prevent another interpretation or possible misinterpretation of the data and will ensure that you are correctly representing the knowledge and understanding your research participants bring to the research process.

Language issues

It is understood that unless you are conducting home-based research with a social group in which you share membership, when conducting fieldwork in the Third World you will find it necessary to learn at least some local language.[5] Mcintyre (1993:46) argues that despite linguistic competence being one of the key assumptions of anthropology, the difficulties and frustrations that accompany language-learning are rarely discussed.

Language-learning, according to Mcintyre, renders the anthropologist mute. In learning a language the anthropologist is 'beholden, ignorant...[and]...impotent' (1993:47). Veeck puts it in even more blunt terms:

> The ability to have all sorts of conversations, to really be able to think in another language, will, in turn, propel our research to new levels. That is a fact. Through fluency, we will not only conduct more successful research because we can hear more voices but also, over time, differentiate issues that warrant our research efforts from less pertinent pop issues with only passing significance. You cannot come to understand the really important issues by spending three months to a year with your mouth shut, or by sitting in your room every night reading the cheesy novels your family and friends send you in care packages. (2001:36)

While the issue of language is often a source of strain for many researchers (Ellen, 1984:106), and there is seldom space for developing language fluency within most Masters or Doctoral programmes (Robson, 1997: 70; Veeck, 2001:34), language-learning has great personal and professional benefits. Knowledge of the local language enables richer and more textured data to be collected and generates greater opportunities to interact and enjoy the company of others in the researched community (Devereux, 1992:44). By contrast, a lack of local knowledge can lead to inappropriate or even invalid data and can generate feelings of frustration and low morale.

How much language?

Once researchers have acknowledged the necessity to learn language, the question of 'how much is enough' emerges. Devereux (1992:44-45) argues that it is important at the outset of fieldwork to weigh up the costs and benefits of language fluency before any decision regarding language tuition is made. He stresses that while there is obviously much to gain from language fluency, the costs, in terms of time and money spent on the endeavor, are generally high. A decision thus needs to be made about whether a researcher can afford to spend the months or even years required to become competent in the language or whether it would be more beneficial to begin other forms of data collection with the aid of an interpreter.

Even when months are devoted to intensive language tuition, issues related to language fluency remain. As language is fluid and constantly evolving and is intimately tied to an individual's social world, a researcher may have to contend not only with dialectal issues between ethnic groups, but also with differences in vocabulary and expression *within* social groups. Moreover, it is one thing learning a language for say travelling or business purposes, but quite another when it comes to conducting research. A stray tense or a misplaced article can have an enormous impact on the data collected and on the relationships a researcher is carefully cultivating.

Unless you are conducting home-based research within your own social group or have prior experience of the research vernacular, it may be a better idea then to reflect on your specific circumstances before launching into months of intensive language-learning. If, for example, you are a person who finds learning other languages fairly easy and who plans to collect data mainly from observation and interviews over a long period of time, then it is probably a good idea to learn the vernacular as intensely as possible. If, on the other hand, you are a person who finds language-learning difficult and who plans to collect quantitative data over a short period of time, then a basic understanding of some of the important vocabulary and cultural norms related to your chosen area of study will probably suffice (Devereux, 1992:45-46). At the end of the day, however, your willingness to learn the language will mean more to your research participants (Flinn, 1990:106) than your ability to handle the subjunctive tense! Regardless of whether you achieve fluency or not, the important message is that you have tried.

For example, during the first few months of Helen's fieldwork in El Salvador, she enrolled in a language school and undertook total immersion language training. This method of language-learning was immensely beneficial for not only the solid grounding it gave her in Spanish but also, for the support and friendship it offered. In addition, the school's commitment to cultural awareness enabled her to make sense of some of the more 'alien' aspects of life in El Salvador. Thus, spending time in a language school provided her with a safety net to test ideas and actions that may have been detrimental to her future ability to relate to Salvadorans in a research situation.

Finally, a good rule of thumb is that if you are exposing yourself to local languages your abilities are likely to improve over time (as will your confidence). So, if worried or lacking, leave surveys and more in-depth interviews until later in the piece.

Conclusion

Arrival and adaptation provide both personal and professional challenges to researchers. Even with considerable planning one is more often than not faced with the harsh and stressful realities of arrival into a foreign setting. Initial shock and confusion may be followed by a more delayed testing period of adjustment and cultural acceptance. There are, however, ways in which to prepare for and deal with these pressures. Above all, it is important to have pre-planned for as many of these trials as possible (see Chapters 5 and 6). Still, nothing can prepare you for your immediate initiation, and it presents an unavoidable challenge. Even for returning researchers and those going home, pressures of research permission, of community acceptance and the logistics of data collection, will always present difficulties. A thorough research design, an initial strategy for adaptation, keeping contact with supervisors and mentors, using diaries, language-learning and having realistic expectations will all go some way to helping you through the anticipated and unanticipated demands that will present themselves from the first hour until the final day of your fieldwork.

Recommended reading

DeVita, P.(ed.) (2000) *Stumbling Toward Truth: Anthropologists at Work* Waveland Press Inc., Prospect Heights, IL.
DeVita. P. (ed.) (1990) *The Humbled Anthropologist* Wadsworth, Belmont.
These edited volumes offer honest and humorous examples of how researchers cope with the challenges thrown up during cross-cultural fieldwork.

R. Sanjek (ed.) (1990) *Fieldnotes : the makings of anthropology,* Cornell University Press, Ithaca.
An excellent resource on writing fieldnotes. Though it is primarily aimed at the anthropologist, *Fieldnotes* is a worthwhile read for all researchers interested in keeping notes and journals in the field.

Devereux, S., Hoddinott, J. (1993) The context of fieldwork. In S. Devereux and J. Hoddinott (eds) *Fieldwork in Developing Countries* Lynne Rienner, Boulder, pp. 3-24
Ellen, E.F. (1984) The fieldwork experience. In *Ethnographic Research: A guide to general conduct* Academic Press, London.
These two chapters provide an excellent overview of the issues facing researchers during fieldwork and prove that some issues do not change a lot over time.

Notes

1. After two weeks Donovan was still despondent ('The dogs barked all night and the train got on my wick') and yet, a week later problems of sleeping in had emerged!

2. While your arrival may be the biggest event of *your* calender, this may not necessarily be the case for others. Dumont's first day went like this: 'When all my gear had been carried safely across the river, Domingo Barrios was suddenly confronted with the absolute reality of my arrival. Once more trousered, shirted, and sunglassed, he welcomed us rather coldly. Our presence was troublesome, because we had arrived right in the middle of the preparation for a *waxpoto*, the festival of the dead, which was to begin that night' (Dumont, 1978: 49). Werner and Schoepfle (1987: 239-40) classify three native reactions to researchers: enthusiastic acceptance, benign neglect, and complete rejection.

3. Researchers are often asked to help with basic medicine, especially if they are seen to have a medical/first aid kit (Bradburd, 1998: 98-110).

4. Or, as Van Maanen bluntly states, understanding why and where one's presence is likely to bring forth an 'oh fuck, here he comes again' response (Van Maanen, 1991:36).

5. Still, language may well be an issue for researchers returning to their own country. Ite (1997: 80-81), a Nigerian, relied on English to communicate with respondents as she could not do so in the local dialect.

8 Ethical Issues

Regina Scheyvens, Barbara Nowak and Henry Scheyvens

Just imagine how easy it would have been for you to have done your thesis in the place where you live, if you didn't have to travel to the other side of the world to learn about other experiences.... I just think about you, how you leave your children, live in a risky situation, because it's dangerous here, how you have to travel so much, to be able to interview us.... I admire this idea of yours and I feel like I've won a prize to have been included in this written work. (Carla Martínez, research participant, 24 May 2001, cited in Cupples, 2002:376)

Introduction

Fieldwork in the Third World can give rise to a plethora of ethical dilemmas, many of which relate to power gradients between the researcher and the researched. Combined with this are complex issues of knowledge generation, ownership and exploitation. Ethical issues which arise in relation to cross-cultural situations thus need to be considered and questioned seriously by all scholars pondering fieldwork in the Third World, and ethical principles should in turn inform all stages of research, from the inception of a research project through to writing up results.

However, for many graduate students in particular, 'ethics' has come to be equated with a gruelling test to write an ethics proposal acceptable to the powers that be within their university. This is not what ethics is really about. Doing ethical research in a foreign setting, as indicated by the starting quote for this chapter, is about building mutually beneficial relationships with people you meet in the field and about acting in a sensitive and respectful manner. There is also a moral imperative which should inform Development Studies research, as recognised by Madge (1997:114) who asserts that 'ethical research should not only "do no harm", but also have potential "to do good", to involve "empowerment"'. Corbridge (1998:49) similarly argues that the interdependencies of the world economy mean that those of us who are privileged should be 'attentive to the needs and rights of distant strangers'. Furthermore, he suggests that Development Studies scholars have an obligation to inform development practice, specifically, 'to provide plausible alternatives to existing social arrangements or patterns of development' (1998:42).

In this chapter, we explore the typical principles under which university ethics committees operate, before moving on to explore a much wider range of ethical issues likely to present themselves to students in the field, including questions of who sanctions one's research, balancing the expectations of different stakeholders, reciprocity, deception, and the safety of the researcher. Specific ethical issues associated with studying 'down' (that is, studying those much less privileged than ourselves) and studying 'up' (those more privileged than ourselves) will be considered in Chapter 9. We also alert researchers to the potentially exploitative relationships that can develop with their research participants. These warnings should not, however, necessarily deter researchers from Western countries from engaging in development fieldwork in the Third World, nor should this deter Third World researchers wanting to conduct research in unfamiliar locations 'back home', as this could seriously undermine the potential for research to broaden our understanding of complex development issues. As noted in Chapter 1, there can be many benefits from cross-cultural research and there are ways to avoid causing harm to our research participants.

Ethics in research

What do we mean by ethical[1] issues in field research? John Barnes writes that ethical decision making in research

> arises when we try to decide between one course of action and another not in terms of expediency or efficiency but by reference to standards of what is morally right or wrong. (1979, cited in May, 1997:54)

Decisions based on ethics are not determined by how successful the researcher will be but rather by whether the research is just or not; by the extent to which the research takes the participants' needs and concerns into account. The research process must ensure the participants' dignity, privacy and safety. What we are most interested in discussing in this chapter is not deliberately unethical behaviour such as falsifying or fabricating data, misappropriating funds, or plagiarism, but rather decisions involved in negotiating field research which are less obvious such as avoiding harm to those involved in the research.

There are two ethical models prevalent in social science research (Denzin, 1997). The first is a traditional model based on Immanuel Kant's (1724–1804) philosophical work. This absolutist ethical model is premised on a set of principles or codes which direct research practice (de Laine, 2000: 23). These principles of research must be adhered to under all circumstances. There is no flexibility regarding guidelines and the ability of the individual to make ethical decisions based on situational and personal circumstances. In other words, there is no ethical relativism. The second model, originating from a postmodern, feminist philosophy, argues for flexibility in ethical decisions. This model contends that the rational objectivity required in the first model is a false reality. Supporters of this model maintain that researchers are not apolitical, neutral observers but rather fully involved, self-aware, interacting people who are (or should be) ethically fully informed, therefore responsible for their actions. Proponents of this model argue that research should not be simply for the sake of research, but rather researchers should be committed politically to empowering those individuals and communities needing help. Research should be in support of soliciting positive change for people, not necessarily the researcher. Thus, ethical issues should be considered throughout the research process (Denzin, 1997). Researchers should be knowledgeable about professional codes of ethics but in the end, ethical decisions should be based on reasoned beliefs regarding the 'goodness' or 'correctness' of what to do. Ethical decisions are reached on an affective rather than intellectual basis (de Laine, 2000:28; Denzin, 1997:276).

To this perspective others counter that 'a loose and flexible system involving "anything goes" so easily opens the research door to the unscrupulous' (May, 1997:56). However, even professional associations with Codes of Ethics recognise that flexibility is critical. The American Anthropological Association for example, says:

> No code or set of guidelines can anticipate unique circumstances or direct actions in specific situations. The individual anthropologist must be willing to make carefully considered ethical choices and be prepared to make clear the assumptions, facts and issues on which those choices are based. These guidelines therefore address general contexts, priorities and relationships which should be considered in ethical decision making in anthropological work. (1998: II)

If codes of ethics are seen more as adaptable guidelines than a rule book, this suggests that there is possibility for compromise between the absolutist and relativist positions. Both ethical absolutists and relativists believe fieldwork must be concerned with ensuring that the research will not have negative implications for the participants. There are a variety of 'good practices' the researcher should remember, many of which follow ideas intrinsic to participatory development. They include:

- respect for the culture, traditions and knowledge of the local community
- consultation with the local community
- involvement of the local community in project design
- research done in partnership with the local groups
- the return of knowledge and information to the community

(Medical Research Council of Canada et al., 1998)

Official ethics procedures

Nowadays ethics approval from a university review board or committee is often mandatory before fieldwork can be undertaken. This fact has not always been welcomed by researchers, who bemoan that the 'recent increase in the extent and range of university bureaucratic controls over research with human subjects often conflicts with, and may unduly delimit, the academic imperative to pursue research' (Casey, 2001:127). Problems can arise for students and other researchers seeking ethics approval if the board does not include anyone with experience in conducting research in Third World settings. Further problems can arise if the ethics board takes an absolutist stance, as discussed above, by adopting a Code of Ethics with specific requirements which must be adhered to. Ethical relativists argue that a research situation is continually evolving, and flexibility must be worked into the process. They would contend that formulating ethical procedures based on a Code of Ethics is helpful as a starting point but rigidity, the inability to shift one's procedures and ideas, might lead to unsuccessful research results and possibly even harmful situations for the participants or the researcher. This is particularly so now that there is not such a clear separation between researcher and researched as in the past:

> The tradition in ethics committees has been to see ethics in terms of what we do to subjects, rather than the wider moral and social responsibilities of simply *being a researcher.*(Kellehear, 1993:14)

> The traditional impersonal and objective ethical model assumed the separation of researcher and researched, but the new fieldwork being practised suggests less distance or detachment between researchers and researched; and a new ethic or moral imperative that is not yet codified. (de Laine, 2000:4)

This section outlines typical concerns of university ethics boards, as well as raising examples of difficulties some researchers have had in gaining approval from such boards. While there are variations, three critical ethical concepts that must be guaranteed by the researcher are of particular interest to those sitting on ethics boards: informed consent; privacy, including ideas of confidentiality and anonymity; and conflict of interest.

Informed consent

Informed consent is when a potential participant freely and with full understanding of the research agrees to be part of the project. It is premised on the notion that the person has a complete and thorough understanding of the aims and processes of the research project, what the research will be used for, such as policy formation and publications, and who will have access to the information gathered. Knowledge of the research comes from the researcher fully and honestly explaining what the research is about and providing an opportunity for the participant to ask questions about the research at any time.

An essential aspect of ethical research is ensuring people's freedom not to participate and that they are fully cognisant of this. Consent must occur without duress or pressure (American Sociological Association, 1997). The researcher must clearly state to the potential contributors that they do not have to participate and if they decide not to there will be no prejudice to their pre-existing entitlements or for any continuing opportunities. Another critical aspect of informed consent is the knowledge of the right to withdraw from the study at any time with the understanding that the information provided will be removed from the pool of collected data.

The researcher should also honestly and fully advise the people requested to contribute to the study about any potential harm or benefits the researcher believes might become of them as a consequence of their participation. This might mean physical harm by others fearful of what might be revealed, it might mean loss of livelihood or it may mean an increase in living standards. No matter what the potential ramifications might be, the researcher needs to disclose them. One risk might be from not protecting anonymity in research notes. The researcher needs to describe clearly how participants' identities will be protected, for example, how the information contributed will be separated from the master list which matches pseudonyms to real names.

Informing potential participants typically occurs via an 'information sheet'. Most university or institutional ethics committees require inclusion of the following information, which should be phrased in language which is simple and easy to understand:

- a comprehensive statement of the purpose of the research
- a description of who the researcher(s) is/are
- the expected duration of the research
- nature of the research procedures and the role the participant will be asked to play
- a complete and honest discussion of the potential harms and benefits that might result from participation; discussion should also point out that a decision not to participate in the research will have no negative impact on people
- a discussion of how data will be stored and the precautions taken to ensure privacy issues
- who will have access to the data
- what will be the final product(s) of the research in terms of publications and conclusions, and who will have access to this/these.

Along with the above points, the information sheet should also include all the basic rights of the participant:

- to decline participation
- to withdraw from the study at any time
- to have privacy and confidentiality assured
- to have any audio or video recording device turned off at any time
- to ask questions about the study at any time, and
- to receive information about the research results and conclusions.

(Massey University Ethics Committee, 2000)

Some ethics committees suggest and even require that the researcher removes himself or herself from the initial phase of requesting assistance from potential participants by having a third party make contact and pass on the information sheet. Committees reason that people might feel pressured if the researcher makes the initial contact. They also suggest that potential participants have an opportunity to read the information sheet and consent form at their leisure before committing themselves. Depending upon the research and the cultural context within which one is operating, this process may or may not be possible or desirable, and would need to be considered for each project. Some communities would prefer, for example, that potential researchers meet with them face to face before deciding whether or not to cooperate with or endorse their research.

While ethics boards or committees generally encourage translation of the information sheet into foreign languages, where appropriate, they do not always recognise that in cultures with a strong oral tradition, and/or where a large proportion of the community to be studied is illiterate, what is written on a piece of paper may have very little meaning for potential participants. In some cases, participants may be very wary of signing a form which could end up in the hands of authorities. This is especially the case where military regimes have made people terrified of official documents. It may be therefore more advisable in some contexts for the researcher to sit down with potential participants and introduce oneself including provision of background information (family members, which country one comes from and what life is like there). After such introductions, a full explanation of the research could be provided, covering the types of points made above in the discussion of information sheets about voluntary involvement, the right to withdraw, and so forth. Convincing ethics committees or boards of the appropriateness of providing oral information rather than a written information sheet may sometimes be difficult, however.

In conjunction with a written information sheet, ethics committees also require 'consent forms'. The consent form spells out all of the participants' rights (mentioned above). At the bottom of the consent form is a place for the participant to sign if he or she agrees to participate. Casey (2001:139) suggests that this requirement of written consent is an example of excessive 'bureaucratic formalisation' of ethics procedures within universities. Most ethics committees or boards now recognise that where culturally inappropriate or where there are good reasons not to record a person's consent in writing, consent can be given verbally. However, they will usually require that this be documented (e.g. on a tape recorder). Not all researchers agree that this is appropriate (Box 8.1). We would argue that in certain circumstances, consent should be achieved verbally in an informal, undocumented way. For example, verbal, undocumented consent may be appropriate where potential participants are illiterate, but ashamed to admit so. As suggested above, in other circumstance signing one's name to a document might have negative implications to people who might fear for their lives or loss of their property if they sign a document. As a researcher it is imperative to be sensitive to the participant's individual and cultural history.

Box 8.1 Appropriate and inappropriate ways of gaining 'informed consent'

A PhD student at an Australian university was asked by the ethics committee to have his informants sign a consent form that showed they understood the nature of the research and were happy answering his questions. The ethics committee was not deterred when told that the informants, who were poor village women, would most likely not be able to sign their name, let alone read the consent form. They instructed the student to use a tape recorder to record the reading of the consent form to each informant and her agreeing to answer questions. The student rewrote the ethics application form accordingly, which was accepted by the ethics committee.

Interestingly, the committee did not inquire about factors that could impact on the welfare of informants in relation to the researcher's proposed activities; such as the length of interviews, the locality or time of day at which they would be conducted and whether the researcher (a male) being seen with local women might raise suspicions of his intentions.

In this case, when in the field the student did not follow the instructions of the committee, feeling that producing a tape recorder before beginning interviews would only cause the women to be fearful. Rather, he asked a third party who the women trusted to introduce him and briefly describe his research, before the women decided whether or not to participate in it.

Many fieldworkers have found that their informants are far less interested in the formal design and goals of the research than the character and disposition of the researcher, and how the research might contribute to their own lives (Wax, 1979: 254). This certainly seemed the case in this instance, when the women's main preoccupation was day-to-day survival.

Ethics boards and committees usually have particular guidelines about obtaining consent for research involving children or the intellectually disabled. In such circumstances, the consent of a parent or guardian is usually required. Once again, not everyone may agree that this is appropriate (Box 8.2).

Box 8.2 A failed attempt to carry out research with child prostitutes in Indonesia

An Indonesian student in Australia studying for her Master's degree sent a proposal to her university ethics board to undertake a study of child prostitutes in Indonesia. She had undertaken a similar study through her former university in Indonesia. For her Master's research she intended interviewing the child prostitutes and their pimps, drawing upon relationships she had built up during her previous study.

The student appeared in a good position to undertake what could have been valuable research. The ethics committee effectively put a stop to her plans, however, by insisting that before speaking with any prostitutes under the age of 18 she gain permission for the interviews from their parents. The child prostitutes did not reveal the true nature of their occupation to their parents making it impossible for the student to approach them.

While we have exposed some problems associated with the application of informed consent, we do not disagree with the principle of informed consent. Rather, as the American Anthropological Association Code of Ethics states, 'It is the quality of the consent, not the format, that is relevant' (1998: III4A). Discussing consent to participate reminds people of their rights and it is also an excellent mechanism to avoid researcher complacency. However, research is a dynamic and continuous process so informed consent at all stages of the research cannot be guaranteed by a pile of signed consent forms handed out early in the research process. The research milieu can change. Relationships between the researcher and participants evolve as might the socio-political environment within and outside the community. Often it is later in the research process that people truly give their consent, by answering questions without inhibition and volunteering information. They can also withhold consent of course, by avoiding interviews or through their silence.

Anonymity and confidentiality

In the research context, anonymity refers to the researcher's responsibility to keep the identity of participants private, if they so wish, so that they will not be personally identifiable in any outputs (for example, theses, journal articles) produced by the researcher. The information sheet should indicate when anonymity cannot be guaranteed and this should be explained to participants at the time of interviews. If, for example, you ask a village leader for his/her opinion of a nearby hydroelectric scheme that is being constructed, you can identify this leader when citing his/her response as long as a) you have received consent to do so, and b) they are speaking in their capacity as a village leader. It would be wrong to assume, however, that all participants want anonymity. Consent should allow for the disclosure of participants' identities (see for example Cassell and Jacobs, 1987, Case 5). Often participants feel very proud of being included in a research project and want direct acknowledgement of their contribution in your writing. This should be balanced with the understanding that even though individuals or communities may want such acknowledgment, the researcher might decide disclosure is inappropriate in terms of future harm.

Confidentiality is a broader term which recognises that a researcher may be entrusted with private information. Thus the researcher has responsibility for ensuring that any fieldnotes, tapes or transcripts will be stored in a safe place and that information contained in them is used only for the purposes of the research. In assuring participants of confidentiality, you must also be prepared to destroy information that someone has provided you with if that person approaches you during or after the information is collected and requests that it be withdrawn. Sometimes this occurs if a participant decides what they have said is inflammatory or just problematic.

Even guaranteeing anonymity and confidentiality, and establishing guidelines that allow for participants to withdraw from the study at any time, may not be enough to make participants feel secure about your research. When a student from the USA went to a country in South America to study local level politics, some of her participants became concerned that she was learning too much, and they became fearful for their positions and their lives. Withdrawing from the study was not an option which would resolve their problem. Their solution was to plant drugs on her. She ended up in a woman's prison before lawyers were successful in achieving her release. The lesson to be learned from this is that no matter what protocols you establish you may never be able to fully protect yourself from unanticipated situations.

Conflict of interest

Research is based on relationships of trust and loyalty with participants, research sponsors, supervisors, universities, and professional organisations and societies. These trust relationships can be put at risk by conflicts of interest. A researcher's objectivity, ethics or loyalty may be jeopardised as a result of a conflict of interest (Palys and Lowman, 1999:4.1).

On the issue of conflicts of interest, the American Anthropological Association's (AAA) Code of Ethics states:

> Anthropologists work in many parts of the world in close personal association with the peoples and situations they study.... They are involved with their discipline, their colleagues, their students, their sponsors, their subjects, their own and host governments, the particular individuals and groups with whom they do their fieldwork, other populations and interest groups in the nations within which they work, and the study of processes and issues affecting general human welfare. In a field of such complex involvements, misunderstandings, conflicts, and the necessity to make choices among conflicting values are bound to arise and to generate ethical dilemmas. It is a prime responsibility of anthropologists to anticipate these and to plan to resolve them in such a way as to do damage neither to those whom they study nor, insofar as possible, to their scholarly community. Where these conditions cannot be met, the anthropologist would be well-advised not to pursue the particular piece of research. (1998: IIIA5)

Conflicts of interest may arise more often in the case of students conducting home-based research. Those who wish to return home to work after their studies in a Western university are completed may find it particularly difficult to pursue topics in which concerns about their government's processes and policies may arise. As noted by Sörbö (1982), local researchers often have long-term responsibilities to their government. They may also find that barriers are put in the way of their research simply because they are not trusted by local authorities, who 'perceive them as potential political adversaries, as radicals' (Cernea, 1982:134).

It is sometimes a good idea to talk problems through with your supervisor or a colleague, as they may be able to identify a conflict of interest which is not apparent to you, or they may be able to suggest a way of handling such a conflict. A solution can sometimes be easier and less traumatic than simply abandoning a particular piece of research, which the AAA code suggests. It might mean altering the direction of the research, for example, or not accepting financial assistance from some sources, as discussed in Box 8.3.

Box 8.3 Financing fieldwork: a conflict of interest

One of the challenges I met while undertaking field research for my MPhil (Development Studies) degree in December 2000, was having to choose between enhancing the validity and reliability of my data and observing Massey University ethics requirements. My supervisors and I had decided that a case study approach would be best for pursuing the study goals I had in mind. In that regard, it was clear that numerous case studies would be more favourable for my study than a single one. However, I had one major impediment: finances. I simply could not afford to undertake more than one case study given the distance between the various potential case study locations and my very limited budget.

Fortunately or maybe unfortunately in retrospect, a former work colleague came up with what appeared to be a potential solution to my financial problems – he would help fund my study on the condition that I would allow him to use and publish my work for his own purposes.

Now while my colleague's proposal may have sounded like a prayer answered, it presented its own set of problems. It would very likely violate several of Massey University's ethical requirements. For instance, I was not sure if my colleague would respect the research participants' anonymity or if he would inform and obtain the participants' permission to publish the work based on them. Furthermore, what was painfully obvious to me at the time was that it would not serve my colleague's intentions to keep the participating company's name confidential.

After weighing up this situation and consulting with my supervisors back at Massey, I thought it best to forego my colleague's proposal. So I limited my research to the one case study I could afford and accounted for my decision in the fieldwork chapter of my thesis.

Source: Khutso Madubanya, MPhil student, Massey University

The value of official ethics procedures

In comparison to the social injustices we may be investigating the concerns of ethics boards can sometimes appear quite trivial, if not totally misplaced. At times it may seem that our academic institutions are far more concerned with their image and protecting themselves from the potential threat of litigation than allowing research into important social issues (Casey, 2001). This is ironic considering that the potential for poorer people, who are often the subject of Development Studies research, to sue a Western university is effectively non-existent.

Ethics boards are of course able to offer sound advice and it would be unfair to portray them simply as one more hurdle that the researcher needs to cross. At the very least, submitting an application for ethics approval should force you to think systematically about your research and the well-being of your informants. Nevertheless, before sending in an application for ethics approval you should contemplate carefully exactly what the board wishes to hear, not just what you consider to be important ethical issues. What are their most likely concerns and how can you allay them? Seek advice from your supervisors and others who have experience submitting ethics applications. No matter how critical you believe your research is it will not receive approval from the ethics board unless they are satisfied with the elementary issues discussed above.

Going through formal ethics channels does not mean you will know all the ethical dilemmas you will face, nor does it mean you will necessarily have the tools to deal with them. Likewise, ethics procedures cannot make unethical research(ers) ethical. Thus we conclude our discussion of official ethics procedures here, and move on to consider a broader range of ethical issues which will be of concern to many people conducting Development Studies research.

Power relations between researchers and their informants

Power imbalances between researchers and research participants exist on two levels: real differences associated with access to money, education and other resources, and perceived differences which exist in the minds of those participants who feel that they are inferior, and researchers who give the impression that they are superior. Whether we like it or not, the nature of much Development Studies research means that we will be in positions of power in relation to most of our participants, a fact which can and should make us engage in some awkward self-reflection about the value of our research (see Box 8.4 for an example of such reflection from Patai's research). This does not mean, however, that we have to be as negative as Patai (1991) or that our research will bring no benefits, an issue discussed further in the section on reciprocity below.

Moving on to the second level of power differentials between researchers and informants, that is, perceived differences, it is important that researchers do not reinforce any feelings of low self-esteem which may be common among marginalised groups. In many societies expressions of sympathy for the struggles of the poor or marginalised by those more fortunate are often merely a matter of show. The poor are considered stupid and their poverty a consequence of their idleness. When approached by outsiders marginalised groups will usually show deference. They may also be fearful, and for good reasons. Having little power within their society they may have many experiences when others have taken advantage of them.

Researchers should avoid reinforcing feelings of powerlessness which our research participants may have by considering carefully both how we interact with our informants and how we behave in the community more generally. Interviews need to be conducted with care. Chambers explains that:

In questionnaire interviewing, power and initiative lie with the interviewer....The status of the interviewer is shown by clipboard and paper, and often by clothing.... Respondents are sometimes intimidated, fearful and deferential. (1997:94)

Box 8.4 Unequal relationships in the field

'It was the summer of 1981 – that is, it was summer in North American terms, but winter in Brazilian terms. In the city of Recife, in the northeast of Brazil, I met Teresa, a black woman who did laundry and ironing for some white acquaintances of mine. She agreed to talk with me and suggested that we go to her house after her morning's work. From the bus stop at the bottom of a hill, we trudged up a muddy road through the slum where she lived. Teresa was not yet 45 years old, but appeared to be much older. Only four feet ten inches tall and weighing perhaps 80 pounds, she looked very thin and frail, and had almost no teeth. As we approached her dwelling, I saw that a piece of metal wire held shut a low and rickety wooden gate in the make-shift fence that surrounded the shack. Teresa untwisted the wire and invited me in. Paintings and statues of Christ decorated the front room, along with pictures of naked women and soccer stars put up, she explained, by her grown-up son, who also lived there. As in many poor neighbourhoods in Brazil, there was no indoor toilet, no sewer facilities, but there was running water (which Teresa shared with a few neighbors who had none, and then also shared the bill) and electricity. Despite my repeated attempts to refuse her offer of food, which perhaps offended her, Teresa insisted on giving me something to eat and drink. She went to the refrigerator and got me a bottle of soda and then brought over a piece of cake – the one remaining piece that was sitting on a plate on top of an otherwise bare counter. I accepted the food, and Teresa sat next to me at the table that occupied most of the front room and watched me eat.

I do not really know how much food there was in Teresa's house on that particular day, but the refrigerator was bare when she opened it, and she herself looked worn out and undernourished. On my return to Brazil two summers later, I learned that she had died suddenly of a heart attack a few months after our meeting.

Thus, long before I began to think about the larger issues of how we use other people in our research, and how inadequate are our usual questions about our purposes or procedures, I was made aware, by that scene in Teresa's house, of the unease of being a well-fed woman briefly crossing paths with an ill-fed and generous poor woman whose life I was doing nothing to improve.'

Source: Patai (1991:140-141)

As Chambers suggests, our outward appearance can also affect the power gradient between researcher and informer. Some things we cannot control, such as our size, sex, and colour. Razavi (1992:156), conducting research in her home country, Iran, felt that being a woman, especially one that was young, single and physically small, redressed to some degree the power imbalances between herself and her informants, who were men of much lower socio-economic status. Conversely, Western men and women conducting research in Third World settings often find that they are considerably taller than the local population, which may simply add to the perceived power gradients. In general, however, power gradients may not be so extreme with female researchers because, as Devereux and Hoddinott point out, 'Women are often perceived as being less threatening than men'. However, they go on to note that because of this women 'may find it more difficult to be taken seriously' (1992:18).

Other aspects of physical appearance we can control, such as the way we dress and our general appearance. We should always be clean and tidy and dress in a culturally respectful manner (see Chapter 6); we should not dress in 'showy' clothes with designer labels nor emulate the dress of, say, government officials if we do not wish to be associated with this group. Thus for example, a researcher arriving on the outskirts of a Kenyan wildlife reserve to interview local people may be perceived as more threatening if wearing a safari suit reminiscent of the dress of British colonial officers or park wardens.

By recognising the power dimension of relationships it is possible to undertake interviews in such a manner that they minimise discomfort felt by participants. Our attitude and the manner in which we conduct ourselves plays a critical role. If we are genuinely interested in the lives and well-being of informants and show we value the information that is being given, then it is more likely that the interview process will be rewarding for both them and ourselves. Chambers (1997) suggests the strategy of 'handing over the stick' by asking residents to teach the researcher local skills is an important means of showing appreciation of their knowledge.

We can also make efforts to reduce power imbalances by placing ourselves in positions in which our informants are comfortable, even if sometimes we are not. Chapter 5 noted that there is sense in living within our comfort zone when conducting fieldwork and that it is not always wise to live in our research sites, however, the converse is also true: it is sometimes very wise to do so, particularly when wanting to overcome power inequalities. Thus we can conduct interviews in the homes of our informants. We can live locally during the period of research, use local transportation and eat at local eateries. This might mean sleeping on the floor of a mud hut rather than in a comfortable hotel bed, being squashed in an overcrowded bus on a seat far too small rather than driving a hired jeep, and eating food that does not always agree with one's palate. In the process of becoming accustomed to this foreign environment we may occasionally make social blunders but to do so merely reveals that we are fallible.

While there are clear power gradients between the researcher and the researched which, for the most part, favour the researcher, it is also important to stress that 'difference' between the researcher and researched is not necessarily a problem in itself. In 1997, Helen Leslie, a PhD student from New Zealand, visited El Salvador to conduct research on women's experiences of the recent civil war and the work of a local feminist organisation for political action in assisting women to reconstruct their identities through the memories of such experiences. She had expected that her presence would be more of a hindrance than of any assistance to both individual women and the organisation itself. Her main activities included participation in self-help groups facilitated by the organisation and conducting in-depth interviews with individual women participants of the self-help groups. Often her experiences participating in the groups and conducting interviews were very emotional as many of the women spoke of their experiences of extreme hardship. Many carried the guilt of the loss of family members and their inability to care for their children during war-time crises such as *guindas* or flights, where they were forced to hide out in the mountains in an attempt to save their own and their families' lives. During one such *guinda* a woman interviewed had lost her small baby due to starvation. While some commentators would warn against the appropriateness of cross cultural research which intrudes on women's personal lives, the reactions Leslie received from her research participants would suggest that they generally had very positive feelings about her research, as seen in Box 8.5.

Box 8.5 Development of positive relationships between a New Zealand researcher and her research participants in El Salvador

Before leaving for El Salvador I had read a great deal of literature on feminist research methods which often led me to doubt both the appropriateness of my proposed research and my own ability to offer something worthwhile to participants in the research process. Such was my angst, that at times, I felt that perhaps it would be a better idea to call the whole thing off! I was extremely surprised and I must admit delighted to find that once I reached El Salvador that most of my worries dissipated. Without exception, all the women I had contact with during the course of my fieldwork, were extremely welcoming and happy to help me with my research. When I first introduced the idea of conducting in-depth interviews with the women of one self-help group I had been observing over a period of 3 months, I could not believe the reaction. A party atmosphere prevailed as the group participants worked out the logistics of my visits to their homes. They all commented during the course of the subsequent interviews that they found it very special that I had come from so far away to listen to the stories of their lives. One participant felt that I was giving her the opportunity to portray the reality of life in El Salvador. The Salvadoran government, she stated, 'tells so many lies'.

In hindsight, I realised that I did have something to offer my research participants and that one should not necessarily assume that feminist treatises on the exploitative nature of cross-cultural research will apply in all contexts and with differing research projects. I realised that the factors most important to my research participants in as far as my being there was concerned, had little or nothing to do with my 'positionality' but more with my ability to engage with and participate in the 'family' they had formed through their self-help experiences.

Source: Helen Leslie, cited in Scheyvens and Leslie (2000:125)

Similarly, Martha Macintyre's work with the Tubetube island people in Papua New Guinea suggests that participants may not find the 'difference' between themselves and the Western researcher to be oppressive. Rather, during her fieldwork, Macintyre (1993) found that the differences that existed between herself and the women with whom she lived, created a bond between them whereby '[her] interest in their lives was matched by their interest in [hers]'.

Gatekeepers

Gatekeepers are defined as 'those individuals in an organisation that have the power to withhold access to people or situations for the purposes of research' (Miniechello et al., 1997 in de Laine, 2000:123; see also the discussion in Chapter 5). Gatekeepers might include village headmen, community religious leaders or heads of kin groups or households. In many instances before they even reach the community researchers will have to apply to and receive permission from government agencies which can control who does research on what topic. Note that gatekeepers sometimes try to have control over who you speak to, and over the research findings. As Valentine warns:

> Beware...when you are relying on gatekeepers for an introduction to members of a social group (for example the chair of the local Women's Institute), that they do not try to direct you to a narrow selection of the members (probably their friends) and discourage you from talking to others. In this situation you may want to make a discreet effort to talk to other people in order to make sure the gatekeeper is not trying to steer you away from them so as to prevent you from hearing a dissenting voice, and therefore distorting your understanding of the issue you are researching. (1997:116)

Gatekeeping controls sometimes conflict with the needs and rights of the researcher and/or the researched. Many researchers have faced problems regarding to whom it is they are obligated. Is it to the people who the researcher lived with and learned from, or is it to the gatekeepers, including the host government (Box 8.6)?

In Malaysia, government officials view themselves as the researcher's host by virtue of granting research visas. The visa establishes a patron–client relationship between the government and the researcher. This can make researchers feel less inclined to make statements that describe the government in a negative light.

But what happens if the researcher's experiences highlight problems with the way government policy deals with the marginalised people the researcher has been studying? To whom does the researcher owe his/her loyalty, the people who initially allowed him or her into the country, or to the people who provided the day-to-day support and answered his or her questions? If the researcher decides on the latter, what impact might this have on future study? It might mean the government will not allow the researcher back into the country. It might mean the government will ban all foreign researchers. This is where ethical considerations come into play, as noted by the American Anthropological Association, which states,

'Anthropological researchers should do all they can to preserve opportunities for future fieldworkers to follow them to the field'(1998:B3). Not only is this then difficult for future researchers but it also means that quite possibly no one will be able to follow up on what is happening to the communities under threat (see Nowak and Laird, 1998, for a complete discussion of this problem). But as Nancy Scheper-Hughes (1992) and Michael Taussig (1987) have both pointed out, if researchers do not speak out against the injustices witnessed they are condoning the injustice. The researcher's position is a position of privilege which should be used to help those in need.

Box 8.6 Community versus government gatekeepers in Malaysia

I applied for a research visa and waited nearly two years to finally hear from the Malaysian embassy granting me the necessary permission. The visa required a significant amount of information, including the name(s) of local people willing to act as financial and political guarantors for my presence in the country. I was warned that the guarantor unofficially must be of Malay ethnicity. Malaysia is a country which remains ethnically divided in terms of economics, typically controlled by Chinese groups, and politics, controlled by Malays. The orang asli (aboriginal) groups, one of which I wanted to conduct research with, remain both politically and economically marginalised.

Some researchers had told me I would need to go to Malaysia to get my visa, that the government did not give permission from a distance. When I received my visa while still abroad I was thus surprised. But there it was, a visa, with two pages of official stamps in my passport. Little did I know that this meant nothing. When I finally arrived in the country, I was told my visa was not valid and I needed to report to the immigration office within 24 hours. The immigration officials informed me that the visa remained invalid until I replaced my financial and political guarantors. The couple who had initially agreed to help were no longer in Malaysia and the guarantor needed to be present there. Was this my fault? I thought not as it took the Malaysian Government two years to process my application! Who could I turn to? I didn't know any Malays in the country. I was lucky and people in the university where I went for assistance were generous and helped me. I got my signatures and statement of agreement to guarantee me within the allotted 48 hours. I was in!

After a few days of considering my next step I was told an official from the Department of Aborigines was going to visit a village in the area I wanted to go to. They offered me a ride. I decided at this point not to go in to the community with all my belongings and say 'Hi, here I am!' Rather, I decided to go in and see what the situation was like, what I would need to live there and if my research would be feasible. I especially wanted to ask permission of the village leader.

I went in and received the permission I was looking for. A week later I moved into the community. I had a terrible time in the village however for the first eight months I lived there. People, while never threatening or mean to me, were never particularly friendly or helpful. I felt as if I had a communicable disease. It took quite a long time for people to want to talk with me, to want to include me, to want to be my friend. I found out months later that the women thought I was a wealthy woman who would steal their men.

> *The villagers taught me a lesson. Although I had received 'official per-mission' from the government run by Malays, it was not the government that was going to help me with my research. It was not the government who would have to put up with my stupid questions and ignorance of their language, it was the villagers! The village leader had no choice but to agree to the government's decision, so when I initially arrived and asked his permission to stay it was a moot point. Even though government offi-cials were the initial gatekeepers, the formidable gatekeepers, the gate-keepers of the information, were the community members. It was the villagers who decided what I would and would not learn.*
>
> *Source: Barbara Nowak, PhD research in Malaysia, 1980-1982*

Reciprocity

Before, during and after fieldwork it is important to consider what you can give back to those who have provided you with assistance. Your informants give up their time and provide you with information, but what do you give back in return? There seems to be a general agreement in the literature that we will gain far more from our fieldwork than those who participate in it (Patai, 1991; Wolf, 1996). We return to our home universities, write our dissertations or research papers, and will most likely seek employment or promotions based on our newly gained information and qualifica-tions. But what is in it for those we study? After three decades as an anthropologist Walcott (1995:135) concludes very frankly that 'I have no evidence that my own research ever helped anyone I thought it might help or intended it to help'. Unless our research is policy-oriented and unless we have built linkages with institutions that are committed to act on our findings, our research will benefit us far more than our informants. Of course, if published our research findings might contribute in some small way towards a certain movement or change in policy over time.

The fact that we will gain more from our fieldwork than those we study should not deter us from embarking on our research programs. It does not make our research unethical. The understanding you gain from fieldwork could lead you down various avenues of activism.[2] Later in life we may find ourselves in positions in which we can influence development policy or practice. Or, we may be able to inform oth-ers in positions of power of the insights we have gained. We should not therefore become immobilised by doubts about the legitimacy of fieldwork. Even Walcott (1995:239) finds enough merit in fieldwork to conclude that it is 'an activity one can engage in – with passion, without apology'. However, it may be good to keep in mind Patai's observation that academics face a fundamental contradiction in their work which often stands in the way of using their research for the public good:

> As I see it, the problem for us academics, who are already leading privileged exis-tences, resides in the obvious fact that our enjoyment of research and its rewards con-stantly compromises the ardour with which we promote social transformation. At the very least, it dilutes our energy; at the most, it negates our ability to work for change. (Patai, 1991:139)

There are various ways that you can give something back and these should be considered before fieldwork begins. You can give something back through the process of research. This has already been alluded to in the discussion on power relationships in this chapter, and was debated in Chapter 4 when considering the value of participatory approaches to research. Some suggest, for example, that collective oral histories from participants can increase their self-esteem (Francis, 1992). When doing home-based research in Nigeria, Amadiume (1993) found that by running an essay competition for school children she could both verify her research findings and instil in them a sense of pride in their culture and history (Box 8.7).

> **Box 8.7 The value of organising an essay competition in Eastern Nigeria**
>
> 'I felt that it was time for me to return to London.... There was, however, one last task for me to do. I organised an essay competition for both the boys' and girls' secondary schools. My intention, apart from encouraging interest in local research into our customs, was to open up a wider discussion on our history and cultural institutions and, more importantly, to have an overall source of data with which to cross-check my own findings and conclusions.
>
> This technique proved an unbelievable success. Nnobi basked in cultural pride for several days. The town was mentioned on the state radio, which reported the names of winners of the essay competition. It advised other towns and villages to follow the example of Nnobi. In Nnobi, elders, both men and women, felt that this sort of thing should be a regular event.'
>
> *Source: Amadiume (1993:188-189)*

Similarly, Box 8.8 provides an example of how Helen Leslie sought to assist women in her research project on post-conflict El Salvador by using the interview process as a way of giving participants the opportunity for further reflection on, and thus redefinition of, their gendered experiences of the war.

The research experience can be rewarding for your informants when you show you value their information and knowledge. Visiting poor households/individuals that would normally be ignored by distinguished visitors (a category you will most likely be placed in, despite any unease you may feel about this) could help raise their self-esteem. You may even develop mutually rewarding relationships that could last a lifetime. If you are doing research in remote areas then at the very least you are likely to be a distraction from the boredom of village life (Goward, 1984:109). And, as you blunder your way through the vagaries of cross-cultural research, you may also provide a source of amusement.

Outside of data gathering activities there will be other ways to give something back. You should consider participating in local activities and learning local customs that show you value the culture of those you study. A visitor to the village of Lesu in New Ireland was told the following about the anthropologist Powdermaker, who had previously done research in the area:

Box 8.8 The therapeutic value of interviews for women in El Salvador

I hadn't really considered the therapeutic value of my in-depth interviews with participants, but as I began to conduct my interviews it became apparent that they were, in fact, constructed as having therapeutic value to the women. Many experiences which were considerably traumatic for participants were recounted in the course of the interview process and these would induce much emotion on the part of the participants, my research assistant and myself. Some time for reflection on gender issues raised in the self-help groups was also part of the interview should the participant desire it and these opportunities, along with the process of expressing emotion, often resulted in women feeling that a great burden had been lifted off their shoulders in terms, for example, of the guilt they felt for transgressing society's notions of the role of a 'good' mother during the conflict.

Source: Helen Leslie, cited in Scheyvens and Leslie (2000:128)

You know, when she [Powdermaker] came here she was so dumb. She did not even know how to speak. She was like an infant. She knew nothing. But now, ah, all is changed. She speaks and she understands us; she knows our magic; she can dance with the women; she has learned our folk tales; she knows how we garden and the different ways we fish; she has been to our feasts . . . . Ah, she knows much. Who is responsible? I am. (Wax, 1979:255)

The villager, recalling Powdermaker's ineptitude when she first arrived in the village, expresses pride in the manner in which she claims responsibility for teaching Powdermaker local customs and practices.

Gift giving is another means of showing appreciation to those who have assisted you or given up their time to speak with you. It is, however, a very delicate issue. Bleek (1979:201) argues against giving presents on the basis that they serve to reaffirm existing socio-economic inequalities. This position is adequately countered by van Binsbergen (1979:207), however, who believes that gifts or services are appropriate when they are to express one's commitment to evolving relationships, not to 'buy off the informant's envy or one's own feelings of guilt'. Before giving a gift careful thought should be given to the nature of your relationship with your informants and the type of offering. Gift giving that results in a patron–client relationship, that is, one in which the receiver expects and becomes reliant on further gifts, can be very problematic. What informants might hope for and what is reasonable, can present another quandary. Francis (1992:91) elected to fund a number of 'sop' activities during which each guest was provided with a small gift. She recognised that some participants expected more of her in hoping that she could help them find employment in the urban centres. Having no influential contacts in the cities to help with finding jobs, Francis could not consider this option even if she had wanted to. Before departing for fieldwork, discussions with nationals or other researchers who have conducted fieldwork in your study country may help. You should seek local advice after arrival as well. In other instances, it may only be during the course of fieldwork that you will become aware of what gift giving gestures are appropriate.[3]

Near the end of two separate village level studies in Bangladesh, Henry paid for dinners of high status food for the field staff of the development organisations he was researching. It was only through discussions with the management of these institutions that he became aware that this was an appropriate gesture of gratitude. For some of his informants who were impoverished women, he offered to take photos and send to them prints as soon as possible. He found that some women would put on their best saris before allowing to have their photos taken suggesting that they valued this opportunity. Of course, such a gift is not going to help these women in their daily struggles. Researchers face the dilemma that the gifts they offer may be little more than a token of their visit.

In some instances you may be able to offer certain practical services. Razavi (1992) found she could provide practical assistance during the duration of her fieldwork by transporting locals in her car. Lewis (1991:62) had access to a photocopier and was able to give out maps of village plots that were normally not accessible to locals.

Truth and deception

The subjects of truth and deception cut at the core of the ethics of fieldwork, and thus not surprisingly have been at the centre of some rather emotive debates. On one side are those who insist that it is essential to be absolutely honest with participants when you expect truthfulness from them. Purveyors of another view argue that 'truth' is a relative concept: even researchers who are strong advocates of telling the truth may choose to withhold some personal information about themselves, which could be seen as deception, and participants certainly are known for manipulating information and telling untruths or partial truths when they feel this is in their interests. There are also those who believe that partially concealing the truth can be more sensitive to research participants (see Adams and Megaw, 1997:220-221), thus supporting the idea that to be open and truthful at all times could undermine not only the research objectives, but the well-being of research participants: 'Ethics say that while truth is good, respect for human dignity is even better' (Bulmer, 1982, cited in Adams and Megaw, 1997:221).

Many researchers in practice sit somewhere between the absolute and partial truth camps. Under most circumstances they are honest, but they may lie to participants if this could improve their access to research information. For example, a single female researcher may feel a lie about her marital status is justified if it allows her access to important information or events in the field, especially if the 'lie' causes no direct harm to participants. Of course, whether or not lies cause harm can be difficult to ascertain, as noted by Raybeck who starts a chapter in his book on fieldwork in Malaysia entitled 'Shady Activities and Ethical Concerns', by stating that:

many ethical decisions require a degree of compromise....While I hope to have done 'right' in each of these instances, I lack full confidence that this was always the case. As you will find, several of my decisions involved obfuscations, some concerned temporizing, and still others included outright lies (honesty is not always the best policy). (Raybeck, 1996:116)

Certainly telling lies, whether about one's marital status, class or religious background, may cause little direct harm but in some cases 'the guilt for those deceiving their respondents with whom they are attempting to create a bond of empathy may cause considerable anguish' (Wolf, 1996:11-12). Furthermore, supporters of the 'absolute truth' camp, would probably suggest that to begin your research with a lie establishes a bad precedent.

A number of researchers have found that when they have been truthful, the negative reactions they expected have not been forthcoming. Schrijvers (1993:148) for example, describes her initial reluctance at revealing the true nature of her present relationship and her personal history to her participants, lest she met with disapproval:

> We had not told anybody in the village that the children were not Peter's; that both of us had had a divorce; that Peter's two children lived in the Netherlands with their mother; and that in that country, too, lived the real father of my children. We knew that in Sinhalese society a divorce was most detrimental to one's reputation. Revealing these facts of life did not seem like the best introduction. But also we did not like to tell lies.

Eventually, however, Schrijvers' sons explained their complex family situation to others in the community, and soon word spread around the village. To Schrijvers' great surprise, '...our scandalous past did not damage our good reputation. Rather it helped us to be viewed as more or less "normal" human beings, people who, just like most villagers, had undergone some serious difficulties in their personal lives'. Further, 'People were most amazed that Peter, who was not the children's own father, behaved like a real father towards them. This greatly increased his moral reputation!' (Schrijvers, 1993:149).

Another situation in which researchers may feel compelled to conceal the whole truth is when dealing with gatekeepers who are protecting their own interests:

> Informed consent may be seen as an obstruction to access gatekeepers can use to protect their interests. In response [ethical] relativists may recognise that something less than full disclosure or lying is necessary to combat 'exploitation' and for promotion of the greater good of the group. (de Laine, 2000:24)

For example, a researcher wishing to examine the social impacts of a new mining project on an indigenous group may disguise this intention in their research proposal presented to the mining company, claiming instead that they want to focus on the economic benefits the indigenous people have gained since the mine was established. While such deception may give the researcher access, it may mean they are more likely to limit publication of their findings to academic forums and less likely to present the full findings of their research to the company, thus failing to give the company the opportunity to reform their practices.

Stacey (1991, cited in Wolf, 1996:20) and de Laine (2000:76-77) talk about deception which stems from befriending participants (see also AAA, 1998:A5). They note that friends may be told private information which is never intended to be included with one's research data. Thus de Laine questions whether it is ethical to become too friendly with people who are participants:

> Informed consent may be procured, yet complicity and 'friend-like' relations between the researcher and the researched may be developed to procure more information than people would want to divulge....The closer the relationship the ethnographer has with participants the more difficult it may be to avoid deception, since protecting what is shared from disclosure is at odds with the research goal. (2000:50)

Researchers who are friends with their research participants may become privy to intimate information such as who is having an illicit affair with who, who is the actual biological father of a person, who is involved in illegal activities. What will the researcher do with this information? Is it acceptable to include it in notes or to discuss the information with others? The researcher has a possible conflict of interest which is the result of his/her dual role as researcher and friend. To publish the information might be viewed as a deception to the person who spoke with the researcher in the role of friend not researcher (de Laine, 2000: 77). Clare Madge confronted such issues of disclosure of information from 'friends' when returning from fieldwork in the Gambia (Box 8.9)

Box 8.9 What to do with 'privileged information' from fieldwork 'friends'

'During my year's stay in The Gambia I learnt much 'privileged information' through my personal relationships with individuals, informally chatting or through daily participation. However, after becoming a friend, I did not feel that I could suddenly become the detached stranger on my return to England and use such information for my academic advancement. For example, I learnt much privileged information about the use of herbal medicines for 'women's' complaints, but although one aspect of my study was the role of herbal medicines to rural Gambians, I did not use the information about women's herbal medicines in my thesis. To do so would have been to betray the trust of my friends, as in this context knowledge is linked to power; I may have disempowered them through the use of such information (I was sending the villagers a copy of my thesis so anyone could have gained access to that medicinal knowledge).'

Source: Madge (1994), cited in Madge et al. (1997)

Issues of truth and deception, like issues of ethics generally, are not as black and white as they may at first appear. Researchers need to be guided by their conscience, which should ideally be strongly influenced by what is in the best interests of those being researched. Regularly considering how we might respond to issues of truth and deception if we were the ones being researched, might help. de Laine (2000:29) suggests that we ask 'would I want others to do this to me?'

Sex and sexuality [4]

There are many viewpoints on the issue of sexuality and fieldwork, from those who propose that field workers put sex on hold for the duration of their work lest they behave in a culturally inappropriate manner, or lest they jeopardise their sense of identity and links with 'home', to those who say that sex is a normal act of human expression and it would be dishonest for the fieldworker to inhibit themselves from behaving in a sexual manner in the field. We do not wish to push any single viewpoint on readers but rather, to make you aware of the gamut of ethical issues involved.

The potential for misunderstanding in cross-cultural contexts, and the unequal power relations between the researcher and most of their participants, means that sex in the field can be both exploitative and unethical. Fieldworkers need to be aware, for example, that sex can take on unanticipated meanings in cross-cultural settings. While in most Western countries, sex outside of marriage is relatively acceptable, this is often not the case elsewhere. Similarly 'trying out' a succession of partners before establishing a more permanent arrangement may be the norm for many Westerners, whereas in other countries establishing a sexual relationship with someone brings with it the commitment of a long-term relationship and ties not just to the individual, but to their extended family. As Killick (1995:90) explains for Korea, 'The notion of a "sexual career", a series of partners tried and rejected until one finds a compatible permanent mate, may seem natural to most Europeans and Americans, but it has not been generally adopted by Koreans, who continue to think of marriage as the normal outcome of any relationship between sincere and well-meaning lovers...'.

The contributors to Kulick and Willson's (1995) volume note, however, that sex in the field need not be seen as inherently problematic and unethical. In fact, they advocate for more openness and debate about expressions of sexuality in the field. That the issue of sexual desire is rarely raised in accounts of fieldwork may in fact speak volumes about ethical concerns surrounding positionality, racism and exploitation which researchers want to avoid discussing (Kulick, 1995:19).

Some researchers find that when in foreign field settings, they become 'asexual' with all thoughts of eroticism put on hold. We call this the traditional 'no sex, we're fieldworkers' approach:

> There seems to be a kind of unwritten, unspoken, and, for the most part, unquestioned rule about the ethics of sex in the field that all anthropology students

somehow absorb during their graduate education. That rule can be summarised in one word: *Don't.* (Kulick, 1995:10)

It seems that at least some of those who choose to remain celibate are motivated by a fear of being rejected by the community in which they are residing, and on whom they are reliant for their research data. Others become nervous that sexual attraction to one's research participants may be equated with neo-colonialist exploitation: for example, they do not want to perpetuate the image of the foreign male wishing to 'possess' or 'exploit' the exotic, Eastern female (Killick, 1995:80). Such concerns need not be limited to male researcher-female participant interaction. Morton (1995) exposes her attraction to Tongan males, whom she describes as 'tall, muscular, handsome, and extremely charming', and bravely reflects on the 'possible overtones of racism' inherent in her attraction particularly when, in the case of one partner, she and he could not communicate well because of language differences.

It has been suggested, on the other hand, that to choose to get close to our participants and share their lives in a multitude of ways *except* sexually, may itself smack of racism:

> The taboo on sexual involvement in the field serves to maintain a basic boundary between ourselves and the Other in a situation in which our goal as ethnographers is to diminish the distance between us…. Refusing to share in sexuality across cultural boundaries helps to perpetuate the false dichotomy between 'us' and 'the natives'. (Bolton, 1995:140)

This may be a relief to those researchers who experience a heightened sense of eroticism in the which may be associated with the freeing up of culturally restrictive norms that dictate behaviour in our home society, coupled with a romantic fascination with the new society in which we are living and those we are engaging with.

We should not assume that by avoiding sexual activity, we will receive greater acceptance and respect in a community. Gearing found that the opposite was true when she had a relationship with a man she met during fieldwork in St. Vincent:

> Contrary to my expectation that my relationship with my boyfriend would provoke comments about my 'loose morals', several of my female neighbours told me they were glad 'I had a man about the house', and that they had been concerned about my living alone. My previous 'standoffishness', demonstrated by living alone and not having a boyfriend, had been a cause for worry and comment. My Vincentian neighbours let me know in subtle ways that by being in a sexual relationship I was finally acting like a normal adult. (Gearing, 1995:200)

It is important to note, however, that in Gearing's case the community's acceptance of her relationship was at least partly based on the fact that she had followed traditional Vincentian protocol of a 'courtship' with her boyfriend, and he had introduced himself to other community members when courting her, rather than behaving in a clandestine manner.

Whether a sexual relationship between a researcher and a local person is widely accepted therefore, will depend a lot on the culture involved, including associated religious beliefs, as well as the way in which the relationship evolves, the terms on which it takes place, and the sensitivity of the researcher to cultural norms. Such relationships need not be exploitative or oppressive.

Safety of the researcher and responsibilities to self

Many discussions of ethics now raise concerns that official ethics procedures pay great attention to protecting research participants, without concomitant attention to protection of the persons doing the research:

> researchers are often well versed in outlining the importance of protecting participants, the ways they intend to do this and the possible consequences of the research process upon the lives of those being studied.... However, the issue of their own or their co-researchers' safety and welfare needs is often thought through in a cursory manner or in an ad hoc contingent fashion once in the field. (Lee-Treweek and Linkogle, 2000:1)

Box 8.10 The importance of contingency plans

In 2001, Ishara was preparing to conduct PhD research back home in Nepal on gender issues associated with rural energy technologies (see Box 6.1, Chapter 6). Following the murders of the Nepalese royal family and the heightened activity of the Maoist led insurgency movement in Nepal, Ishara and her supervisors (Barbara and Regina) discussed the possibility that Nepal was not a safe place for research. Discussion included whether or not an alternative location, with similar critical factors, could be substituted for the original location if things got worse. An alternative was agreed upon and the sponsoring agency was contacted for agreement for the change of research location, if necessary.

A few months later Ishara and her supervisors felt the situation in Nepal was calm enough and research went ahead as originally scheduled. In the early stages of field work the ceasefire between the Maoists and the government fell apart however; the government declared a state of emergency. Ishara and her supervisors thus had to continually reassess her safety and the appropriateness of continuing her fieldwork in Nepal, particularly when 16 policemen were killed in a raid by Maoists very close to her field site.

There are various aspects or types of risks researchers face including physical, emotional, ethical and professional risks (Lee-Treweek and Linkogle, 2000).[5] Research on communities under threat, high crime communities such as gangs or street children, research in war zones or regions of civil unrest, all present immediate and potential dangers for the researcher both from those people involved in the 'illegal' or dissident activities as well as from those in authority (for example, see Jipson and Litton, 2000; Nordstrom and Robben, 1995). In places where there are insurgents researchers need to be cautious of being suspected of spying for the military or supplying the rebels (Green, 1995; Howell, 1990: 96; Nash, 1976; Oglesby, 1995). Even if you are not going to an area to study conflict, violence or a dissident group, you may accidentally find yourself in the wrong place at the wrong time. Supervisors and an ethics committee may suggest or even require the establishment of particular research protocols to ensure the researcher's safety (see Sluka, 1995, and Box 8.10). At other times, it may simply not be possible to continue with your research as originally planned. This has been the experience of Helen Sherpa, a New Zealander married to a Nepalese man who has been doing grassroots development work in Nepal while also trying to complete her Masters degree (Box 8.11).

Box 8.11 A safety-first approach to research: protecting participants and self

The following derives from emails sent by Helen Sherpa to her supervisor.

Well the weeks and months pass and I achieve little progress on my thesis research. I have read extensively on civil society and the different aspects and issues. If you ever follow the news from Nepal you will be aware that the civil war here has gone from bad to worse. The death toll has now passed the 6,000 point. The government has collapsed and the king has seized powers and installed a puppet government. Local government and all elected government have ceased to exist. The Maoists routinely execute political leaders, teachers and social workers. The dangers on the ground are great and I find my work extremely stressful as I try to ensure the safety of a large staff working in many different districts.

Sadly my thesis seems to be a disaster. For my field research I carefully selected VDCs (Village Development Committees) in Makawanpur that represented hill and Terai, accessible and inaccessible, Brahmin and Chettri and oppressed minority communities, etc. These very VDCs were subjected to terrible floods and landslides this monsoon. Over 60 people died and 120 families lost all their homes and lands in just one of the four research VDCs. Since then the Maoists have taken over the VDCs. I still have work projects going on there but research on civil society participation looks dangerous for anyone, myself or an assistant.

Your advice a while ago was to wait and see if the conflict abated or if possible include what continues to work even in a conflict situation. The second idea has a certain amount of appeal but just collecting information is the problem. Visits by foreigners asking questions put locals at risk and draws unwanted attention from both the Army and Maoists to the community.... If I need to hurry this along to meet a fixed deadline I think I need to change topics. Otherwise I can start my research here on the Valley rim and experiment with collecting the data and then look for a second relatively safe area outside the valley in which to replicate it for comparison.

Source: Helen Sherpa, extramural Masters student, Massey University, 2002

Another physical danger in the field which is more often faced by female than male researchers is that of sexual violence (see for example, Moreno, 1995). Many female researchers have found that images of them have been tainted by Hollywood movies which portray Western women as having few morals and being sexually available. As noted in earlier chapters, it pays to present a professional image if you want to be treated professionally, but even smart, conservative dress style may not dissuade men from giving you their unwanted attention.

Female researchers may have particular difficulty when unwanted attention is directed at them from males in positions of power. Gearing's experience during research in St Vincent, when government officials played important gatekeeping roles, is indicative of this:

> Suggestive remarks and invitations to go out for drinks were more difficult to dismiss as mere annoyances when the power relations between us were reversed, and my research depended on gaining access to government records or getting permission to conduct interviews. After several unpleasant encounters, I learned to rely on my personal network and obtained information through indirect channels. (Gearing, 1995:193-4)

Researchers in conjunction with their supervisors and even ethics committees might jointly work on finding a safe way to do research. When a Masters student was preparing a thesis on gangs in New Zealand, for example, the university ethics committee was very concerned about the student's safety, a point she had not fully considered. Together they established safety mechanisms. Before going out to meet with participants of the study, the student wrote down the name(s) of the people she was scheduled to meet and where she was going. She would place this information in a sealed envelope and leave it with a trusted person. This person would only open the envelope if the student did not return at an agreed upon time. When the student returned, she would destroy the envelope. These guidelines resolved the conflicting needs of participants' privacy and the student's safety.

While researchers need to be aware of potential risks and cognisant of ways of protecting themselves, it is worth noting that dangers in particular fieldsites can be exaggerated, especially by those 'locals' who have limited understanding of places they only hear about through the press. During his doctoral research, Donovan, one of the editors of this book, found squatter settlements much safer than tourist areas in Manila, even at night.

Conclusion

This chapter has unearthed a range of ethical dilemmas commonly faced by Development Studies researchers, from dealing with powerful gatekeepers to hiding truths from research participants, from ensuring reciprocity in relations with participants to deciding whether to follow up on one's sexual interests in the field. While to some, their own strong moral convictions may place them in the 'ethical absolutist' camp and make responses to the above dilemmas clear cut, many researchers find themselves adopting an 'ethical relativist' position which means they are constantly debating, negotiating and reflecting on such dilemmas in the course of their fieldwork.

Only one thing is clear: while satisfying the requirements of a university ethics committee may encourage you to think through some ethical concerns before engaging in fieldwork, it will almost certainly not prepare you for a range of other ethical dilemmas which will crop up once you are actually doing your research. While a general code of ethics which covers informed consent, confidentiality, and conflicts of interest, can provide you with useful guidelines, in many cases it is your personal characteristics – ideally, a combination of integrity, maturity and sensitivity to the local cultural context (de Laine, 2000:28) – which you will need to call on to guide you.

Recommended reading

de Laine, M. (2000) *Fieldwork, Participation and Practice: Ethics and Dilemmas in Qualitative Research* Sage, London.
An excellent text which deals comprehensively with issues of ethics associated with qualitative research.

Dowling, R. (2000) Power, subjectivity and ethics in qualitative rsearch. In I. Hay (ed.) *Qualitative Research Methods in Human Geography* Oxford University Press, Melbourne, pp.23-36.
A succinct and clearly written chapter which introduces the reader to university ethical guidelines, while also drawing attention to the need to move beyond these guidelines and take a stance of 'critical reflexivity'.

Patai, D. (1991) U.S. academics and Third World women: is ethical research possible? In S.B. Gluck and D. Patai (eds) *Women's Words: The Feminist Practice of Oral History* Routledge, New York and London, pp.137-53.
This chapter provides a useful reminder to Western researchers of the power relations inherent in cross-cultural research, focusing particularly on research targeting women in Third World countries.

Notes

1. The word ethics originates from the Greek word *ethos*, meaning character, custom or usage.

2. See the discussion in Chapter 9 on 'Advocacy and activism'.

3. Chapter 10 provides a further discussion on gift giving with relation to leaving the field.

4. Chapter 6 has touched on some issues of sexuality (see the section on 'Families in the field' which includes a discussion on homosexuality).

5. Physical risks are discussed in detail in Chapter 5 in a section entitled 'Health and safety', material which will not be repeated here. Likewise, readers interested in the emotional challenges of fieldwork are directed to Chapter 6, which drew attention to the stress and personal difficulties often associated with fieldwork and strategies for dealing with these in practice.

9 Working with Marginalised, Vulnerable or Privileged Groups

Regina Scheyvens, Henry Scheyvens and Warwick E. Murray

Introduction

By now you will be well aware that fieldwork in the Third World can present difficult practical, ethical and personal challenges. When the subjects of research are marginalised groups, the challenges look even more foreboding. How should you behave when you are interacting with people who are obviously much poorer than you, or who are minority ethnic groups,[1] lower class women, or children? How will they react to you? We must be sensitive if we are to carry out ethical and worthwhile research involving marginalised peoples. hooks indicates that for too long research on the marginalised has been carried out in an oppressive manner:

> Often this speech about the 'other' annihilates, erases: 'no need to hear your voice when I can talk about you better than you can speak about yourself. No need to hear your voice. Only tell me about your pain. I want to know your story. And then I will tell it back to you in a new way. Tell it back to you in such a way that it has become mine, my own. Re-writing you, I write myself anew. I am still author, authority. I am still the colonizer, the speak subject, and you are now at the centre of my talk. Stop'.
> (1990:151-152)

Efforts should be made to ensure that our research is not merely a self-serving exercise. This can be achieved in various ways, from nurturing respectful and friendly relationships with our participants, to forms of activism, as will be discussed later in this chapter.

Another group with whom we have to take special care in our research are the privileged – those who are rich and/or powerful. While some people may feel that research involving the poor is more of an immediate priority in development studies than research targeting the rich, this overlooks the importance of understanding the culture and practices of those occupying powerful positions. It also ignores the value of understanding various social constructions, such as class or ethnicity, from the perspectives of both poorer and wealthier people (Wolf, 1996:37). 'Studying up' is thus now considered a highly credible form of research as it allows us to gain a greater understanding of how differentiation and power are reproduced and used as tools to exacerbate marginalisation of the weak.

While a section of this chapter is thus devoted to researching the elite and powerful, the first four sections will examine special considerations for researchers working with groups whose members are often marginalised or vulnerable, that is, women, children, minority ethnic groups, and the poor. We realise that the groups we have chosen do not cover the gamut of marginalised social groups with whom researchers may come into contact – the physically or mentally disabled and the aged are obvious groups not specifically discussed due to space constraints – but we try to make up for this somewhat by suggesting general principles to apply when working with disadvantaged and vulnerable groups (see Box 9.7). In choosing to focus on these groups we also do not wish to suggest that women, children, minority ethnic groups, and the poor are universally oppressed, nor that men, adults, majority ethnic groups and the very rich are universally oppressive. Rather, members of the former social groups are more often in less powerful positions, and thus face reduced opportunities to access resources to improve their well-being.

When working with marginalised or privileged groups which are differently positioned from ourselves,[2] we need to examine carefully our motivations for fieldwork, as discussed in Chapter 6. It has been suggested, for example, that some researchers are merely hopping on a popular bandwagon by choosing to study yet another excluded minority group (Matthews et al., 1998). Wolf (1996) urges that researchers 'need to critically and self-consciously examine their positionality, if only to better understand their role in the global arena or their self-appointed "do-gooder" role' (Wolf, 1996:35). Therefore those of us who are motivated by emotional responses to poverty, human rights abuses and other social injustices need to consider carefully how we present ourselves to the subjects of our study. A danger is that rather than valuing our informants and the knowledge they possess, we pity them if they are marginalised, or, in the case of elites, we mistrust or even despise them. We view our informants not as people who lead multi-dimensional lives – laughing, crying, celebrating, grieving and hoping, just like the rest of us – and who hold information that could increase our understanding of a particular topic, but as people we feel a need to help or that need to be taught something or to be taken down a peg or two. Our attitude towards people who face economic and other hardships should not be so shrouded by pity that we fail to see things of value in those we study. Neither should our attitudes to the elite be clouded by suspicion or anger before we have even met them.

This chapter therefore provides an examination of the importance and concerns associated with both research involving the marginalised and the privileged. Our aim is to help researchers prepare for the challenges of such research so they are able to work in a responsible, sensitive manner and make the most of the opportunities that are available.

Researching women

As suggested in the introduction to this chapter, women are not all vulnerable or disadvantaged in relation to other members of society. However, societal structures which vary from culture to culture mean that many women do face specific forms of oppression in their daily lives and are less able, in general, than men to be able to access resources to improve their quality of life. Furthermore, many researchers are aware of the need to consult women, especially because past research efforts so often ignored women or misrepresented them, and such misinformation was often used to inform development policy and practice (Rogers, 1978; Tomm, 1989). However, there are often difficulties associated with research involving women in the Third World. In fact it has been suggested that the sensitivity of ethical issues in development research is often intensified when participants are Third World women (Scheyvens and Leslie, 2000).

Using research to reveal what women are thinking and hoping for can be a process fraught with difficulties. It may, for instance, be very difficult for the researcher to gain access to women, partly because they are often extremely busy, and time to sit and talk may be restricted to the late evenings when it may not be appropriate, or practical, for a researcher to visit women's homes. In addition, women are rarely given roles as official spokespersons for a community thus they are not the first people outsiders are likely to encounter. Women's freedom in public domains may also be constrained, meaning it is unlikely that they will attend community meetings, or, if they do, they will sit quietly at the back and not express opinions or ask questions. The notion that only certain individuals are qualified to speak out in public exists in many Third World contexts. Because women have been consulted so little in the past, there may be genuine surprise and suspicion in the minds of community leaders if a researcher asks to speak to women. If such permission is granted, men may 'loiter' when focus groups or interviews with women are held, at least until they feel comfortable that the issues being discussed are either a) not threatening to them, or b) 'only' women's business.

Even when means are found of talking to women, many may be reluctant to express themselves in front of an outsider due to low self-esteem. As noted by Keesing, a sense of inadequacy can certainly influence what women will tell a researcher about themselves:

> Reflexive autobiography is possible only when subjects believe that their own lives
> are important enough to deserve recounting, and when social support is provided....
> If a people's dominant ideologies, expressions of male political hegemony, define
> what women know and do as secondary and unimportant, then creating a context
> where women can and will talk about themselves and their partly separate realms of
> life and expertise may indeed be difficult. (1985:37)

It is perhaps not surprising, therefore, that a researcher working with women in a traditional society in Papua New Guinea found that most women preferred interview sessions at night, in contexts where the lighting was dim. Some women admitted to the researcher that they felt more relaxed under these circumstances than they would during the day as they did not want him to look at their faces or to identify who was talking (Lagisa, 1997).

Development research with women can also be sensitive if it reveals aspects of women's disadvantage. Critical research examining issues such as gender inequities in household decision-making or the impacts of an agricultural extension programme on men and women, for example, can inherently challenge the status quo. If the purpose of such research is made public, it may upset power brokers within a society and others who benefit from women's disadvantaged position.

Difficulties in conducting fieldwork with women should not provide an excuse, however, for researchers to avoid engaging in such research. It is possible to create contexts in which either socially repressed, introverted or less accessible women are willing to open up their private worlds to view (Keesing, 1985). As long as researchers are informed of and sensitive to local socio-cultural contexts, the difficulties discussed above can often be overcome, and women can become very enthusiastic participants (see Box 8.5, Chapter 8):

> For people who do not usually have the opportunity to voice their concerns, research can be very positive and enabling in itself because it can encourage such people to articulate their needs. (Pratt and Loizos, 1992:17)

Even those concurring with the above conclusion may be less certain about the place of men conducting research with women in the Third World. Essentially, should one's sex determine if an individual can carry out research with Third World women? A number of writers suggest benefits arising from same sex researchers and participants, with Oakley (1981) for example arguing that female research participants respond more freely and openly to a female researcher. Similarly, Reinharz (1992:19) suggests that women interviewing women 'is an antidote to centuries of ignoring women's ideas altogether or having men speak for women'. On a more practical note, Sollis and Moser (1991) suggest that in gender-segregated societies where there is sensitive information to collect about women, it is best to use a female researcher. The example in Box 9.1, and the following quote, lend further support to this viewpoint:

> in many developing countries the world of women is not open to men so that translating the needs and desires of women into research problems and vice versa can best be done by women. (Boesveld, 1986: 46)

But do these authors suggest that there is no place for men in conducting research with Third World women? Indeed, if a man carries out interviews and then interprets the findings which are later published in a report, does this constitute 'men speaking for women?' Is a man able to access women's opinions?

Such challenging questions have led to reluctance on the part of many male researchers to directly engage in research with women in Third World contexts. Some have changed their research topics accordingly, or employed female research assistants to conduct the necessary research with women. In other cases, however, males have effectively carried out research with Third World women on their own. One example is research for a Masters thesis which was conducted in Lihir, Papua New Guinea (PNG), by a male PNG student from a New Zealand university. While the student, Leonard Lagisa, was not from Lihir and thus did not speak the local language or understand all of the people's cultural traditions, he was from the broader New Guinea Islands region in which Lihir is located, and both his society and Lihirian society are matrilineal.

Box 9.1 A male anthropologist tries to research 'intimate issues' in Nepal

'I recently returned from my fourth trip to Nepal's Nubri Valley in my capacity as an anthropologist specialising in demographic processes.... During a more ambitious and infinitely more naïve period of field research I had actually attempted to elicit responses from women regarding their ages at menarche and menopause, familiarity with contraception, and even went so far as to try to prompt them to describe birthing experiences. Those who knew me well remained silent on the issues yet managed to cast a sardonic smile my way indicating a sympathetic tolerance for such brazen and invasive questions. Those who did not know me so well pointed to the door and signified in no uncertain terms that it was time I made use of it.

Things took a dramatic turn for the better last October when I went with Dr Sabra Jones (MD) to Nubri in order to collect more demographic data, and more importantly, to gather detailed information about reproduction and childbearing from women's perspectives... Dr Jones' interviews revealed fascinating insights about the plight of women who spend much of their adult lives either pregnant or nursing newborns, are often afflicted with vaginal infections for which they have few remedies, witness the deaths of too many of their infants and desire to somehow delay or prevent births yet lack the means or knowledge to do so.

One immediate result of this research was that we managed to organise a program in Kathmandu (January 2001) through the NGO SEEDS (www.nepalseeds.org) at which Tibetan and Nepali women doctors provided basic training on how to prevent many of the problems that were uncovered. It was most gratifying to witness field research being translated into positive action within a matter of only a few months.'

Source: Geoff Childs (2001:2) Demography Program, Australian National University

---

In Lihir, Lagisa examined women's involvement in decision-making regarding a major mining project which was in its construction phase, and considered the initial impacts of the mining development on women's lives. Most of Lagisa's fieldwork consisted of group interviews, as it would have aroused suspicion had he attempted to talk alone with village women with whom he was not formally acquainted. Many of the women were quite shy and unused to talking with those from outside their village area; however, they participated actively in these interview sessions, somewhat to the surprise of Lagisa. As he later reflected, this may have been due to the fact that they felt he could help them to overcome some of the disadvantages they were facing (see Box 9.2).

While the example in Box 9.2 may seem to suggest that men can only gain access to female participants if they trade on their status as authority figures, this tells only part of the story in the case of Lagisa's research. He also found that his position as a man helped him to gain insights into local gender relations and male perceptions of females, especially through participant observation. When staying with one family, for example, he witnessed an argument between a woman and her husband which occurred when the wife, an employee of the mining company, came home late. The husband was upset that food was not ready; thus he scolded his wife, saying:

> What sort of work do you people do that you come home this late? Do you remember that we have children to look after? Tell whoever your boss is to remember that some of you are mothers and should come home early to cook for the family. . . if you come home late again I will come and physically abuse you and your boss. (cited in Lagisa, 1997:158-59)

This provided a poignant reminder to Lagisa of the burden of the double day which female employees of the mining company faced, and the ways in which men's attitudes impeded women's development. It is unlikely that the man quoted above would have spoken to his wife in this way, however, had the researcher staying with them been female or from a foreign country.

Box 9.2 Benefits of a man conducting research with women: a PNG mine site example

In hindsight, it appears that the women responded a lot more openly to me than I had thought they would because they saw me as an authority figure, as someone with access to authorities, who could help to alleviate the problems they faced. In this way, being a man may have actually assisted in gathering information.

The thing that struck me most during my interview sessions with them [Lihirian women] was their interest in wanting to know what I would do with the information I was collecting from them. I tried my best to make them understand that my research was strictly educational but I promised them that I would write a special report which I would send to LMC (Lihir Management Corporation) in the hope that they would act upon it. Lihir women were clearly interested in changing their disadvantaged position and they hoped that my research would, in some way, help to achieve this.

Source: Lagisa (1997:104, 106)

Hence, while it has been drawn to our attention that 'Male and female interviewers will not necessarily see or be allowed to see the same social worlds' (Women and Geography Study Group of the Institute of British Geographers, 1984:135), this should not necessarily be interpreted as meaning that men will not be able to conduct effective research with women.[3] Neither should it be assumed that women researchers will be able to build better rapport than men with female participants, or that they will be likely to gather more meaningful data. Being the same sex as one's participants will not necessarily lead to immediate bonds between a researcher and those being researched, as Schenk-Sandbergen (1998) found out when working with women in a complex cultural setting within India. Restricted access to certain domains should certainly not deter men from engaging in sensitive research projects in which consulting women on their ideas, knowledge and experiences is vital. Not only is it possible for male researchers to talk to women in many circumstances, there are likely to be advantages in having male researchers working with Third World women, listening to their ideas and exposing information on gender roles, gender relations, and local interpretations of masculinity.

Clearly there are arenas of difference other than gender, including ethnicity, class, age, marital status and sexual preference, all of which can affect our behaviour in the field, who we are able to access in our research and how openly they respond to us (Crick, 1993).

Researching children and youths

None of the authors involved in this book has conducted research that focused specifically on children. This makes us no different from most people doing research in the Third World where the trend has been to consider children indirectly, if at all: 'Choosing to study children in development is in itself a major challenge to the researcher, for it is often not considered a worthy subject. It is rather a category taken for granted – seen but not heard, acted upon but not with' (Bowden, 1998:282). In this chapter we have identified children as an important, less powerful group in society whose voices deserve to be heard if their interests are to be served. Thus we support the current trend among social researchers which views children as meaningful actors in their own right who can speak for themselves and express multiple ideas and opinions (Valentine, 1999). Below we consider appropriate ways of working with children and youths.

Guidelines for researching children and young people in Box 9.3 provide some pointers regarding ways to ensure research minimises harm and maximises benefits to them, including suggestions as to how involvement in the research can be made more fun and interesting for our participants. Any potential benefits from the research should be made clear from the outset. Perhaps the most important guideline for those conducting research with children to abide by is to allow sufficient time to build trust and rapport. This can be achieved through repeated visits in which the research proposal is carefully explained, before any actual data collection goes ahead. In some cases it may be appropriate to establish on-going relationships with the children or young people, whether by writing occasional letters or re-visiting them for research or just out of interest. This will help to overcome a serious concern identified by Matthews et al. (1998:316), that is, that sometimes research with children has turned into 'a "raid", whereby the investigator moves in, plunders the results, swiftly moves out and in this process, the children are denigrated to little more than tokens'. It is also suggested that researchers should pay particular attention to accessing the views of less confident or less articulate children, particularly girls (Gordon, 1998; Matthews and Tucker, 2000:300). Researchers overcame this problem in Nepal by encouraging girls to sing songs, which helped to make them more comfortable and gave the researchers insights into girls' present perceptions and future goals (Johnson et al. 1995, cited in Gordon, 1998:67). Using visual methods may also prove a valuable means of encouraging child-led participation in research, as Young and Barrett (2001) discovered when conducting research with street children in Kampala.

Box 9.3 Guidelines for research involving children and youths

• Clearly explain the purpose of the research to children and young people in terms they can understand, and what their participation will involve. Also inform their parents or guardians and, where appropriate, the wider community.

• Allow sufficient time to build rapport with young participants – this is vital if you wish to develop their confidence and encourage active participation from them.

• Give children and young people the chance to opt into the research without pressure from parents or friends. Assure them that they can withdraw from the research at any time.

• Find ways of enabling children and young people to exert some control over the research e.g. giving them control of the tape recorder during interviews so they can turn it off if they feel uncomfortable.

• Assure the children and young people's privacy and confidentiality and their right to remain anonymous in the research.

• Ensure that participation in the research is enriching and mutually beneficial for yourself and your participants. This can be achieved through use of child-friendly research methods which are more rewarding and less intimidating than conventional questionnaires or interviews, such as making posters, drawing, story writing, keeping oral or written diaries, or role play. It is important to utilise methods appropriate to the group one is working with, however, as not all children will be comfortable holding a pen or crayon in a drawing or writing exercise, for example.

• During long research sessions such as workshops, provide recreational activities such as singing or dancing, to rejuvenate children's energies.

• Show respect for all children and young people involved in your research by taking their views seriously.

• Consider appropriate ways of providing feedback and inform all participants as to when feedback will be provided.

• Show appreciation for young people's participation but do not raise unrealistic expectations among participants.

• Provide acknowledgement of young people's involvement in your research.

Source: Based on Haque (1998:77-78); Matthews and Tucker (2000:300, 302-308); Robson (2001:137, 138)

Matthews et al. (1998) urge us to ensure that our research involving children and young people does not misrepresent them, and neither should it be embarrassing, harmful or intrusive. While such a statement is easy to agree with in theory, Robson found that her research, which was intended to reveal the difficulties facing young people caring for sick relatives in Zimbabwe, was seen by some to be very harmful (Box 9.4). In retrospect, she believes the research was still of value, but we do not know if the carers would share her view.

Box 9.4 Emotional research with young carers in Zimbabwe

In 1997 Elspeth Robson conducted research on young people involved in caring for sick relatives – many with HIV/AIDS-related illnesses – in Zimbabwe. She engaged a Zimbabwean woman researcher to carry out interviews with nine participants who were between the ages of 15 and 17. Robson later became concerned about this research, however, because participants became distressed during the interviews: 'For the young carers in Zimbabwe, telling their story was at considerable emotional cost to them, to their family members present and also to the interviewer' (Robson 2001: 136). One participant, for example, had watched her mother, whom she had cared for, die only one month previously. Thus the interviewer later described the interviews as 'unfair' and 'cruel', which led Robson to reflect carefully on the research process.

Eventually she concluded that the research was still valuable in highlighting the voices of young carers from Zimbabwe and could lead to positive interventions in the future. She also felt that the research was not as harmful as it had been suggested for several reasons: 1) some young carers withdrew from the interviews because of distress, thus expressing their agency and exerting control over the interview process; 2) 'tears are a form of "voice" that should be listened to' (Robson, 2001:137); and 3) it can be therapeutic for young people to talk to a supportive adult about something which has caused them grief.

Source: Robson (2001)

When the research subjects are children, it is also very likely that the researcher could be viewed with suspicion and seen as a threat to the safety of those they are studying. Thus Matthews and Tucker (2000:301) make the important point that if you are carrying out research on children in public spaces, you must inform authorities beforehand and carry identification and copies of any research permission documentation with you.

Some researchers are now utilising children to conduct research. Heyer (1992), for example, employed school children as research assistants in her work in Kenya, asking them to keep time budget diaries of their own households and those of their neighbours. While this can be a way of teaching research skills to children and helping them to understand how information can be collected and processed in order to aid our understanding of important issues, Heyer does not mention how the children could have benefited from involvement in her research, and she completely ignores ethical issues associated with employing, or 'using' children. Save the Children Fund adopted a rather different approach in Vietnam where they planned to train street children to conduct research with children in their own community. They hoped to empower children through raising their skill levels and through recognition from adults about children's ability to conduct research (Theis, 1998:85).

Despite the depth and breadth of ethical issues concerning research with young people, if we exclude them from research we may marginalise them further: 'If we do not allow children to participate, there is a price to be paid. Not only are we denying ourselves the benefit of their uniquely different experiences and perspectives, we may actually be having a negative effect on their well-being' (Ivan-Smith, 1998:262). Ivan-Smith (1998) cites the example of water projects which ignore children's role in water collection, thus siting a new water source in a place that is dangerous for them or providing heavy equipment which is difficult for them to use. There is definitely a need then for more sensitive, well-thought out research with children and young people in Third World settings, because '…children need allies…and vulnerable, invisible, poor, minority children…in the global South desperately need allies with long-term commitment in both academic and political worlds' (Robson, 2001:140).

Researching minority ethnic groups [4]

Anthropologists, in particular, have a long history of conducting research with minority ethnic groups. Other social scientists have often found that their interest in topics such as the creation of national parks, cultural tourism or the impacts of logging or mining has brought them directly into contact with these groups. In the past it was assumed that those hailing from Western academic institutions had a 'right' to engage in such cross-cultural study. The power relations inherent in this research were not considered important enough to warrant comment. Now the increasing political awareness of minority ethnic groups, combined with a good deal of self-reflection on the part of academics (as discussed in Chapter 1) has led to important changes in the ways in which such research is carried out.

Many indigenous groups, in particular, remain wary of outside researchers because their historical experiences have been framed by imperialism, their knowledge colonised for the benefit of Western science (Smith, 1999:19). Most of us are familiar with the term 'research problem', but Smith turns the meaning of this term around to suggest that to indigenous peoples, research is the problem:

> indigenous peoples are deeply cynical about the capacity, motives or methodologies of Western research to deliver any benefits to indigenous peoples....Because of such deep cynicism there are expectations by indigenous communities that researchers will actually 'spell out' in detail the likely benefits of any research. (1999:117-8)

As Chapter 1 asserted, too often researchers have been preoccupied with their own agendas and have offered little that is of benefit to those they are researching: research has been a one-way process of extraction of information. A researcher may have received the government's permission to conduct research, but not that of the community they plan to work with (see Box 8.6, Chapter 8), and they may have given the community no opportunity to influence the questions being asked or the way in which the research is conducted (see also Chapter 5). Because of such concerns some governments have put in place specific rules about working with ethnic groups within their borders. Box 9.5 provides a summary of regulations regarding research in the Pacific Island country of Vanuatu, which is home to around 180,000 people speaking 105 distinct languages, a testimony to the country's ethnic diversity (Stanley, 2000:791). Note particularly the need to gain the permission of the community, not just the central government, and the pro-active role taken by the Vanuatu National Cultural Council in terms of initiating research ventures, encouraging training of and research by indigenous people, and ensuring that communities get tangible benefits from research, not just a copy of the completed thesis or an academic paper.

Box 9.5 Summary of regulations regarding research in Vanuatu

Evaluation
All research proposals must receive the approval of the Vanuatu National Cultural Council and the local community. An explanation of the proposed research project to the local community by the researcher and/or the Cultural Centre is a prerequisite to the local community giving approval.

Encouragement of ni-Vanuatu performed research
With a view to maximising opportunities for ni-Vanuatu (the indigenous people of Vanuatu) to conduct research it is the responsibility of the National Cultural Council to: a) initiate research ventures to be undertaken by ni-Vanuatu, including cooperative ventures with expatriates; b) ensure input by ni-Vanuatu into all research projects; and c) ensure that a

research proposal received from a foreign national does not conflict with research undertaken by a ni-Vanuatu, which will involve identifying the possible research aspirations of ni-Vanuatu scholars in training.

Training
There must be maximum involvement of indigenous scholars, students and members of the community in research, full recognition of their collaboration, and training to enable their further contribution to country and community. The National Cultural Council may nominate individuals to be involved in research and/or trained.

Benefit to the local community
All research projects will include a cultural product of *immediate benefit and use* to the local community. Such products could include booklets of kastom information, photo albums of visual records, simple educational booklets for use in schools...programs for the revitalisation of particular kastom skills in the community, training workshops in cultural documentation, etc.

Accessibility of products of research
The researcher will be responsible for the translation of a publication in a language...used in education in the local community.... Researchers are also required to submit an interim report of not less than 2000 words no later than 6 months after the research period has ended giving a reasonable précis of their work. This should be in one of the national languages and in 'layman's terms' so as to be of general use to all citizens.

Benefit to the nation
Having a trained person working at a local community level is an opportunity from which the nation can gain significant benefit, and the National Cultural Council, the Cultural Centre or the national government may therefore request the researcher to perform certain services additional to their research work. For instance, researchers could provide assistance to government by [doing] ... health surveys, [or providing] information on the viability of certain development projects.

Source: see http://arts.anu.edu.au/arcworld/vks/contre.htm *for a copy of the full Vanuatu Cultural Research Policy*

Concerns about outsiders dominating research projects have led to the call that more research on ethnic minorities or indigenous groups should be conducted by members of the groups concerned. As Smith explains with relation to New Zealand Maori:

Increasingly...there have been demands by indigenous communities for research to be undertaken exclusively by indigenous researchers. It is thought that Maori people need to take greater control over the questions they want to address, and invest more energy and commitment into the education and empowering of Maori people as researchers. (1999:178)

There is a specific need for more research by indigenous researchers in cases whereby ethnic groups have been misrepresented in past research by foreigners. This was part of Amadiume's (1993) motivation for going home to do research in Eastern Nigeria on Igbo women.[5] However, in addition to the fact that shared ethnicity will not necessarily make researchers 'insiders' when they conduct research (see Narayan, 1998), there can be significant constraints to research being conducted by indigenous researchers. As Hau'ofa explains, limited funding has undermined a good deal of indigenous research in the Pacific region:

> because of the intense interest in and preoccupation with material development, and the consequent emphasis on practical and applied studies, there is a danger that thorough ethnographical and ethnological research by indigenous anthropologists in Tonga and in much of the South Pacific may be postponed for a long time to come. Under these circumstances, in-depth cultural and social investigation will continue to be in the hands of foreign universities and academics. (1982:215)

One possible way around this is to encourage more collaborative research, particularly where Western researchers can gain access to grants to support fieldwork carried out with indigenous researchers. Such collaboration can also be important in terms of mentoring indigenous research assistants. A collection of works by indigenous anthropologists in 1982 suggested that there is value in work done by both indigenous researchers and foreign researchers, thus exposing '...the superficiality of the belief that the cure for the excesses of colonial anthropology lies in its replacement by indigenous anthropology' (Madan, 1982:16).

It is clearly important that research which gives voice to the interests and concerns of minority ethnic groups and indigenous peoples is carried out, especially where these groups still face political repression or subversion of their rights. However, researchers must be very sensitive and aware of the politics of such research because otherwise they may endanger themselves and/or the groups they are studying.[6]

Some ethnic minorities and indigenous groups have decided to give an unequivocal 'no' to outside requests to conduct research. The most well-known example of this in New Zealand is Te Kohanga Reo National Trust, which is the administrative body for a large number of Maori 'language nests' for pre-school education (Smith, 1999:178). In such cases, we must respect the wishes of the group concerned, just as contemporary ethical guidelines insist that we instruct our research participants that they have the right to withdraw from participation in our research at any time.

Researching the poor

The majority of researchers conducting fieldwork on development-related topics will come into contact with people who are much poorer than ourselves and who have difficulty in sustaining even a basic livelihood. Yet there seems to be very little in the literature either on the practical challenges of conducting sensitive research with the poor, or on how we might prepare ourselves for the emotional shock of coming into contact with extreme poverty. This applies both to Western researchers and to Third World students from middle or upper class roots who have not been directly exposed to various forms deprivation or oppression before. Walcott rightly observes that during our university education we are protected from some of the harsher realities of life: 'All those statistics we read – poverty, illness, accidents, violence, abuse – may suddenly materialise for a fieldworker whose most traumatic experience to date had been a ticket for speeding' (Walcott, 1995:93). Chapter 6 presents some useful advice in this regard under a section entitled 'Preparing for discomfort and depression', while Chapter 7 provides guidelines for recognising and dealing with the culture shock which may ensue in such circumstances.

A particularly challenging issue to address is how should we respond if our fieldwork brings us into contact with people who are struggling to meet even their basic survival needs. Here we are not talking about gift giving as an expression of gratitude (as discussed in Chapter 10), but whether we should provide assistance for humanitarian reasons to people who are destitute. When Henry (one of the authors of this chapter) conducted PhD fieldwork in Bangladesh, his subjects were poor village households who were already participating in programs initiated by local development agencies. Because these organisations were attempting to instil in program participants a sense of self-reliance, it would have been inappropriate for Henry to offer material assistance. Instead, he felt it was best to write reports informing these organisations of his findings and making recommendations that he believed were practical. However, encounters with severe poverty, such as that described in Box 9.6 can be a difficult experience and it would be wrong to suggest the search for an appropriate response is an easy task.

Box 9.6 Twenty-five times the price for two eggs

On one occasion, Henry's interpreter was very moved by the impoverished state of one household they visited. As a Bangladeshi national who had participated in similar village level studies before, poverty for the interpreter was not an unusual sight, indicating just how extreme the hardship this household faced was. The household owned a few ducks and the sale of eggs provided one of its sole sources of cash income. The interpreter offered to buy two eggs and paid about 25 times the usual price for them. The following day an elderly couple, hearing of this incident, approached the interpreter for a loan.

Source: Henry Scheyvens, doctoral research in Bangladesh, 1998-1999

How appropriate was the interpreter's action? We would not like to be the judge. Some argue against charity. Certainly, we would not wish to undermine the efforts of committed development organisations to build self-reliance among the poor. Wilson provides the following sound advice on how we should respond to people who are destitute:

> Fieldworkers should know the destitutes in the community studied as part of understanding the economy and society of the area. On the basis of such knowledge, fieldworkers can then make appropriate contributions to their welfare, in the same manner as other members of the society do, including, for example, giving transport to a clinic, a listening ear and an occasional gift of food or clothing. Such aid should be given quietly, but not necessarily secretly, and in the manner deemed appropriate in that society. (1992:194-5)

Wilson's quote suggests that even if charity is inappropriate, in some instances you may be able to offer practical services (see Chapter 8 on 'Reciprocity'). Razavi (1992) found she could provide practical assistance during the duration of her fieldwork by transporting locals in her car, while Lewis (1991:62) had access to a photocopier and was able to give out maps of village plots that were normally not accessible to locals.

In terms of data collection, there are a number of other issues you should consider when researching the poor. The data you seek, you may not find. Poor households may be forced into activities that are frowned upon within their societies and may hide these from the researcher. Lewis (1991:57-8), for example, examined the practice of kutia in which a poor farmer takes a loan from a rice mill owner to buy rice for husking at the mill, but he found that his informants were reluctant to reveal whether they had taken loans from informal moneylenders. The village rice mill owner was happy to discuss these loans, however.

Those undertaking social surveys will have to familiarise themselves with indicators relevant to local contexts, which will in turn depend upon having a good understanding of what matters to one's respondents or informants. In the US, weekly household income may be a good gauge of socio-economic status. In villages in Pakistan, however, how many times the household enjoys fish or chicken each week – or month – may be a better indicator. Reading studies that have been undertaken in the country or specific area you are conducting research in by government agencies, research bodies, NGOs and other institutions, should provide direction on what are useful indicators. In addition, sensitivity is needed in many instances when asking questions about income. Firstly, sources of income are likely to be so erratic for people living from day to day that asking them to estimate how much they earn daily or weekly may be inappropriate, and for agricultural day labourers there is also the problem of seasonality. Secondly, asking about a poor person's meagre income may simply reinforce their feelings of ineptitude as providers for their families.

This section concludes with Box 9.7, which provides principles regarding research with marginalised groups in general. These principles draw attention to the way in which research is conducted, the respect accorded to the participants, and the benefits of the research for them.[7] Importantly, appropriate means of disseminating the research findings should be of concern to all researchers working with marginalised groups.

Box 9.7 Principles regarding research with marginalised groups

• The research must be based on respect for the knowledge, skills and experience of people in the group being studied.

• Marginalised groups are active subjects rather than passive objects of the research.

• The research questions should be centred around issues of interest and concern to the group being studied.

• The researcher's participation with the marginalised group should be characterised by committed involvement rather than impartial detachment.

• Research findings should be shared with the marginalised group in a means deemed appropriate by the group, e.g. public meeting; workshop allowing for discussion, feedback and modification of findings; summary sheet; report; not necessarily a thesis or academic papers.

• There should be positive outcomes of the research for the marginalised group, and any anticipated negative outcomes should be eliminated if possible.

Source: adapted from Hall (1992) cited in Martin (2000:193-4)

Researching the elite and powerful

There is a large gap in the literature that investigates the elite and powerful in developing societies. In terms of methodological writings the overriding focus has been on scenarios where the researcher is more powerful than the researched. In a groundbreaking special issue of Geoforum, Cormode and Hughes (1999:299) argue that the lack of attention accorded to elites can be attributed to at least two factors. First, researchers of development often hold a political commitment to working with the less privileged in society. Second, gaining access to elite groups is often difficult, and this is amplified when the data being sought is qualitative. Past studies of the elite, focused in particular on business managers, have tended to be quantitative in nature and provided less access restrictions (Healy and Rawlinson, 1993). Given the increasingly complex nature of the global space-economy, and the shift to post-positivist epistemologies required to capture this complexity, researchers have argued the need for richer, ultimately more ethnographic, interpretations of the motivations and rationale of the elite (Herod, 1999; Hertz and Imber, 1993; Schoenburger, 1991). It is crucial then that we have an understanding of the practical and methodological issues relevant to such research.

The relative silence of development studies with respect to researching the elite represents a significant challenge for the subject. But why should we be motivated to study the elite? At least four linked points can be offered.

1. The gap between the elite and the non-elite is getting wider in global society, and arguably some elements of the elite increasingly determine social and economic outcomes as their relative power increases (Cormode and Hughes, 1999). Understanding what drives the elite is thus essential.

2. Given the above, there has been a divergence of elite and non-elite opinion with respect to the implications of development in practice, in particular in the context of the impacts of neoliberalism, free trade and globalisation (Mullings, 1999).

3. Elite networks are increasingly glocally constituted. That is to say that local elites often now operate in both global and local spaces and that the separation of the two is problematic. Understanding local outcomes in developing areas requires an understanding of how elites act as vessels of global scale processes and imperatives and how power relations in given territories influence outcomes on the ground.

4. Linked to point 3, and influenced by dependency/structuralist worldviews, it can be argued that the elite and non-elite are two sides of the same coin. For coherent representations we need to understand both sides. It may be that any given project will require the gathering of data from both the elite and the non-elite. Or it may be, and this is perhaps more likely with student research, that the focus will remain in one of these two camps – to be later integrated into an increasingly bi-focal literature.

But what do we mean by 'elite'? This is a definition which is fraught with difficulty. Herod defines the 'foreign elite' in the context of his work as 'foreign nationals who hold positions of power within organizations such as corporations, governments, or, in the case of my own research, trade unions' (1999: 313). He does not intend this to be a catch-all definition however and it is hardly adequate for our purposes here. Herod is referring to what we understand in the West as the 'elite'. But what of socio-cultural systems of which Westerners have little understanding? For example, a traditional Fijian chief can hardly be defined as having any influence over global networks in the way Herod's definition suggests. Such chiefs are demonstrably part of the elite within the context of their own societies however and wield enormous power (and arguably are important transmitters of global processes). It may be necessary then to distinguish between global, glocal and local elites, and each of these raises different methodological questions.

The above differentiation is further complicated by the fact that the researcher's perception of what constitutes a member of the elite is heavily contingent upon the various axes of their own identity. For example, the researcher's status as a Western, middle class, male doctoral candidate may in the eyes of male, middle class and educated interviewees put the researcher in a closer social space to themselves than an uneducated, female, Third World national. A final complication is that qualitative research is a social process whereby power relations are fluid across space and time, thus the relative position of the researcher and interviewee will change, sometimes in the course of one interview. All of the preceding demonstrates that the 'elite' is in no way a fixed entity.

But why all this fuss? Is there anything inherently different about researching the elite? Echoing McDowell (1992, 1998), Cormode and Hughes suggest that a researcher studying the elite is often, 'a supplicant, dependent of the cooperation of a relatively small number of people with specialised knowledge, and neither a potential emancipator or oppressor' (1999:299). Further, they argue that:

> Researching 'the powerful' presents very different methodological and ethical challenges from studying 'down'. The characteristics of those studied, the power relations between them and the researcher, and the politics of the research process differ considerably between elite and non-elite research. (1999:299)

Herod (1999) agues that, in the case of researching 'foreign elites', methodology is complicated by two factors. First, there are problems of transcultural communication and misunderstanding which need to be considered (it could be argued that this is the case for 'foreign' research in general). Second, it may be particularly difficult to access foreign elite institutions where the organization is relatively unknown to the researcher. In general then there are two sets of overlapping issues which are specific to researching elites; 1) practical issues; 2) issues of positionality.

Practical issues in elite research

Gaining access to the elite, be it representatives of a corporation or Fijian chiefs for that matter, can be particularly problematic. Why should such people, for whom it is often said 'time is money', grant an audience to a student or any other researcher? There is perhaps a feeling in business circles that academics are somewhat, well, 'academic' (in the sense that everything is hypothetical), and that exchange with them is likely to produce little of practical use. This can be turned to the researcher's advantage, as being perceived as non-threatening can help win access to information that might otherwise be considered sensitive.

The lack of seriousness which interviewees may accord an encounter can often lead to last minute cancellations and many interruptions during the interview process (Mullings, 1999). Pursuing personal interaction under such circumstances can be frustrating. It is very important that personal contact is made however. Warwick (one of the authors of this chapter) constructed a questionnaire for thirty multinational fruit export companies as part of his PhD research and sent it out by post. He received three replies, two of which said that the companies could not help! When these companies were approached again through telephone calls and informal drop-ins virtually all of them agreed to grant personal interviews (see also Chapter 5, 'Establishing contacts'). This was undoubtedly assisted by being extremely nice to secretaries – an important skill worth cultivating. Not only did access rates improve, the quality of the data was far richer through the utilisation of open-ended interviews which retained some of the closed ended attributes of the original questionnaire. It is essential when negotiating access to strike a balance between impersonal and personal interaction.

The use of networks is an important way of achieving access and gaining the cooperation of interviewee. Herod (1999) suggests that using a flow chart, which traces all of the individuals who put you in contact with other individuals in different institutions, can be very useful. A very good way of starting an interview is to say 'I was given your name by…'. Likewise, some contacts may 'phone ahead' for you. This will help establish your legitimacy, reduce the perceived threat, and may also please the interviewee in that it is implied that they are recognised within their relevant networks. This is particularly useful in societies where personal links are paramount. In many Pacific Island nations for example without explicit names you would be very unlikely to gain access. Meanwhile in Chile, the age-old system of *pitutos*, which constitute networks of semi-formal contacts that interact reciprocally, must be understood for the researcher to operate effectively. Warwick found that the only way to gain access to local civil servants in the countryside was to quote the name of a friend who worked for the Ministry of Agriculture in Santiago who had an established system of *pitutos* across the country. This is in no way intended to say that 'developed' countries do not operate like this – of course they do – but it is important to understand how these networks operate in the context of your particular country of study.

A final practical issue is that, just like non-elites, the participants in research may wish to see copies of the work you finally do. You will have total power of the final writing up of your work. If you are somebody who becomes critical of the elite within the context of a particular study, this may present a problem. It is possible to be selective with what you choose to feed back to the groups you worked with, but this is not advisable. We have already argued that the world is becoming smaller and if this doesn't catch-up with you it may make access for others in the future difficult. It is best to be as critical as you feel you should be based on the evidence you have before you (see the section on 'Advocacy and activism' below).

Positionality in elite research

As discussed in the introduction to this chapter, it is important to examine our positionality in relation to our research subjects, but we should be aware that notions of 'insider' and 'outsider' are more accurately understood as existing on a sliding scale or continuum, rather than being seen as binary opposites. With respect to elite research, most authors agree that the problems of self-positioning are considerable, however, how they should be dealt with is contested.

In the context of foreign elite research Herod (1999) argues that being an 'outsider' and playing up this aspect of one's identity can actually work in the favour of the researcher. As a foreigner doing research in Eastern Europe he was surprised by the seriousness with which he was taken. In particular, the fact that he had come from many miles away (the USA) combined with the notion held among the interviewees that he was a 'foreign expert' acted in his favour. 'Outsiderness' he argues was perceived in this particular situation as non-threatening and even encouraged small talk. Furthermore, as an outsider he felt more comfortable asking for things to be clearly explained and in this way was able to maintain a crucial critical distance. Warwick found similar things in working with the elite in Chile. The fact that somebody from an academic institution in the Western world should be interested in particular individuals and their opinions was often considered flattering. When asking fruit companies about their operations and relationship to small farmers, he would often play up his ignorance and ask flattering questions such as, 'how do you explain your enormous success in securing good supply?', or 'what is it about Chilean companies that has allowed this export miracle to take place?'. Naturally whether such tactics solicit faithful responses and not exaggerated boasts is uncertain, but it certainly stimulated flowing responses.

In the context of elite research in Jamaica, Mullings (1999) takes a different stance to Herod. She argues that with the central goal of encouraging participation the optimal strategy was to attempt to occupy 'shared positional spaces'. Towards this end she argues that it is good to present yourself to elites as a temporary insider – someone who knows the ropes of the particular issue under concern and is therefore an intellectual equal. She also argues, that as a black, female, US resident researcher in Jamaica, it was advantageous to put various aspects of her identity to the fore at given times. There can be little doubt that your gender, race, nationality and sexuality has the potential to influence the research process to the extent that you make these things visible and how they are perceived by the interviewee. Ultimately Mullings argues for cultivating insiderness for elite research:

> recognising that the information that we as researchers receive will always be partial makes our claims circumspect and our stance more reflexive. This is a consideration that is particularly important for researchers whose identities rest upon axes that are not only different, but in many circumstances may be disempowering. Identifying aspects of difference which may stultify dialog and seeking spaces where some level of trust can be established, to me, is the only way that researchers can gather information that is reliable (1999:349).

A central issue then is how we represent ourselves to gain access and information (see Chapter 8, 'Truth and deception'). Of critical importance perhaps is striking a balance between being an insider and an outsider and cultivating the ability to represent oneself according to the situation. You must be able to move up and down the sliding scale of intimacy as Herod (1999) calls it. Is this tantamount to deception? In the sense that one puts particular axes of identity on display at a certain time to achieve self-interested goals, perhaps so. However, who does not alter their speech register, their appearance, and their behaviour in different social situations?

Moving up and down power structures presents particularly salient problems. In many cases, as noted earlier in this section work will involve interviewing both the elite and non-elite. How do you scale hierarchies successfully and ethically? Working with the elite in this context presents a particular problem, often such groups may actually be able to prevent access to the non-elite if they are not satisfied what you are doing is in their interests. The researcher has to remain flexible and learn to improvise where necessary in this respect. Recognising that one's positionality is inevitably and necessarily ever-changing, and learning to cultivate shifts where this is required is perhaps the first step in being able to negotiate these tricky problems satisfactorily.

Advocacy and activism

Research with marginalised or privileged groups, as discussed above, is often driven by a concern for matters of social justice. How to take the next step – to use one's research to actively promote change – is a matter to which we now turn.

Kobayashi (1994:78), writing about her research with the Japanese-Canadian community said, 'I am deeply convinced that no social scholarship is independent of political action, and I am personally committed to acknowledging my research as political and to using it most effectively for social change'. It is not the norm to find such strong convictions espoused by academics, although the recent publication of a text devoted to emancipatory research (Truman et al., 2000) suggests this is perhaps becoming more common. There are several bodies of thought which have contributed to the development of emancipatory research, the key ones being humanistic psychology, critical theory, feminist theories, and poststructuralism (Humphries et al., 2000). The field of development studies has been particularly influenced by Paolo Freire's (1972) work which suggests that research should be an empowering process for participants, an opportunity for education and a stimulus for social action (Humphries et al., 2000:7). This accords with the point made in Chapter 6, that many researchers of development issues are motivated at least in part by their moral conscience. They want not just to better understand the world, but to enable people to improve their living conditions and overcome inequalities.

If as a researcher you are motivated by a desire to conduct emancipatory research, which may involve advocating on behalf of disadvantaged peoples or challenging those abusing positions of power, there are issues you should consider. Advocacy will require effort outside that directed towards attaining academic qualifications but the personal gains can be very rewarding, in particular, giving you the sense that you are able to 'make a difference'. Yet your enthusiasm for 'changing the world' may need to be tempered if you are to carry out effective research.

> Contributing to social change involves deliberate attempts at mobilising opinion in a particular direction. If the conclusions, however, are predetermined by the activist's own predilections and ideas, without taking into account the situation, perceptions, and wishes of those on whose behalf we seek to help bring about change, we can easily end up either being irrelevant, pompous imposters or authoritarian manipulators. (Kishwar, 1998:293)

For those wanting to become involved in advocacy, their research itself is not a form of activism but a means by which they can gain greater knowledge to be better advocates. There are types of research, however, which are a form of activism that students should at least be aware of. Action-based research, involving the researcher intervening in the community being studied and observing the changes that take place, is one example. Many of the rural development models that are now implemented in Bangladesh were based on this approach. The two-tier rural cooperative system, for example, emerged from experiments that date back to the 1960s by researchers led by the late Professor Akhter Hameed Khan at the Bangladesh Academy for Rural Development (Hye, 1993). The well-known Grameen Bank model of micro-credit delivery emerged from experiments by Professor Muhammad Yunus and his students dating from the second half of the 1970s (Counts, 1996).

Participatory research is another method of inquiry in which the research process is a form of activism (Chambers, 1997). Under this approach participants play a role in the collection and analysis of data, and on the basis of their findings engage in action to transform society (Cohen-Mitchell, 2000:146).[8] Thus researchers who adopt a participatory stance inherently take on responsibilities with regards to their research:

> Supporting or enabling participation in the strongest sense becomes a political act through establishing partnerships between the researcher and the researched, whereby ownership, empowerment and responsibility for accountability are shared throughout the research process. [Thus] PR [participatory research] can play an important role in fostering or stimulating community activism at both the individual and collective levels. (Dockery, 2000:95)

Cohen-Mitchell's research with disabled women in El Salvador led to collective action when the women she was interviewing on an individual basis expressed a keen interest in meeting as a group: 'they saw a support group as a place to share and solve problems, and also do community outreach to identify and incorporate other disabled women...' (Cohen-Mitchell, 2000: 163).

Researchers choosing to conduct action-oriented or participatory research need to be led by practical considerations, not just by their ideals. For example, you need to ensure you have time and resources to do advocacy or activist work, or to take a participatory approach to research, if this is secondary to your agenda of writing your thesis. In addition, in the case of both types of research, strong institutional support in the study country is usually necessary. Also, while local involvement can have benefits for our research, it may also result in pitfalls. Some of these might be foreseen and avoided. Megaw's account of his research in Ghana is illuminating (Box 9.8).

If you are considering advocating on behalf of your informants you will need to address the issue of representation (see Chapter 11 on 'Writing and representing'). The question of 'who speaks for whom?' is often raised in relation to cross-cultural studies and needs to be treated carefully (see the quote by hooks (1990) in the introduction to this chapter). Women in the Third World, for example, have queried whether women in the West can represent their interests if they have never experienced double or even triple oppression based on gender, class and ethnicity. It is not necessary to experience the struggles of another group, however, to sympathise with their plight. It is the task of the researcher to interpret these struggles in the peculiar social and political context that has given rise to them; not to superimpose inappropriate conceptual frameworks drawn from their own experiences and societies. Interestingly, the poor or otherwise marginalised groups who have no effective voice in their societies do not seem to be as concerned as academics are with the issue of representation. If you are in a position to bring their concerns to the attention of decision-makers, then with the exception of politically sensitive situations when this could lead to further oppression, they most likely will wish you to do so. An extreme post-modernist viewpoint becomes an easy excuse for not engaging in advocacy.

Box 9.8 The pitfalls of being an activist

After several weeks of ethnic conflict in northern Ghana, Megaw was asked by the leader of a small indigenous NGO to assist with relief and rehabilitation. Later he attended and even chaired meetings held between a consortium of Western NGOs and the local NGO. This activism had mixed consequences for his research. Megaw's direct involvement with the NGO placed him in a good position to observe the evolving relationship between Western and indigenous NGOs. However, as the leader of the NGO wished him to advocate on the organisation's behalf, he attempted to hide its shortcomings.

Megaw was also asked to run trivial errands because of his access to a 4-wheel drive vehicle that interfered with his research. Eventually, he decided to distance himself from the NGO. Factionalism within the NGO community was creating problems and being aligned so closely with one NGO restricted him from moving freely between different organisations.

Source: Based on Adams and Megaw (1997)

More conventional research can also be both a means to gain a greater understanding of the injustices being examined and a medium to give voice to those suffering these injustices. Applied research, that is, research intended to bring about a change in policy, has a long history in the social sciences. One of the earliest applied studies, by Booth and his colleagues, described the conditions of working class families in London using a combination of ethnographic and survey research. According to Wax (1971:25) it 'stirred the contemporary social conscience' and played a part in the passing of the Old Age Pension Act of 1908.

Researchers may be in a position to advocate by disseminating research findings through various channels. Writing reports for development organisations is one possibility, which is further discussed in Chapter 10. This will require work that in no way directly contributes to your qualifications or career; hence you may be tempted to keep putting this off. However, if your findings are to have any impact, the sooner you report on them the better. Postgraduate students should tell their supervisors that they are writing a report and ask them to allow for this when judging the progress that is being made on writing up. Writing reports for non-academic institutions requires special skills. The report should be free of jargon, succinct and make at most a few clearly argued points, supported with sufficient data from your fieldwork. If you are advising a change in policy or practice, then consider carefully how to do so in a constructive fashion. You are not merely engaging in academic debate. Any criticism could be taken very personally, though sometimes this may be impossible to avoid. You may also find an opportunity to give an oral presentation, for example, at a village meeting or at the office of organisation that has assisted you. Such opportunities can be invaluable for providing feedback on your data and analysis.

If you are advocating a change in development policy or practice, there may be a temptation to overplay data that supports your views and understate data that does not. Our arguments will be all the more persuasive if they are based on a rigorous investigation rather than if we are only willing to see those facts that concur with our views. Wilson (1992:182) argues that a good researcher is not the most vocal and eloquent advocate for a particular cause, but a person who wishes to get to the 'bottom of things'. And in 'getting to the bottom of things' we must be prepared to listen carefully to the multiple, often contradictory voices of those we are studying:

> We should not assume that because we subscribe to an ideology that we believe is in the best interests of the people whose lives we are looking into, or because we genuinely believe we have their interests at heart, this will automatically give us greater insight into their situation, or that our perceptions are necessarily superior to their own regarding the possible solutions to their problems. (Kishwar, 1998:310)

Kishwar (1998) suggests that if our research merely confirms our preconceptions about a particular development issue and fails to unearth any surprising or contradictory information, there was really no point in doing fieldwork.

The possibility of acting on someone's behalf in your study area may also exist but needs thorough thinking through. To remain neutral during the duration of fieldwork on every issue that concerns us may be extremely trying and even inappropriate. Yet, in our desire not to offend anyone we may be overly concerned to always portray ourselves in a non-threatening fashion. You should not expect to be friends with everyone. Wilson (1992:189) makes the valid point that living in another society does not mean we should suspend our own moral code. In one instance he felt compelled to remonstrate with a woman who, among other deprivations, was making her elderly father sleep outside. On another occasion his field assistants went to 'rough up' a man who had abandoned his partially blind wife and their baby to slow starvation.

Conclusion

This chapter has examined the difficulties, and rewards, which can stem from research involving marginalised and/or privileged groups. The ethical and practical constraints associated with conducting research on these groups should not provide us with an excuse to avoid such research, rather, this should force us to reflect carefully on our motivations for research, to conduct our research in a sensitive manner, and to ensure that our research will have beneficial outcomes – particularly for those who are marginalised.

Some commentators are now starting to suggest that participation in the research process can, in itself, be an empowering experience for research participants, especially those who face significant social disadvantage (Humphries et al., 2000). Acker et al. (1991) posit that interviews can raise some women's consciousness, leading to their emancipation. And when poor people are aware that the researcher has travelled from afar specifically to speak with them, not just those of higher social status in their communities, it can add to their sense of self-esteem (Scheyvens and Leslie, 2000). Cotterill (1992) also asserts that research can be therapeutic, and Opie (1992) claims that this is especially true if interviewers encourage participants to reflect on their experiences and to understand how the system which disadvantages them can be challenged. England (1994:85) also supports this viewpoint on the basis that, '. . . many of the women whom I have interviewed told me that they found the exercise quite cathartic and that it enabled them to reflect on and re-evaluate their life experiences'. Thus it appears that research projects which seek to elicit and project previously silenced voices can be empowering for participants (Pratt and Loizos, 1992).

This chapter has also argued that those interested in emancipatory research should not shy away from research focusing on or involving elite groups. If we do not understand the motivations or actions of this group we will never devise strategies for dismantling privilege and building more equitable societies: 'Understanding global inequalities is a key stage in the process of overcoming them' (Taylor, 1992:20).

Recommended reading

Boyden, J. and Ennew, J. (1997) *Children in Focus: A Manual for Participatory Research with Children* Radda Barnen, Swedish Save the Children, Stockholm.

This manual provides excellent practical advice and case studies on appropriate research with children in Third World settings.

Geoforum (1999) Volume 30(4).
This special issue is devoted to concerns associated with elite research.

Humphries, B., Mertens, D.M. and Truman, C. (2000) Arguments for an 'emancipatory' research paradigm. In C. Truman, D.M. Mertens and B. Humphries (eds) *Research and Inequality* UCL Press, London, pp.3-23.
A useful starting point for those wanting to ensure their research has emancipatory potential.

Journal of Contemporary Ethnography (1993) Volume 22. Special Issue: Fieldwork in Elite Settings.
Another very useful special edition of a journal devoted to elite research, containing a number of articles pertinent to research on development issues.

Smith, L.T. (1999) *Decolonizing Methodologies: Research and Indigenous Peoples* Zed, London.
Written by a Maori woman, this book provides insights into appropriate methodologies for engaging in research with indigenous people, and stresses the importance of indigenous people conducting their own research.

Wolf, D.L. (1996) Situating feminist dilemmas in fieldwork. In D.L.Wolf (ed.) *Feminist Dilemmas in Fieldwork* Westview Press, Boulder, pp. 1-55.
Wolf's opening chapter of her edited book provides a comprehensive examination of ethical issues associated with feminist fieldwork, many of which apply to cross-cultural research with women.

Young, L. and Barrett, H. (2001) Adapting visual methods: action research with Kampala street children. *Area* 33(2): 141-52.
Provides interesting examples of ways to facilitate child-led participation in research using visual methods, and also reflects on ethical issues involved in research with children from an excluded group.

Notes

1. 'The marginalised' in this chapter is a term used to embrace groups which have been socially constructed such that they lack access to power, resources and privileges in society in relation to other groups.

2. It is increasingly recognised by all but the most dogmatic positivist that we come to research and writing from a particular position – the axes of our identity leave an imprint on the construction, organisation and execution of the academic process. In considering the nature of positionality, and the methodological problems it raises, researchers have often been conceived as 'insiders' or 'outsiders'. The 'insider-outsider' binary is not helpful. After all, to argue that insiders or outsiders should be better placed to conduct research with certain groups falls into the positivist trap of assuming that there is 'truth out there' waiting to be discovered by those with the most appropriate culture and identity and that representations of certain voices are closer to 'reality'. Rather we all sit on continuum between the 'insider' and 'outsider' extremes and shift endlessly as the contexts and individuals are reconstituted along this sliding scale.

3. The reverse scenario, women researching men, need also not be problematic. When Ravazi carried out research in her home country of Iran, she found that it was not so difficult to

enter the realms of males in a sex-segregated society as many would anticipate. Ravazi suggests that the view that a female will not be able to research males in such settings '...ignores a subtle relationship between gender and other variables. Factors such as class and outsider status can interact positively with gender, thus reducing its constraining influence on the researcher's accessibility and freedom' (Ravazi, 1992:158).

4. The term 'minority ethnic groups' does not necessarily refer to numerical minorities, rather, it is used more broadly to include ethnic groups which are politically, socially and/or economically marginalised. Thus while ethnic Fijians in Fiji are not in any numerical sense a minority, they may be considered somewhat economically marginalised in relation to Indo-Fijians and Fijians of European heritage. In some cases, minority groups may make up a larger proportion of the population than the ruling group. Indigenous peoples in many countries – both Western and Third World – also fall within the category of 'minority ethnic groups'.

5. Note, however, that international students conducting home-based research are often not members of ethnic minorities or indigenous groups, in which case they may be seen just as much as 'outsiders' as foreign researchers.

6. The section on 'Truth and deception' in Chapter 8 provides further insights into this issue.

7. With respect to the fourth point, 'the researcher's participation...should be characterised by committed involvement', not all readers may agree: being a temporary 'insider' could, for example, be regarded as patronizing.

8. Participatory research should not necessarily be equated with PRA techniques, as discussed in Chapter 4. We are referring here to an approach to research, whereas most of the criticisms levelled at PRA in Chapter 4 were referring to arbitrary use of the techniques or tools used by PRA advocates, often without attention to the overarching philosophy behind PRA. See www.goshen.edu/soan/soan96p.htm for many links to websites with information on participatory research.

PART IV

LEAVING THE FIELD

10 Anything to Declare? The Politics and Practicalities of Leaving the Field

Sara Kindon and Julie Cupples

Introduction

There are two universal processes we share as human beings – arriving and leaving (Maines et al., 1980). Within the context of development studies and fieldwork we are encouraged to spend a great deal of time and effort on preparing to arrive in our field site and to carry out fieldwork in appropriate and ethical ways. But what about leaving the field? How do we prepare for this aspect?

Leaving involves us in both a physical relocation and a sociological transformation. We leave a particular geographical space with which we have become familiar and also leave distinct social spaces and relationships in which we have performed particular identities, sometimes over prolonged periods of time. Through the combination of less frequent contact with the geographical space and our research participants, and the acts of analysis, writing and re-presentation once back at university, the field and the meanings of the space and the relationships formed in it become actively transformed over time. Leaving the field is therefore not a benign or passive phase of research, but often plays a dramatic part in shaping our experiences and understandings (Maines et al., 1980).

As the previous chapters in this book have shown, there is a great deal to think about in terms of research design, ethics and methodology before we set off for and while we are in the field. Yet, arriving and leaving are intimately connected processes and one should not be thought of without the other. Arriving, how our research work evolves, what relationships and commitments are made, the kind of person we become to our participants and others over time (Maines et al., 1980), and contingencies like mistakes, conflicts or betrayals (Shaffir et al., 1980), all influence how we (are able to) leave and how we can later write once back at university.[1] As Wolf indicates:

> The manner in which one leaves the field, and the issue of whether or not one stays in touch, will depend very much on how one got there in the first place and the personal relationships and public identity one maintained while in it. (1991:211)

Consequently, it is important to recognise that all phases of the research process influence the experience of leaving. Thinking before we arrive in the field about what we hope to achieve with our academic work, what relationships we may establish, and what commitments we might realistically be able to meet upon our departure, is critical to the pursuit of ethical and rewarding research. It will also save a lot of anxiety and frustration later on!

In a sense, leaving is but a further stage in the ongoing interplay between ourselves and the people or issue we are investigating (Shaffir et al., 1980), and we remain psychologically and emotionally connected to the field even when we have left it physically. From Letkemann's (1980:301) perspective, 'the research field consists essentially of human beings who can continue to enrich the researcher's life long after the original data is forgotten', and for Bailey 'we don't so much terminate our field relationships as continue them in another form over greater distances' (1996:86, see also Stebbins, 1991).

There is no 'right' way to negotiate the complex web of human relationships which make up the field (Cook, 2001, Hyndman, 2001, Katz, 1992, Stebbins, 1991). There are, however, a number of things to think about and consider before and as we act. Box 10.1 contains some questions that we think are useful starting prompts and you may think of others as you read through the rest of this chapter.

Ultimately as Maines et al. (1980:273) note: 'the problems, concerns, and ease of field exiting are not uniformly distributed across research settings', and what actions or decisions are appropriate will vary according to the specific geographical, cultural and institutional contexts in which we are working. It is often harder for us to extricate ourselves if working with vulnerable or marginal groups (see Chapter 9) than it is if working with people in positions of power or people more like ourselves.

Box 10.1 Questions to ask about leaving *before* arriving

• How and when will I know it is time to conclude my fieldwork?

• How do I wish my experience of fieldwork to end?

• How will I manage the personal relationships formed with my research participants? For instance, do I wish to cultivate ongoing associations, or should all relationships be research-dependent and end when the fieldwork ends?

• How will I manage the social, political and ethical implications of my research? For example, what commitments (practical, emotional, academic) can I realistically make and maintain at the end of my stay?

Source: Adapted from Letkemann (1980), Taylor (1991) and the authors' own experiences

---

It is also important to remember that we will form other types of relationships with people aside from those primarily structured by our research, and that we are returning to university and another set of personal and professional relationships with family, friends and supervisors. The clearer we are about the power relations between ourselves and others with whom we interact while in the field, as well as their expectations of us, the easier it is to avoid misunderstandings, end our field-work and negotiate changes in relationships with goodwill.

Hence, this chapter is not and cannot be a 'how to' guide to leaving the field. We all have to negotiate these processes in ways most appropriate to our own cir-cumstances. However, what we do want to share here is some 'food for thought' from our own experiences carrying out qualitative and participatory research in Costa Rica, Nicaragua, Indonesia and Aotearoa New Zealand, and the experience of one of our colleagues who has undertaken fieldwork in Thailand. The chapter also integrates some ideas and reflections from staff and post-graduate students in the UK who have worked in various countries in Africa, Latin America and Asia.[2] This wide range of experiences comes not only from 'western' researchers carrying out fieldwork in the 'third world' or with indigenous people in a postcolonial con-text, but also from 'third world' researchers carrying out fieldwork in their own countries and returning to 'western' universities to write. As such, the issues raised here we hope will strike a chord with most readers of this book.

In the following sections we look at the reasons for leaving the field and fac-tors which can influence our experiences of leaving it. We then explore a range of possible feelings that researchers may experience and discuss strategies for manag-ing them and departure from the field. We focus particularly on exploring researchers' ethical responsibilities to our participants and others with whom we have developed relationships and provide some handy reminders about practical considerations such as planning, packing and presents.

Reasons for leaving

Unless researchers choose never to embark on fieldwork or to 'go native' and remain in the field without completing research or writing about it, the process of leaving a research site is inevitable. It is a methodological imperative (Maines et al., 1980:274). However, when, why and how we leave can vary enormously depend-ing upon the nature and type of our research, the 'field' context and the relation-ships we have formed during our fieldwork. In particular, why we leave often has a huge influence upon when we leave, how we leave, and how we feel about leaving. It also informs the feelings of the people we leave behind.

In many cases, why and when we leave is related to pragmatic reasons or what Letkemann (1980) has called external factors: the time allocated for field-work is up and either our funding or research permits are running out or have expired. We may face strict university/departmental deadlines for submission of our thesis or contractual obligations to provide reports to funding agencies. More personally, we may need to get back to meet private and family obligations.

Hopefully, we also leave because our methods have exhausted possible sources and are generating little or no new information. We reach 'theoretical saturation' as Glaser and Strauss (1968) put it and our fieldwork yields diminishing returns (Taylor, 1991) as we hear the same information over and over again, or there are no new people to talk to about our topic.

Alternatively, we may find that no new information is generated because our research design and methodology aren't working. The relationships we have established and/or the approach we have adopted don't enable us to get below a superficial understanding, or may actively work to prevent us getting detailed information. We need to try other approaches or accept that it is time to abandon our particular focus and leave our field site. It is important to acknowledge that fieldwork may not always be a positive or rewarding experience.

We may also realise that it is time to leave because we have become so immersed in our field site that it is becoming difficult to analyse it with any clarity (see Box 10.2). We may feel that we are losing our sense of self in the immediate cultural context and putting our ability to do research and write about it at risk.

Box 10.2 Knowing when it is time to leave

'The final months of fieldwork are generally the best and most productive: the months of laying groundwork pay off in the increasing intimacy and comfort in your relationships and in the depth of the insights you are able to reach. This fact made me ever more reluctant to say that my research was "finished". I kept extending my stay at the factory; it became something of a joke, as the older women would tease me about my parents, whose "neck must be sooooo long"' the expression one uses to describe someone who is waiting impatiently. "You must have found a boyfriend," they would tell me, or laughing, they might suggest, "Why not find a nice Japanese boy and settle down here?" I laughed with them, but I continued to stay on as research became more and more productive, until one event convinced me that the time to depart was near. At a tea ceremony class, I performed a basic "thin tea" ceremony flawlessly, without need for prompting or correction of my movements. My teacher said in tones of approval, "You know, when you first started, I was so worried. The way you moved, the way you walked, was so clumsy! But now, you're just like an ojosan, a nice young lady"' Part of me was inordinately pleased that my awkward, exaggerated Western movements had finally been replaced by the disciplined grace that makes the tea ceremony so seemingly natural and beautiful to watch. But another voice cried out in considerable alarm. "Let me escape before I'm completely transformed!" And not too many weeks later, leave I did.'

Source: Extract taken from Kondo (1990:23-24)

In other cases, we may have to leave unexpectedly because aspects of our personal or field circumstances change. There may be a death in our family or among our research participants, or there may be problems in our personal relationships or illnesses of people we care about that require our attention. We also may become ill and need evacuation at short notice. Alternatively, the relationships or context of our research may change dramatically beyond our control. There may be personal or institutional responses to events or information 'exposed' through our research and permission (informal or official) for us to remain and work may be revoked. Or there may be a 'natural' disaster, political upheaval or civil unrest, which places either our participants or us at risk and forces us to leave.

All these scenarios are possible (see Box 10.3), and you may be able think of others depending on the specific area(s) in which you are proposing to work. Clearly, there is no singular time or way to leave or one way to feel about it. Much depends upon the specific relationships between our research topic, processes of arrival and implementation, geographical, cultural and political contexts, and, most importantly, our personality and attitude.

Factors influencing experiences of leaving

Leaving is likely to be less complex if we have adopted a topic that is not contentious, or if we have implemented a research design and epistemology that has required us to remain somewhat distant from our research participants (an observant outsider). It can also be more straightforward if we have only been involved in short periods of fieldwork and relatively functional relationships.

If we undertake a survey of government or NGO officials in a capital city for example, we may be involved in interviewing and also be responsible for the co-ordination of local research assistants who administer the survey. Our research interactions are likely to involve a series of short encounters with a range of relatively well-educated people. Here, the acts of arriving and leaving research participants can occur within a relatively short time period associated with the interview and we remain clearly positioned as outsiders (see Chapter 2 for a more detailed discussion) throughout. Our obligations to them may be limited to the professional realm such as providing a summary report of our research findings.

Leaving our research assistants, however, may be more challenging and require different strategies because we will have got to know them quite well over a period of time (see Chapter 7). In this case, some of the strategies discussed below may be more appropriate to the changing nature of our relationships with them.

In other cases, our research design and methodology may involve us in periods of ethnographic or participatory work where we become more involved in the lives of our participants, and where we occupy a more ambivalent position as insider/outsider. In situations like these, leaving can be more complicated as the acts of arriving and leaving may be further apart or our need for acceptance by our participants may increase the likelihood of problems in ending or changing relations later (Roadberg, 1980:283). We, along with our participants may 'forget' that we have to leave to write about our experiences and participants may place greater expectations upon us as a result of our longer and/or deeper involvement in their lives. Our obligations may be both professional and personal and extend well beyond the period of fieldwork (also see Chapter 11 for a discussion of these aspects).

In addition to the factors of time, research design and methodology, our characteristics and those of our participants also influence the process of leaving. It is important to remember that their influence will be greatest when working with vulnerable groups (see Chapter 9) where power relations are most unequal, and when we are involved in more participatory and long-term action-oriented research (see Box 10.3).

Box 10.3 Factors influencing experiences of leaving

- Nature and topic of research
- Research design, methodology and methods adopted
- Length of time spent in one place
- Nature of research and other relationships formed
- Degree of immersion in the field
- Degree of similarity or difference between researcher and participants
- Commitments and obligations made to research participants
- 'Success' or otherwise of fieldwork
- Expectations and feelings of family members and friends
- Perception and feelings associated with returning to university
- Cultural norms and expectations associated with leaving
- Time available for the leaving process

Not surprisingly, leaving is always going be problematic for researchers working in the 'third world' because of the potentially sensitive nature of topics we tend to research and the often implicit desire for change as a result of our work. We are also likely to encounter greater power differentials between our participants and us because of our status as 'western' or western-educated academics who have the ability to leave once the fieldwork is completed. Such problems give rise to a range of feelings and emotions associated with leaving which we discuss in the next section.

Feelings/emotions associated with leaving

There are many feelings, emotions and psychological difficulties associated with the processes of disengaging and leaving (Gallmeier, 1991). These may occur to varying degrees of intensity during fieldwork as we move from one place to another, and as we prepare to head back to university. The important thing is to recognise them and find ways to work with them, rather than pretend that they don't exist, or wish that they would somehow go away. As researchers, we inevitably establish multifaceted relationships with the places and people in whom we are interested, particularly if we spend a period of extended time in one place. We develop a familiarity with another culture (or a specific part of our own culture), experience different aspects of our selves and often, though not always, come to care about the people and places where we are based. The complexity of these relationships often makes it hard to define their exact nature and how we feel about them, which in turn complicates the imperative we have to leave (Maines et al., 1980). For example, Gallmeier (1991) following the work of Roadberg (1980) described feelings of guilt, alienation, sadness and ambivalence on leaving his research site. However, we are just as likely to experience relief, satisfaction and a sense of achievement.

Reluctance or resistance

It is often only when we come to leave that we find we do not want to go, and realise the extent of our immersion in the field (Wax, 1971:44). If we have been trying to maintain a more distanced 'objective' position in relation to our research participants, these feelings can come as a surprise. As Shaffir and Stebbins (1991) note leaving presents us with both a psychological and a tactical problem which we may want to avoid.

Disappointment, sadness or loss

Depending upon how our research process has gone and how our relationships with our participants have developed, we may feel disappointment or regrets as we get close to leaving. However it is important to remember that we have acted to the best of our knowledge at each stage of our fieldwork and that 'everything is always clearer in hindsight'. Being realistic, accepting the limitations of our work and finding ways to integrate them productively into our writing often provides food for thought in later analysis (see Chapter 11).

In most cases, there is also an element of sadness, loss or grief that accompanies leaving as relationships and routines change irrevocably, and we return to other ways of living and being. In particular, we may begin to miss the freedom from institutional pressures at university or long for our identity as a 'researcher' and the unique status and opportunities it affords us. Others may have developed a particularly intimate or sexual relationship with someone in our field site or local area, which can complicate the leaving process and prove emotionally traumatic.

For those of us researching in our own cultures, feelings are likely to be even stronger as we face the prospect of returning to university in a foreign place. Piyachatr Pradubraj's (Pui's) experience of leaving Thailand to return to New Zealand after a period of fieldwork in 2001–2002 is common (see Box 10.4).

Box 10.4 The difficulties of leaving: Pui's experience

Perhaps it was being back in my 'home' environment during 2001–2002 that reminded me of the old days before I had decided to do a PhD and that made leaving less fun than other times when I had travelled overseas. It was a mixture of missing 'my old days' in Thailand and of fearing my life as a PhD student in New Zealand. I didn't want to experience the worry, depression, stress, confusion and disappointment that the PhD had caused before I returned home for this period of fieldwork. However, my desire to stay was sometimes replaced by the thought that I could not have 'things' back the way they were pre-PhD and this helped me to carry on, and to leave.

The process of wrapping things up was particularly tense when I realised that there was less than a month left. It required a big 'push' to take the 'final step' of data collection. I experienced two contradictory feelings: One was to follow my wish to do a proper research job, and the other was to compromise so that I could enjoy the time I had left at home. Sometimes I told myself that I shouldn't care as much so that I could have an excuse to come home again later to collect more data!

As the time of packing approached, I had to tell myself to 'be strong'. Saying good-bye to family and friends was unbelievably tough. It was even harder when they said they would wait for me to come back with a 'Dr' title. At the time, I really wanted to tell them that I was not at all sure if I would be able to do it...

The day I flew out was particularly bad because I wasn't ready and I didn't want to leave. Four hours before my flight, I was still packing and hadn't eaten breakfast. I finally burst into tears, afraid of missing the plane. Part of the stress was also because I was not sure about my future in New Zealand. It was exhausting thinking about coming back here again. I thought about having to find a place to stay; cope with windy, chilly weather; get back into a 'sit-read-write' habit; work non-stop from dawn to dusk; and exercise like crazy as a way of getting rid of stress. I knew I would also miss home where I could buy food anytime without having to go to a supermarket.

On the way to the airport, I was thankful that my mum agreed not to see me off. (She lives outside Bangkok). I intentionally asked her not to because I was afraid that I might cry in front of her this time (I haven't before). However, calling her and hearing her voice on the phone was even worse because I knew that I probably wouldn't be able to see her again for at least a year. When the plane took off, however, the nervousness, anxiety and sadness gradually disappeared. I took a breath. It was time to get back on my own feet again and understand that all of this suffering was to support one dream - a PhD.

Source:Piyachatr Pradubraj, PhD candidate in Environmental Studies, Victoria University of Wellington

Alternatively, we may feel sad because our participants and others we have come to know do not seem to care much about whether we stay or leave. However, it is important to recognise that our participants may be very familiar with researchers or development workers and their cycles of arrival and departure. We shouldn't take it personally if people aren't as disappointed as we are about the fact that we are leaving!

Guilt

As we begin to recognise the extent of our emotional attachments to people with whom we have spent a great deal of time, or as we come to comprehend the expectations our research participants have of us (or that we created – directly or inadvertently), we may experience guilt. If we have been based in one place for any period of time, research participants may implicitly insist that our lives continue to mesh with theirs, and to expect us to live up to our personal commitments permanently (Maines et al., 1980; Shaffir et al., 1980). They may also be unhappy with the removal of privileged status gained through their role in our research, or they may be saddened at the loss of us as a confidant, friend, ally or lover (Maines et al., 1980).

In some cases, 'When our subjects become aware of our diminished interest in their lives and situations, they may feel cheated – manipulated and duped' (Shaffir et al., 1980:259) and these feelings can be hard to negotiate as a researcher. However, on completion of our research, the nature of our commitment to our research participants unavoidably changes. Its intensity subsides as we have less regular contact with them and other considerations inform our lives such as analysis and writing, working and family obligations. That said, it is important to bear in mind that our participants who are left behind may have to face the consequences of their [associations] with us (Mies, 1983:123 quoted in Hays-Mitchell, 2001:320). In some cases these may be positive, i.e., an increase in status perhaps. In other situations, they may be shunned because of their relationships with us.

Anxiety

> every time I have been in the field and become truly involved I have had to struggle with an impulse to stay longer than I should have stayed. By this I mean that I felt an almost irresistible urge to gather more data rather than face the grim task of organizing and reporting on the data I had.(Wax, 1971:45)

Anxiety is a common emotion to experience as Pui mentioned above and it is often associated with our confidence (or lack of it!) as researchers. According to Kleinmann and Copp (1993), our data can begin to feel like a huge monster or burden. Yet, we may also experience anxiety about losing it, a fear that Jackson (1990, cited in Kleinmann and Copp, 1993) has suggested ironically represents a secret desire to get rid of this burden! It is helpful to remember that in almost all cases, we are likely to have more than enough information with which to write upon our return (see Chapter 11).

Relief

Alternatively, or simultaneously, we may experience relief at the prospect of leaving. Relief may be particularly acute for researchers working in their own cultures where, 'the schizophrenic life style [of repeated cycles of cultural immersion and withdrawal] may be methodologically useful but emotionally draining' (Posner, 1980:211). It may also be the most significant feeling for anyone whose research has 'turned to custard' or for whom the whole experience of living and working in another culture has been unpleasant or traumatic in some way.

Even for others who have enjoyed the experience, relief may be associated with being beyond the grasp of powerful key participants or gatekeepers (Altheide, 1980) and back in the institutional support of a university. We may also feel relief at being able to leave behind the difficult working/living conditions or the harsh realities of our participants' lives, although such feelings may be accompanied by guilt as we face the explicit recognition and experience of our privilege and ability to leave our participants behind.

Satisfaction/accomplishment

So far most of the feelings and emotions we have discussed can be painful or difficult to negotiate, however, many of us are also likely to experience a sense of accomplishment and satisfaction associated with the completion of our fieldwork. Living and working in different cultures, or with groups of people somewhat different to us, is demanding even for relatively short periods of time, however, it can also be extremely rewarding (Roth, 2001).

Ultimately, leaving is likely to result in a range of emotions associated with the different experiences we have had throughout our time in the field and the various relationships we have formed in it. Some are perhaps inevitable while others can be managed by carefully considering our 'exit strategies' and ethical responsibilities in advance.

Leaving strategies and ethical responsibilities

To some extent, how we leave the field is related to how much time we have spent there and with which individuals. It is also a personal decision, which depends upon how we view our research participants and the relationships developed with them over that time (Taylor, 1991). We cannot usually be a friend to everyone, but we can be 'a friendly researcher' (Letkemann, 1980:297) who is sensitive to the diversity of research relationships formed and able to negotiate different ways of closing or transforming those relationships at the end of our fieldwork.

Managing information and confidentiality

A way of minimising anxiety is to think carefully about what might be missing from our data before we wrap up our fieldwork (Taylor, 1991). We can do this by trying to imagine what information we will need when we come to write about the places and people involved in our work and making a check list of key facts and figures, people names, positions and/or institutional history. If we prepared some kind of 'research plan' prior to our fieldwork (see Chapter 2), being able to tick off the tasks we have accomplished may also provide some reassurance. The issue of confidentiality must be resolved before leaving the field (Wolf, 1991). This means clarifying the use of real names or pseudonyms with our participants as well as the use of any images in which they appear (see also Chapter 11).

Managing departures ethically

It is often easiest to manage departure where external factors determine the end of fieldwork such as the expiration of funding or visas, personal crises or changes in the research environment (see earlier sections on reasons for leaving and factors influencing our experiences of it). In these cases, the reason for departure is relatively clear-cut and can avoid confusion or disappointment among research participants (Letkemann, 1980). However, Thurston (1998) points out that when we are involved in longer term research, our hosts and participants are likely to construct kinship relationships for us which imply particular responsibilities and appropriate actions on our behalf (also see Keyes, 1983).

Understanding and employing local cultural patterns associated with leaving and the ending of personal relationships (Maines et al., 1980:262) is therefore critically important. For example, if working with a small community or community organisation in some places in the Pacific, it will be appropriate to throw a feast upon departure. However in other parts of the region, the onus may be on the participants to throw the feast and for researchers to give gifts.

One way of thinking about how to manage our departures therefore is to consider the different status of, and relationships we have with, our research participants and the expectations they have of us, then devise culturally-appropriate strategies for each of them. For example, Letkemann (1980) suggests that researchers can avoid bad feelings when leaving if they consciously maintain the distinction between associations which were entirely research-based and ended naturally with the completion of an interview or study and others, which continue based on friendship and mutual interests. However, such distinctions may not always be so easy to make.

It may be appropriate to adopt a gradual exit strategy with participants who have been directly involved in our research or with those whose participation has been more indirect, progressively reducing the frequency of contact with them through cycles of arrival and departure. Such 'periodic leave taking' can remind participants of our 'visitor' status in their lives and be a useful strategy for generating more information as our absence can provide an opportunity to ask 'catch up' questions upon our return (Altheide, 1980, Gallmeier, 1991).

A gradual exit involving periodic visits before the final visit can also enable new relationships based on diminishing frequency of contact to replace former relationships based on regular personal contact (Roadberg, 1980). Periodic or return visits can be problematic however, as local situations change and new avenues open up for possible research. Participants may want us to take up new causes or lines of enquiry, or become confused about the nature of their relationships with us as we begin to distance ourselves from them to write.

Alternatively, it might be more appropriate to 'drift off' from the field (Strauss, 1968, cited in Maines et al., 1980), moving loosely in and out of our research site without an apparent 'formal goodbye' or final visit. This may be acceptable in the context of work or research involving relatively short visits to field sites or when conducting a more formal survey. It may also be appropriate in some longer-term participatory work such as Sara's work with Ngaati Hauiti (an iwi, or Maori tribe) (see more detail in Box 10.6).

In cases like this one, the informality of drifting off 'suspends' rather than 'terminates' the research and keeps the option open to return and continue work at a later stage. Clearly such a strategy works well if we are able to easily maintain physical contact with our research site and participants, but is perhaps less appropriate where we have to relocate over large distances or return to another country at the end of fieldwork.

In other contexts, it may be most appropriate to exit quickly and formally by holding an event such as a presentation or leaving 'do' where there is a clear and explicit acknowledgement of the termination of the fieldwork. Making a presentation of research findings to date and explaining the process of writing and sharing information is a useful strategy to close relationships and give something back before we leave (see Box 10.5 and below for more discussion). It is particularly important where we know disseminating information will be difficult or impossible upon our return, or our participants are illiterate and have limited access to communicative technologies.

In all cases, the process of leaving will be easier if we have negotiated a realistic and understandable 'research bargain' with our participants (direct and indirect) at the beginning of our fieldwork and renegotiated this regularly throughout our stay.

Managing ongoing ethical responsibilities

Our presence in areas of socio-economic deprivation is complex and problematic (Abbott, 1995) and our roles and identities as researchers might not be fully appreciated by our participants. It is important to think about the pressures, which might result from these misunderstandings as our fieldwork draws to a close and to monitor what expectations might be raised by our departure.

Box 10.5 A quick and formal exit strategy: an example from Costa Rica

I worked for four months with a small women's jam-making cooperative in central Costa Rica with another UK graduate (Carol Odell) to undertake an analysis of current and future business practices using a questionnaire and interviews. We knew we had a finite period of time in the field and would not be able to return with a report on our work so we decided to present our 'findings' orally and in the form of cartoons with simple accompanying text in Spanish. We followed this up with a leaving party for anyone involved in our lives. At these formal events we were able to give something back to participants and practice culturally appropriate ways of saying goodbye with exchanges of gifts, stories and tears. Upon return to England, we wrote a report for sponsors. This was not sent back to cooperative members, although we did keep in touch with letters and photographs for a number of years.

Source: Sara Kindon, Royal Geographical Society-sponsored expedition research with Acosta Women's Association, Costa Rica, 1990.

Participants might expect us to give them leaving gifts, or leave them our belongings or do some fundraising for them when we get back to university. Others might expect us to share our preliminary research findings with them before we leave. They might expect us to keep in touch via letters and email or send back copies of published material. People might ask us when we'll be back. It is important that we do not make promises we cannot keep and that we do keep the promises we do make. (Box 10.6 describes two ways in which Sara negotiated various responsibilities associated with leaving fieldwork sites in Indonesia and Aotearoa New Zealand.)

Sending photos and letters after our return is also a valuable way of giving something back and keeping in touch. In areas of high socio-economic deprivation not many people own cameras and therefore receiving photos could be invaluable. Julie took photos of the son of a teenage mother she worked with, both as a baby in 1999 and again as a toddler in 2001. These were the only photos she had of her child.

Box 10.6 Negotiating responsibilities to research participants by sharing our work: Sara's experiences

In Bali, I was part of a Canadian-universities' project to construct a sustainable development strategy for the provincial planning agency. I had specific responsibility for gender and development research and undertook participatory fieldwork in three villages over 18 months with a local research partner. We gave oral summary presentations to research participants at the end of each period of village research and

*wrote summary reports and conference papers in Indonesian about infor-
mation that had been generated through the participatory exercises. We
also facilitated meetings between villagers and government officials so
that development needs identified during the course of our work could be
shared and met. Back in Canada, I wrote my Masters thesis independently and while this was sent back to Indonesia, it was not specifically distributed to participants in the three villages, or to government officials
more widely. I have maintained contact with families in two villages and my
research partner, writing and sending them photos and visiting as often as
I can.*

*Currently, in Aotearoa New Zealand, I am part of an ongoing partici-
patory video project involving a north island iwi (Maori tribe) and an audio-
visual ethnographic specialist. Together we are exploring relationships
between place, identity and social cohesion in their place-based communities and communities of interest through the production of videos and an
audio-visual record of our collaborative research process. Because I live
and work only three hours away from the tribal area, it has been possible
to go back regularly for meetings and to analyse information, write papers
or reports and edit videos together, which are for both tribal and academic use. It is also an obligation I committed to at the start of the project that
members of the iwi have a right of veto on anything written about them, or
how they appear in video footage. I am currently writing my PhD about the
methodology we developed and its implications for geographic research.
In contrast to my previous projects, I anticipate sharing multiple drafts of
my academic writing with my research participants and to giving them a
copy of it once it is completed.*

*Source: Sara Kindon, MA and follow up research in Bali, Indonesia, 1991-
2, 1994 and 1998; ongoing doctoral research with Ngati Hauiti in Aoteoroa
New Zealand, 1998-present.*

There are of course ethical implications if our participants receive clothes,
money, photos or gifts and are therefore favoured over other members of the same
community (see Box 10.7). Our actions could also impact on future researchers in
the same communities. However, it is important to understand the cultural context
in which requests for fundraising and gifts are made. In some cases, these requests
constitute a way of saying goodbye and should not therefore be a source of anxiety.

Once we get back to university and are getting on with our lives and careers,
it is easy to postpone sharing our work, writing letters, sending photos or fulfilling
commitments to 'help' with ongoing development in our field site. We might find,
for example, that fundraising for a development project is not compatible with our
academic commitments at university. We need to be realistic about what we can
commit to and if there is any possibility that we might never get around to these
things when back at university, it is best to do them while we are still in the field.
We need therefore to be flexible enough to respond to participants' expectations
ethically and to be honest about what is possible. We also must allow sufficient time

to meet our obligations, and if we know that a return visit is unlikely, then it is important to say so (Bradburd, 1998). Finally we need to think ahead about keeping in touch and sending back published material (see Chapter 11). Honouring any agreements we make is absolutely critical and should be seen as part of conducting ethical research and aiming for more reciprocal research relationships.

Box 10.7 Saying thanks and giving gifts: Julie's experiences

As my six months of fieldwork into the experiences of single motherhood in post-revolutionary Nicaragua came to an end, the demands for personal clothes and toys that we would not be taking with us became overwhelming. I had to make decisions about what I was going to do with our personal belongings and whether I wanted to take them or leave them. I was more than happy to leave my children's clothes and toys with research participants but had to be careful not to be seen to be favouring one family over another. As a result, I found myself dividing our belongings among a growing number of families.

Leaving gifts are often welcomed, but can be politically difficult where those that participated in the research benefit over non-participants in the same community in similar circumstances. I consulted Nicaraguans working for development NGOs on this issue, and opinions were mixed. Some felt presents were necessary and a valuable gesture, others felt presents were all right as long as they were for the children, others felt presents or food donations were appropriate but gifts of money or cash were not. One person felt that giving gifts would generate expectations that participation in a research project should be rewarded and this would complicate research for other researchers, particularly Nicaraguan ones who might not have the resources to provide gifts.

I developed numerous ways of saying thank you such as providing afternoon tea, throwing a party, and going out for icecream. I tried to decide on 'thank yous' that did not set dangerous precedents or divide the communities in which I worked. In some cases, the best thing I could offer was time. As such, I tried to spend some (non-interview) time with research participants so they could feel valued and friendships could be cemented.

Source: Julie Cupples, doctoral research with single mothers in Nicaragua,

---

Practical concerns

Having considered the emotional, cultural, academic and ethical dimensions of leaving in the previous sections, practical matters may seem relatively straightforward. However, they can cause a great deal of stress and last minute panic and anxiety if we haven't thought about them in advance and planned enough time for them within our fieldwork schedule. In Box 10.8, there are a number of questions, which should prompt you to think about logistical matters associated with leaving.

Checking our information, organising packing, transport, flights and gifts can take a lot of time, especially if we are also trying to leave appropriately (as discussed in the section on leaving strategies) and cope with our feelings about the whole process (as discussed in the earlier section). From our experiences, leaving enough time for personal priorities such as visiting places or doing things specific to the cultures in which we are working is very important in terms of managing stress and easing our transition out of our field sites. Unfortunately, these aspects are also often the first things to be sacrificed when time gets tight. Planning ahead and leaving enough time to accommodate our ethical and academic responsibilities alongside our personal desires is important and will enable us to feel more satisfaction upon our departure. In addition, it is quite likely that people with whom we have been working will want to do things with us before we leave, so planning a timeframe that can accommodate last minute requests or invitations is also worth keeping in mind.

Box 10.8 Practical questions to ask when leaving

Managing information

Last minute checks on data:
- Have I got everything I need in terms of essential contextual facts, figures or photographs of key places and people that I might need?
- What are the addresses, telephone and fax numbers, etc., for people I want to keep in touch with or send information to?

Exporting information:
- How safe is it to carry data with me (tapes, field notes, diaries, etc.)?
- What information may I need to email or send back?
- How safe is it to send information using local mail services?

Personal priorities

- How long will it realistically take me to say thanks or goodbye to everyone I want to/need to?
- How much time can I leave open to respond to last minute invitations or requests?
- How long and what will it cost to have photos developed before I leave (if I intend to give these away)?
- How much can I afford to spend on gifts for those I worked with (if appropriate), and/or contribute to NGOs or other organisations?
- What places or things do I want to visit or do before I leave?

• What presents do I want to take back, how long will it take me to find them and what are they likely to cost?

• What might some of the ethical issues be associated with buying particular goods?

• How am I going to carry or send them?

Packing, travel and taxes

Packing, shipping and weight allowance:

• How am I going to get my materials (and any gifts, etc.) back to university?

• How much can I carry with me on the plane?

• What goods can I or can't I import?

• How long will air-freight or sea-freight take to arrive? How much will it cost?

Confirming plane bookings and getting to the airport:

• How many hours in advance do I need to confirm my flights?

• What time do I need to be at the airport and how long will it realistically take me to get there?

Departure tax:

• How much do I need to keep for my departure or other taxes?

Source: Adapted from authors' own experiences

Conclusion

Leaving is a dynamic, challenging and critically valuable part of any fieldwork experience. It is also essential. It informs our understandings of our research site and participants, impacts upon our ongoing relationships with participants, and indirectly affects the future relationships they may have with other researchers. More fundamentally, it confronts us with our own privilege as educated researchers, and demands that we consider the ethical praxis of our work. It is therefore worthy of considerable thought and planning.

This said, there is no 'right' way to leave the field. Each fieldworker, the nature of his/her research, the types of relationships formed and the contexts in which s/he is working will vary, demanding different approaches and strategies. What we face in common are emotional as well as intellectual responses to leaving, and the imperative to negotiate the implications of our presence in people's lives and our departure from them in realistic and ethical ways (see the figure in Box 10.9). This chapter has given you some insights and tips about how to prepare for leaving – the rest is now up to you!

Box 10.9 Leaving strategies

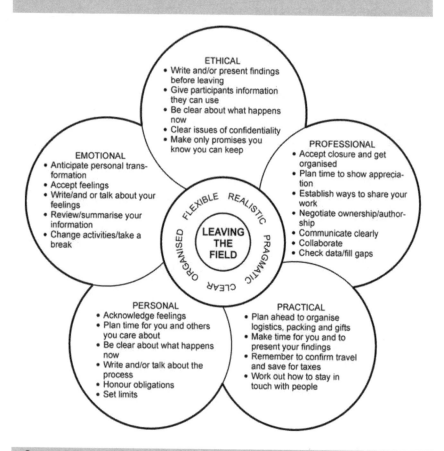

Source: Adapted from participatory diagrams generated in a workshop Sara facilitated for post graduate students and staff in the Development Studies Research Group at the Department of Geography, University of Durham, 14 March 2002.

Recommended reading

Shaffir, W. and Stebbins, R. (eds) (1991) *Experiencing Fieldwork: An Inside View of Qualitative Research Sage, Newbury Park.*
Part IV 'Leaving and Keeping in Touch' deals specifically with the question of leaving and contains five contributions. These include the difficulties and risks of leaving a closed secret society, the question of revisiting and staying in touch, our responsibilities to our participants and the implications of secondary fieldwork involvements.

Notes

1. William Shaffir et al. (1980) describe these activities upon arrival and during our fieldwork as 'the research bargain'. Haas and Shaffir (1980) also note that such a term can abstract and fix into a discrete stage early on what is in fact an ongoing process and negotiation throughout the research.

2. We are grateful to members of the Development Studies Research Group at Durham University who participated in a workshop facilitated by Sara on the themes of this chapter in March 2002. We particularly appreciated comments on drafts of this chapter and Chapter 11 from Emma Mawdsley, Janet Townsend and Marloes van Amerom.

11 Returning to University and Writing the Field

Julie Cupples and Sara Kindon

Introduction

This book has encouraged you to consider the field not as a bounded geographical location but as a space, which is actively constituted through the social and spatial practices of the researcher and his/her relationships with participants. As such, when we return to university to begin the process of 'writing in'[1] our research, the field will continue to 'leak' (Cook 2001: 104) into our everyday lives and will continue to be constituted throughout this process. As Maines et al. have stated:

> it is often difficult to specify when one is 'in' or 'out'. The writing up of results phase isn't even a diagnostic test for indicating when one has departed, since the recording of conclusions, hypotheses and theoretical statements is a continuing process. (1980:264)

When we write up and publish our research, we are forced to make clear decisions about how the places and peoples we have visited are represented. We have to do this without the frequent contact we had during fieldwork and at a time when new pressures, commitments and responsibilities will arise. We must therefore negotiate and balance our ongoing commitments to research participants with those we have to the university authorities or funding agencies, to supervisors and to the editors of the books and journals in which our work will appear. This chapter focuses on the 'post-field' stage (Wax, 1971) and explores the feelings, emotions and identities associated with returning to university and how to meet the exigencies of organising data, writing and publishing our work.

Many researchers plan to move quickly onto the writing process shortly after their return. There are however a number of practical and emotional issues which might affect our motivations and our ability to set and stick to deadlines. Fieldwork can be a deeply emotional experience, which often involves not only finding out about others but ourselves. It is likely to be an experience in which our identities and sense of ourselves shift, possibly in ways that could not have been predicted. Our collected data might compose a series of interviews or survey material, statistical information, photos, newspaper articles, archival material and field notes. It will also contain a series of half-understood issues and events whose relevance to our thesis will not be readily apparent. To move quickly onto writing without allowing time to digest, process and reflect upon what might have been a life changing experience is not always possible. The importance of our field sites to our personal and professional development, our shifting motivations for having chosen to pursue a particular topic in a particular place and the interactions and relationships we had while in the field, will all impact on how we feel about being back at university and how we manage writing.

Hobbs (2001:285) refers to the post-fieldwork period as postpartum, 'when the thrill of being in the field wanes and it is replaced by the grimmer challenge of paying the piper and publishing'. When one of the author's of this chapter, Julie, was pregnant for the first time, she was so wrapped up in the mechanics of pregnancy, labour and giving birth that she barely gave a thought to raising a child and how she was going to do it. She had a very similar experience with her fieldwork. Going to Nicaragua for six months with her children to collect data was in itself so enormous, so anxiety provoking, so overwhelming, that she did not stop to consider very much at all the writing process that would follow it. It can however be extremely fruitful to carefully consider the 'postpartum' phase and to be prepared for unexpected feelings associated with returning. This can motivate us to move onto managing data and writing.

This chapter explores the dynamics of writing and publishing our work and considers how we negotiate our shifting identities between the field and home or the university, how we manage our data and time and negotiate competing responsibilities.

As well as examining our feelings and shifting identities, there are a number of issues which we should consider before we leave the field which will facilitate the writing process (See Box 11.1)

Box 11.1 Issues to consider before leaving the field

- How am I going to manage my data? Do I need time for transcribing and data analysis before writing can commence?
- How am I going to write about my experience and what I learn in ways that are ethical?
- What should I include and what should I leave out?
- How much personal information should I include? How reflexive should I be?
- How do I balance my commitments to my research participants with commitments to supervisors and editors?
- Is a return visit to the field possible, if necessary?

Source: Authors' own experiences

Managing shifting feelings and identities about returning to university

Many students from Euro-American societies who do research in Africa, Asia, Latin America or the Pacific expect to experience some kind of culture shock when they travel abroad to do their fieldwork, as discussed in Chapter 7. However, coming home or returning to university might also entail a reverse culture shock and one that might be unexpected. While many of us might feel a sense of personal accomplishment at having completed an important stage of our research, these feelings might well be mixed with anxieties about failure or an inability to write. Such anxiety about writing may be particularly acute if we are required to write about our work in a foreign language.[2] In addition, we might also have difficulty in readjusting to life at home or back at university. We might find it hard to communicate the intensity of our experiences to family and friends back home or even to find other people who are interested in or care enough about our work or who understand what we have been through.

> **Box 11.2 Phil's experience of returning 'home'**
>
> *I had always thought that going to Papua New Guinea for my research would be a challenge. That was part of the attraction of an overseas trip. I'd need to be independent, sharp and prepared for every eventuality. I was particularly careful to prepare myself for communication issues as I knew that language barriers and cultural gaps would provide significant limitations. But fitting in to PNG was much easier than fitting back in to New Zealand. If I were to sum up the first few weeks and even months following my re-entry 'home' with one word it would be 'disorientation.' In fact, I now regard that re-entry period as the most difficult part of my entire research – by a very long way. I expect that expectations had everything to do with it. I had mentally prepared myself for entering PNG but for NZ I thought it would be like it always had been. It wasn't.*
>
> *There are a few things that stand out for me as being particularly significant in those first few weeks back: the shift in the relationships with friends, my shared house feeling like it was no longer my space, jumping straight into my work (transcribing – the most tedious part of the whole research process), and the fact that I had personally 'shifted' – I simply no longer was the same self I had been three months previously. A friend researching international education once told me that he had found that many international students upon their return 'home' felt that they were walking into a movie that was already half way through. That was how I felt. I knew there was much that had taken place previously, but I never found out exactly what it was.*
>
> *I think that the actual process of re-entry was hard. But what made it much harder was that I did not expect it to be like that. I should have been ready, because I had been warned. But I was sure that it would be a cinch! I had thrived for three months in a remote part of PNG, how hard could little old windy Wellington be? I was wrong because I assumed it was about place. Actually it was all about space: my personal emotional space, my un-met expectations as to what constituted my space, and my failure to be prepared for an altered space of being despite my familiarity with the place.*
>
> *Source: Philip Fountain, MSc Student in Geography, Victoria University of Wellington (2000-2002)*

The longer we are away from our field sites and the more difficult (or impossible) it becomes to visit, the more likely it is that we will experience anxiety about our ongoing relationships and obligations to people we met there. We may also feel a sense of loss related to the shift in routine from being a researcher in the field with daily interactions and patterns of behaviour, to being back at university as a graduate student with a different set of interactions, expectations and behaviours.

Moving back and forth between our field site and home or university, our research agendas, relationships and even our understandings of ourselves change. Being in the field changes us and we never return 'home' quite the same (Hyndman, 2001; Wolf, 1991) and we do not know who we will become during the research process (Till, 2001). According to Sanders (2001:89) fieldwork involves negotiating a disjunctive identity 'between who I am in the field and who I am at home' and the challenge we face when we leave the field and return home is to find ways to connect our researcher-selves to the selves we portray at home. Sanders argues that this disjuncture of identity follows us home from the field and that our careers are shaped by how we resolve it. Whether our experiences of fieldwork are largely positive or negative, it is inevitable that returning to university will involve negotiating and understanding how our identities have shifted in the course of our fieldwork. Philip Fountain's experience provides a useful insight into this process (see Box 11.2).

Fieldwork experiences might be very intense and have a defining influence on what we subsequently become. As Sanders (2001) says, some of us never really return from the field. Fieldwork is also different from other forms of travel because of the need to spend a substantial amount of the following months and years writing up the research. Julie certainly had a number of life-defining experiences in Nicaragua (see Box 11.3). These experiences in many ways became intensified as she wrote her thesis. She was back at university, at 'home', but was still there, listening to her participants' voices on the tapes as she transcribed them, processing data, information and experiences, trying to make sense of a vast range of ideas in terms of the existing literature, and debating the merits and ethics of representing her participants in particular ways. There is subsequently a need to reorient ourselves to our 'new' cultural context and this can take time.

Box 11.3 Julie's experience of getting back and beginning to write

I did my initial period of fieldwork over six months in the second half of 1999. I planned to complete an initial draft of the thesis over the following year and make a return visit to the field in January 2001. My field site was already a place in which I had had a number of intense experiences associated with romantic involvements, unexpected pregnancy and political activism in support of the Nicaraguan revolution. My fieldwork experience was no different. As well as feeling deep intellectual satisfaction associated with getting on with my PhD, I also had to negotiate a long term separation from my partner, I had observed my children become proficient in

---

> Spanish and also experienced the tragic death of my host and close friend. All these experiences added to a vast quantity of rich and fascinating data collected through interviews, the media and in fieldnotes.
>
> Making sense of these experiences as well as all the information collected was difficult. I found that for a few months all my time was taken up thinking, reading and transcribing and I was unable to begin writing until the end of that year. Consequently, I made my return visit to Nicaragua a few months later than planned with transcriptions complete but only three chapters drafted.
>
> Source: Julie Cupples, doctoral research with single mothers in Nicaragua, 1999

How we deal with these issues and feelings will depend to a large extent on our fieldwork experiences, our personalities, the support we have for our work back at university and the possibilities which exist for future visits to our field sites. While it is important not to romanticise our fieldwork experiences and run the danger of living in the past, we do need to allow time for mental and emotional processing. The time we can allow for this will depend on individual circumstances but it is valuable to develop strategies to deal with our feelings on return (See Box 11.4).

Box 11.4 Strategies for adjusting to being back at university and/or home

- Expect return culture shock so it is less of a shock.

- Think about how our fieldwork experience may have caused our identities and subjectivities to shift.

- Work out personal support networks and find people with whom we can talk about our work and experiences.

- Join a graduate email discussion list such as PILAS (Postgraduates in Latin American studies) or a university/department social or support group for international students in which ideas can be shared.

- Continue to write 'field notes' or some kind of research journal upon return in which not only ideas but also feelings can be documented.

- Keep in touch with participants in field sites via letters and email (if possible) to maintain regular contact.

- Eat food and watch movies from our field sites and share these with friends.

Source: Bailey (1996) and the authors' own experiences.

Managing data, time and supervisors

While it is possible to feel that not enough data have been collected (see Chapter 10), it is much more likely that we will feel overwhelmed by the quantity of data obtained and experience anxieties about to make sense of it. Kleinmann and Copp (1993) warn that the fear of analysis experienced by some researchers may become paralysing. However, it is important to realise that this 'postpartum' phase is also a time when 'a lot of the unfamiliar experiences and strange events in the field somehow become understandable' (Lawless et al., 1983:xii).

When setting timetables and deadlines, it might be wise to allow some time for processing in which transcribing or other forms of data collation can take place. Such time can also enable the intensity of fieldwork experiences to settle as well as the potential of data gathered to emerge before we commence writing.

Inevitably many graduate students, because of time and funding constraints, cannot permit themselves to spend too long reflecting and analysing. In the first month it should be possible to read through research notes and identify preliminary findings on which subsequent chapter outlines can hang and be refined. Reviewing books on research and data analysis can then help us to decide how best to organise and analyse our material. It is worth bearing in mind that transcribing and data analysis invariably takes longer than expected (Jackson, 2001) and timetables will often have to be reworked to allow for this. It is also important to think about how our work is to be stored and what back ups we have in the event of computer failure.

It is important once writing has commenced to develop good study habits. In this respect, developing timetables and arranging regular meetings with supervisors is critical. Good relationships with supervisors are often crucial in setting goals and deadlines and maintaining motivation. While supervision arrangements vary widely between departments and institutions, it is important to communicate how you would ideally like to be supervised and the frequency, length and style of supervision meetings. It is reasonable to expect drafts of your work to be returned promptly by supervisors and for them to be clear and specific about their criticisms. You must not, however, rely on your supervisor to motivate you and guide your research. It is a good idea to think of ways of rewarding yourself for sticking to deadlines, such as a weekend away for completing a chapter draft on time.

Writing and representing

While we have argued that it is important to allow time for the fieldwork to settle, it is an excellent practice to start writing before you are ready. Keeping a research journal once you are back from the field is a valuable way of making sense of field notes or other data and does of course constitute writing. Remember that anything we write can be subsequently revised or expanded. It doesn't have to be perfect first time. If you are suffering from writer's block or having trouble getting started, try and write a bad chapter or part of a chapter. Alternatively, what Sara has found helpful is to write 'letters' to her supervisors, which are a form of thinking out loud about thorny issues within her thesis. Using this strategy, she is not tied to thinking about a chapter, but can be free to think about the issues and themes she wants to explore, later working them into chapters where appropriate. Writing to someone concrete and known to her, she has also found helps her to picture her audience (or at least one audience) and sustains her in a dialogue with someone real and supportive.

This process can be encouraged if we see writing and researching as mutually constitutive processes (Berg and Mansvelt, 2000). Many of the insights gleaned from the field experience come only after we return home and begin to take into account the role played by serendipity in the success of our fieldwork (Gade, 2001). As Richardson (1994:516 quoted in Bailey, 1996:104) has argued:

> Although we usually think about writing as a mode of 'telling' about the social world, writing is not just a mopping-up activity at the end of a research project. Writing is also a way of 'knowing' – a method of discovery and analysis.

Thus, the meanings attached to our field sites and our participants are neither pre-given nor decided during the course of fieldwork, but are invented and reinvented in the writing process. As Hyndman (2001) has argued, field experience does not necessarily stand in for knowledge but it allows us to tell certain kinds of stories and there are often a number of different stories (or theses) that could be written from our data and experiences in the field.

Many of the possible stories involve ourselves and the written account of any fieldwork always includes the writer more than we'd like to admit (Lewis, 1991). Many disciplines within the social sciences are now recognising the value of research, which reflexively accounts for the conditions in which it was produced, partly because writing is more convincing if the limitations of the research are made explicit by the researcher. According to Geertz (1988 in Lewis, 1991), it is through writing that fieldworkers persuade others that they have truly 'been there', an ability which he calls an 'offstage miracle'. Whether we can pull off this offstage miracle successfully depends on how we represent our field experience in our written work and negotiate competing responsibilities.

The analyses we make during this process are crucial not just in terms of producing a coherent thesis, but will also impact on how our field sites are constructed and the possibilities which exist for us or other researchers to do further research in the same area. It is therefore important not to lose sight of these responsibilities in the interests of submission or completing written work. We must take care to 'prevent spoiling the field' for ourselves and others (Mikkelson, 1995:277). However, as Stevens (2001) has argued, accountability becomes harder to achieve with the passing of time and there is a particular tension when we consider that writing generally takes place away from the field and must also be done in a way which is meaningful within our disciplines and in terms of the broader literature. As times passes, we also increasingly run the risk of romanticising our fieldwork experiences in ways which compromise our arguments or evoke inappropriate understandings of our field site.

Sangarasivam (2001) has discussed the need to critically examine our motivations in researching particular peoples and communities. To do so is an integral part of respectful scholarship. The writing process provides an opportunity in which these motivations can be examined. Often we are attracted to our field sites because of perceived absences in our own lives, the lure of exoticism or to gain cultural capital. A critical examination of such motivations can help us to avoid or at least expose the neocolonial pretensions in our writing (see Bondi, 1997).

As well as thinking about our motivations and how we write, we also need to consider carefully the visual representations of our fieldwork and the ways in which we are going to use photos, maps, slides and videos. As Goin (2001) argues when using photos, we must not overlook the politics of representation as how a subject is represented is as important as the subject itself. The inclusion of photos of 'third world' places or peoples in first world publications, while satisfying to the reader or invaluable for illustrating certain points, can be politically tricky. If it is not done with care, we can open ourselves to accusations of Othering, exoticism or aestheticising suffering or poverty. Photos of people are particularly problematic as they might breach confidentiality. Making return visits to our field site to seek permission to publish photos might be a practical impossibility. It is therefore best to clarify issues of confidentiality and permission to use and publish photos before leaving where possible (see Chapter 10).

We also need to consider how we are going to contextualise any images we use. According to Goin (2001), it is important not only to take the cultural frame of reference into account, but also to be aware that the meaning of the photograph will change with the addition of text. We must therefore ask ourselves what it is we hope to achieve with the inclusion of an image and the possible meanings and interpretations it might convey to readers.

Reciprocity, confidentiality and sharing the field

Clearly issues of confidentiality are critical when considering the use of photographs. However, we must not lose sight of the importance of reciprocity, confidentiality and thinking about what we owe to our research participants throughout our writing. While some researchers feel that their work should directly benefit the researched community (Stevens, 2001), it is often difficult to match the particular needs of our research participants with the theoretical concerns of the academy. However, sharing the field is essential both in terms of the training of future researchers and as a means of giving back something to those who have helped us (Price, 2001; Stevens, 2001).

We must therefore make decisions about how we are going to share our work with our participants and consider the validity of passing on copies of reports, articles or theses. As discussed in Chapter 10, we can hold workshops before leaving the field in order to share our research. A number of authors have described the benefits of passing on their work to research participants. Donovan Storey recalls returning to a participant's house many years after the fieldwork in the Philippines was completed and was delighted to find a well-thumbed copy of his thesis in a bookshelf with notes written in the margins of nearly every page. Similarly, Brian Miller, who conducted research with gay fathers in the USA, quotes from a letter from a participant to whom he had passed on published material.

> I just read the article you sent of your study. Wow, did I see myself! It's like you peeked at my diary or read my mind. Scary. I'm surprised I was so open in the interview. [...] I loved reading about other gay fathers' situations too. It's a relief to know there are more in my shoes. I'm going to give some of their suggestions a whirl and see how they work for me. (Miller and Humpheys, 1980:220)

It can be common to experience feelings of guilt associated with the process of writing depending upon what commitments have been made to participants about how they will be represented, or whether any publications will be shared with them. For instance, Roadberg (1980) experienced guilt about the length of time it seemed to take him to write up his dissertation and furnish this to the research subjects that had given permission for his study. He was concerned that his apparent 'delay' or tardiness would mean that his research subject would think that the study had been a waste of time and would lose respect for him as a researcher. When he finally did provide a report of his research, he felt an enormous weight lifted.

It is important, however, to think carefully about which writings a researcher should share. Till (2001:53) writes that 'sharing rough drafts and interview transcripts in politically charged settings can evoke anxiety, damage research relationships and even jeopardize attempts at confidentiality'. In some cases, sharing a wieldy thesis (especially if it is written in a foreign language) or theoretically intense articles might not be the most appropriate way to give something back to the field. It might also make the less quoted participants feel less valuable than the more quoted ones.

However, there are other ways of sharing your research in a way which is accessible to research participants. Julie found that passing on copies of interview transcripts was particularly valuable in terms of reciprocity. Many women in my study were delighted to receive what in some cases amounted to detailed written life histories. A couple of women said how they had always wanted to write it all down but had never found the time. Others said it would be useful to show to their children. Other ways of sharing research might be to write short articles for publication in local newsletters, radio programmes or circulation to community groups. Cartoons can work well where literacy levels are low (see Chapter 10). Working through locally produced publications and media outlets can also be very effective. Another strategy is to actually write something with our research participants (see Box 11.5).

Box 11.5 Sara's experience of writing together with research participants

In my research I work very closely with members from an iwi (Maori tribe) with whom I have been researching the relationships between place, identity and social cohesion in Aotearoa New Zealand over the last four years (see also Chapter 10). Together we decide how to write about our research and what it means for different audiences. Usually, I write a loose draft that all parties then work on together. It is a very rewarding process, but it is time-consuming and it demands that we find ways of expressing differences and using language that is accessible to all of us. We also still have to grapple with issues of confidentiality and how we represent others in the iwi who are not co-authors with us. However, I find the process stimulating and worthwhile because of how it enriches our understandings and relationships. It also supports the publication and dissemination of different voices and perspectives, which in turn challenges the dominance of white, western voices in academic research.

Source: Sara Kindon, doctoral research in Aotearoa New Zealand, 1999-2001

If we are going to pass our written work onto participants, or get involved in some collaborative writing with them, it is important to evaluate how this might impact on how we write. Knowing that our research participants expect to read final reports or articles may influence our selection of material within them. We are conscious of the fact that our participants might be able to recognise their own contributions, especially through direct quotations, and we can rarely give equal attention to all and simultaneously handle our material responsibly.

Many of us also consider our research participants as friends and passing on written work might involve a degree of censorship. Friendships and the whole process of liking others are, as Sanders (2001) indicates, unscientific concepts and might lead us to suppress uncomfortable observations. In this respect, ongoing friendships can simultaneously enhance, distort and generally complicate the writing process.

We need therefore to consider whether passing on work means we are going to be less critical of a researched community than we would otherwise be. If so, what are the theoretical implications of such a position? According to Letkemann (1980), it is important to consider the following issues. Would some people be offended if they were quoted less often or not at all? Is passing on our work going to make it difficult for others or us to do further research in the same place? Could people be identified or persecuted in some way as a result of what we write?

Problems associated with the potential identification of research participants in our written work can be addressed by the use of pseudonyms or by not giving full copies of work to people, but giving them an abstract with details of where the publication can be found. This fulfils the responsibility to make participants aware of the material without forcing it on them, and enables researchers to symbolically leave the field as they have left it physically months or years before. However, another problem is that not all participants are equally interested in providing feedback or in having their identities concealed. Letkemann (1980) issued copies of his PhD thesis to informants for comment and discovered that not all participants were happy with the assurances of anonymity given. Some wished to be identified as a means to obtaining some kind of official recognition while others were able to identify individual participants from the quotes used.

There are other issues to consider in terms of the expectations we might be generating. Evidence of publications or reports might lead a researched community to believe that we are going to take up respondents' causes or that we have the power to influence policy or other outcomes. We might also be implicitly suggesting that we plan to do further research in this area.

Sending written and published material to participants can of course be valuable in terms of keeping in touch. Moreover, if our participants are willing to provide us with feedback, this might also provide us with benefits such as enhanced triangulation, longitudinal insight or unanticipated avenues for further research (Miller and Humphreys, 1980). These benefits are important in considering the rigour of research, especially if the topics being researched are particularly sensitive as respondents may have been guarded or misleading first time around. They are also important for yielding deeper analysis of a situation, providing more layers and complexity. Also, with more information over time, the tendency to want to fix data, categories and people can be resisted and the impacts of the research can be assessed more fully.

Negotiating competing responsibilities: participants, audiences and careers

When we engage in academic research, we stand to benefit both personally and professionally. It can be hard over time and distance to maintain commitments and meet obligations to research participants. Once we begin to anchor our work within the broader literature, consider publication outlets for our work, or select external examiners, our notion of our audience might begin to shift and we can find ourselves writing for others. As a result of this shift, Wolf (1991) sees the writing process as a balance between protecting the vested interests of the researched group, exposing moral or social injustice and advancing one's professional career. Negotiating what Nietschmann (2001) has called intellectual property rights and academic espionage is a complex process. John Van Maanen (1988) points out that writing-up is in fact a re-representation of what occurred or was learnt in the field. He questions the direct link between fieldwork experience and the written version.

The writing process is a time to consider how what we write could potentially harm our participants (Wolf, 1991) and to think beyond the confines of data collection about the effects that our research can have on our participants (Hays-

Mitchell, 2001). For example, Hyndman (2001), in her research with UNHCR employees, admitted that to write about certain issues brought up in interviews might have breached confidentiality and jeopardised careers. We must at the very least ensure that our participants are no worse off for having let us study them (Taylor, 1991). Box 11.6 describes how Eleanor Grourk negotiated these competing responsibilities.

As we move onto submitting or publishing our work, we might find academic conventions on the concept of authorship limiting in terms of recognising participants' contributions to our work. Masters and PhD theses are always singly authored regardless of the contributions made by participants and you will need to be inventive if these contributions are to be acknowledged, while confidentiality is maintained. It might be possible to acknowledge co-authorship in subsequent publications, or to plan to write collaboratively as Sara mentioned in Box 11.5. A good example of co-authorship being granted to informants is Townsend et al's., 1995 publication *Women's Voices from the Rainforest, a text* that also addresses the methodological complexities and politics of representing women's voices.

Publication of research is important for many reasons. It can be a way of repaying a 'debt' to participants as a group, a means of providing external confirmation of the value of the information generated, and a process that evaluates the researcher's ability to do justice to it (Letkemann, 1980:299). Where and how we publish our research and in what language however are not such straightforward decisions. Publication can result in positive or negative feedback. Information can be used, misused or not used. As stated above, alternative publications are a good way of reaching a larger audience. However, they might jeopardise academic careers. For example, some tenure track professors in the United States are forbidden by their departments from writing in anything other than refereed journals and the Research Assessment Exercise (RAE) in the United Kingdom does not include articles published in Spanish in Latin American journals. Getting an academic job after completing a thesis might depend on us publishing in the 'right' journals. Alternatively, we might feel pressure to write in ways which correspond with mainstream or 'politically correct' views. These are professional constraints which often compromise our desire to make our work accessible to wider audiences and to fulfil commitments to research participants. Publishing is a personal, professional and political issue, which forces us to examine whether we are writing for our researched communities or our careers or whether we are able to do both.

Box 11.6 For whom do we write research?

My Masters research sought to explore the cross-cultural production of knowledge within participatory processes of development focusing upon a case study of the New Zealand Official Development Assistance piloting of Participatory Impact Assessment. The case study involved three groups of actors who were simultaneously the audiences for my research; New Zealand development practitioners and civil servants, members of a South

Asian Non-Governmental Organisation and members of communities with whom they worked. Each audience 'spoke a different language' (literally and culturally), so in which language should I have written my research?

The people from each group who participated in my research did so mainly through extended interviews and participant observation. I felt a strong responsibility to make my research accessible and pertinent for them, particularly as many extended incredible generosity towards me. However, as they came from a very diverse range of cultures and levels of literacy, the text and format of an Executive Summary, let alone the text and format of the research thesis, while accessible to some would potentially be inaccessible to others.

The desire for a practical application of my research was my main motivation. Yet, the academic structure of writing (locating and qualifying my research within the wider body of research) presented quite rigid boundaries of acceptability. These boundaries had to be met to fulfil the examination criteria and to provide legitimacy for me to present my work to a wider audience. However, academic texts are not always accessible outside of academia! In addition, my academic audience was in itself diverse; not all academics work and write within the same discourse and the framework embraced by one examiner can be problematic to another.

Clearly whatever text I wrote was going to either constrain or enable understanding for different audiences. Therefore, short of writing about four different texts in the 'languages' of my various audiences, how could I effectively communicate my research? Well I didn't find another solution other than to distil the essence of my research and to 're-write' it in the language of each audience. From my thesis oriented towards the academic community, I have rewritten other versions for the New Zealand Development practitioners; the South Asian NGO and the communities with whom they work. Each version emphasises slightly different points and uses language appropriate to the audience.

I have found that my desire to engage in applied research has explicitly required my writing process to be equally applied. Whilst this application is a process fraught with potential conflict, I have also found that re-presenting my research in different ways for diverse audiences has served, overall, to clarify and consolidate the research itself.

Source: Eleanor Grourk, Masters of Development Studies Student, Victoria University

Returning to the field

The writing process after we return to university and the ability to maintain responsibilities to participants will inevitably be influenced by the possibilities we have to return to our field sites. If we feel that some follow-up research is required once writing and analysis have begun, we need to work out whether this is financially or practically possible. These considerations are important in terms of acknowledging in our written work the limitations of our study.

Returning to the field forces the researcher to acknowledge how shifting social and personal relations affect our understandings of the research project (Till, 2001). Till (2001, following Bogdon and Biklin, 1998) points out how conducting follow-up research can be emotionally difficult, time consuming, costly and professionally risky. As Stevens (2001) indicates, returning again and again to a field site changes the dynamics and experiences of fieldwork and while it creates new demands, it also brings rewards.

For Julie, however, follow-up research enhanced her project and better enabled her to meet responsibilities to participants. For Sara, return visits to her field site are also part and parcel of ongoing collaborative relationships. While asking for feedback can be an imposition (Patai, 1991) and not all participants expressed an interest in doing this, a return visit can provide a space in which participants can reflect on their participation in the research. On Julie's return visit, one of her participants, for example, requested another recorded interview. Julie had not planned to interview her again as her transcripts were detailed and extensive but was more than happy to record her responses to reading through her transcripts. This interview proved crucial in both methodological and theoretical terms. First, the woman reflected on how she had focused on the sad and tragic aspects of her life and wanted to express her positive sense of subjectivity, her personal achievements and lack of regrets. Second, she clearly expressed how she felt she and other Nicaraguan women should be represented in Julie's thesis.

Some researchers only return to their field sites once their research is completed. Often they wish to demonstrate their commitment to and interest in their participants beyond their participation in their study. Even though the research may be completed, it may not be possible to completely abandon the researcher identity one had in the field. Lektemann (1980) describes feeling relieved when his research was completed and published because he thought he could then return to visit participants as a friend. He discovered however that his 'friends' were not as pleased with his new role as he had expected, given that they repeatedly provided him with new research ideas and encouraged him to write another book (Letkemann, 1980). For some, returning can be very disorienting, particularly to urban sites in which a great deal of change might have taken place in the intervening period. Returning might be a disappointment and leave the researcher longing for the past. If, when and how we return all have differing implications for our sense of self and ongoing research imperatives.

Conclusion

It is useful not to lose sight of expanded notions of the field and the impossibility of real closure. While deadlines must be met and theses submitted, we are likely to have ongoing personal and professional relationships with research participants and the places in which we conducted fieldwork. We might continue to do fieldwork in that part of the world, we might go back just to visit friends and we might be publishing from our data over many years. It is therefore important to remember the interactional, situational and ever changing nature of fieldwork relationships even when nominally outside of the field (Miller and Humphreys, 1980).

One of critical points in this chapter, as with Chapter 10 before it, is that the experiences of leaving and writing, depend to a large degree on the experiences of arriving and establishing relationships with both the field site and its inhabitants. In a sense, this chapter brings us back full circle to the issues and ideas discussed at the beginning of the book. It highlights the iterative, cyclical and interconnected nature of research and the webs of relationships which exist. We suggest that you now re-read the opening chapters of the book and think through the ideas and recommendations there with new eyes, ones that are reading for the implications of their decisions with respect to the processes of leaving and writing.

Recommended reading

Kitchin, R. and Tate, N J. (2000) Writing up and dissemination. In *Conducting Research in Human Geography* Harlow, Pearson Education, pp.270-89.
Covers the mechanics of writing including the writing process, thinking about audiences, presenting data, editing and referencing.

Boyle, P. (1997) Writing up – some suggestions. In R. Flowerdew and D. Martin (eds) *Methods in Human Geography* Harlow, Longman, pp.235-53.
Looks at starting to write, structuring and presentation.

Berg, L. and Mansvelt, J. (2000) Writing in, speaking out: Communicating qualitative research findings. In I. Hay (ed.) *Qualitative Research Methods for Geographers* Oxford University Press, Melbourne, pp.161-82.
Explores styles of presentation, situated knowledges and questions of validity and authenticity.

Butler, R. (2001) From where I write: The place of positionality in qualitative writing. In M. Limb and C. Dwyer (eds) *Qualitative Methodologies for Geographers: Issues and Debates* Arnold, London, pp.264-78.
Considers the question of positionality in relation to writing with suggestions on how to include the presence of the researcher in written work as well as how theory, ethics and writing styles might be combined.

Notes

1. Berg and Mansvelt (2000:162) prefer the term 'writing-in' to 'writing-up', because writing-up implies that writing is an unproblematic process, which reproduces 'the simple truth(s) of our research' and fails to recognise that 'writing constitutes how and what we know about our research'.

2. See Chapter 10 for more discussion of feelings associated with leaving our field sites.

12 Afterword

Donovan Storey and Regina Scheyvens

Reflections on the value of fieldwork

Despite the invocation that 'anyone who is not a complete idiot can do fieldwork' (McCall and Simmons, cited in Clarke, 1975:105) there are a range of potential challenges facing researchers. Undoubtedly 'Fieldwork inevitably involves a lot more than just sitting around watching things and asking questions' (Ellen, 1984:102). For example, if this book is anything to go by, fieldwork would seem to involve planning and foresight, hard work and a broad combination of skills, both academic and personal. This does not mean, however, that we necessarily agree with Shaffir and Stebbins, who have stated that:

> fieldwork must certainly rank with the more disagreeable activities that humanity has fashioned for itself. It is usually inconvenient, to say the least, sometimes physically uncomfortable, frequently embarrassing, and, to a degree, always tense. (1991:1)

There is no doubt that fieldwork is a baptism of fire for some, regularly punctuated with trials and tribulations, as several personal anecdotes herein have demonstrated. Nevertheless, fieldwork need not be a negative experience for either researchers or participants. This book has highlighted the positive relationships and experiences of the authors, as much as the difficulties: fieldwork still remains a great learning experience for researchers and it can provide a number of rewards for participants as well.

Fieldwork continues to remain a central element in development research. Though recently criticised in terms of irrelevance, exoticism, and its perpetuation of imbalanced researcher/researched relationships, fieldwork remains the primary means by which researchers place themselves in 'foreign' contexts through which they explore and seek to understand other perspectives. We believe it remains a core component in any serious development-related curriculum, especially at the postgraduate level.

Fieldwork remains, above all, both an intensely personal experience and a test of intellect and character. Balancing these demands is not easy and there are no magic bullets, although below we draw out some key themes which emerge from this book. These themes provide an alternative to the simplistic prescriptions students were often offered in the past. As Clarke (1975:105) notes, the common advice was that, if all else fails, 'behave like a gentleman, keep off the women, take quinine daily, and play it by ear'.

Key themes

Although this is an edited volume, and therefore involves variations in emphasis and advice, there are some key themes which recur, notably:

• Good design allows for flexibility. It is not possible to predict from library research your fieldwork environment or the data that will emerge. While thorough preparation is indispensable for fieldwork, it will not guarantee that it will be trouble-free. You will need to design your fieldwork so that you have direction and goals, but you are able to respond to, and envelop, change. Your capacity to cope with the uncertainties and rigours of fieldwork will be as important as your intellectual capabilities.

• Flexibility involves a degree of sensitivity to change, but sensitivity to personal relations is also important in cross-cultural research. You may have one of the most stimulating research questions known, and the highest Grade Point Average in the department, but without sensitivity to others you will return home with very little. An ability to react to situations with tolerance and a sense of humour will assist you greatly.

• Research methodologies reflect different worldviews to a point, but they are a means to an end and not an end in themselves. Whether you are using deductive or inductive research, or qualitative/quantitative techniques, good design and flexibility is critical. Choose methodological tools that can best answer your questions, are compatible with the kind of researcher you are (or want to be!), and are suited to the logistics of your research. This may involve using one set of methods, or combining several (for example, some participant observation, a PRA exercise and a survey).

• Codes of ethics and university ethics procedures provide a useful starting point for those who want (or need) to ensure that their research meets appropriate sanctioned guidelines. But ethics goes beyond these regulations to the very heart of appropriate conduct and respect for the norms and values of other peoples. Ethical Development Studies research is research which involves informed consent, confidentiality and which does no harm, but which also aims to do good.

• Development research may involve research with the poor, the marginalised or the remote, but equally valid is research on the powerful, wealthy and urban. Research on each group will demand a different mind-set and preparation on the part of the fieldworker.

• Though fieldwork may appear to be a discrete period in the life of your research, correlated to the arrival and departure dates on your ticket, it will undoubtedly influence you (and often your participants as well) for many years hence. The way in which you established relationships at the start of your fieldwork will affect how hard it is to leave.

• When leaving the field one of the most important issues confronting researchers is how to deal with relationships established with participants. This is a very personal matter but it should be remembered that as researchers we are the privileged ones in that we can choose when to come and go. We then bear the responsibility for negotiating ethical means of ending or continuing our fieldwork relationships.

• While many researchers feel happy about returning to the apparent 'safety' of their university at the conclusion of fieldwork, it is not uncommon to experience reverse culture shock and/or to have trouble with writing about one's findings. Though researchers are often obsessed with validity and reliability, a key issue regarding 'writing the field' which they may overlook is representation. In this regard some researchers have found it valuable to consider sharing authorship or editorial responsibilities with their research participants. In all cases it is important to keep in mind responsibilities to our research participants. It can be very easy to be seduced by the all-encompassing task of writing a thesis, for example, while ignoring the obligations we have to make our findings accessible to, and meaningful for, our participants.

As this collection has demonstrated, much can be learned through the reading of others' experiences. This is as true for the personal experiences of fieldwork, of ethics, logistics, and relationships as it is for learning about the application of methods. 'Stories' from the field have an important place in development research writing, and should not be marginalised as they have been in the past. We hope that the trend of researchers, whether first-timers or old hands, of writing about their fieldwork experiences for others to share continues.[1]

The future of development research

While not seeking to nominate exhaustively where all research is going, or what topics should be of more interest than others, we thought it may be interesting to indicate some possible future trends and issues:

• Research design and outcome is clearly becoming less positivist and more focused on exploring multiple views and discourses. This makes fieldwork and post-field-work writing and analysis more demanding and complex, but ultimately more rewarding. However, research should not hide behind relativism which obscures the obligation researchers have to say something of worth.

• Though increasing globalisation has led to a widespread belief that we are all the same, and increasingly share a similar worldview (i.e. a Western one) development research will continue to demonstrate diversity and difference, emphasising the importance of situating oneself in other worlds, and of being informed outside the square.

• The subjects of development research are likely to be much more diverse than 'the poor'. Wealthy influential classes, institutions and even individuals (including perhaps Western consultants) are increasingly of interest as actors who are shaping development policy and priorities, or setting the parameters within which other social groups may act.

• Technological advances in computers and software are likely to have some impact on research strategies and logistics. However, as this volume has indicated, the best technology in the world cannot transform poor research design or inadequate methods in real world research. For the foreseeable future researchers will most likely continue to rely largely on the same technology as they did a decade ago.

• Research in conflict and post-conflict environments will increase. There is considerable interest now in humanitarian and post-conflict development. This will affect research in terms of logistics and, of course, safety.

• Safety may also become more of an issue given recent high profile global incidents and threats (September 11, 2001; Bali bombings, 2002). While the direct danger to researchers may still be lower than from car-related accidents, the atmosphere in some regions may have changed considerably. More than ever, it is important to plan and prepare for your fieldwork destination thoroughly and to build into your research contingency strategies.

• Finally, while there are few examples in this book of such research, development fieldwork in the Western world is likely to play a greater role in future. It will be interesting to track the fieldwork experiences of researchers applying 'Third World' concepts and approaches to their own societies.

We believe there is a healthy future for development research. It is particularly inspiring to see donors like the UK's Department for International Development (DFID) recognising the relevance and value of sponsoring research into development problems which they wish to address, rather than just asking consultants to carry out reviews and evaluations of their existing projects. Therefore both to ensure adequate funding for development research, and to increase the likelihood that research findings will be put into practice, it is important for researchers to consider building relationships with both government and non-governmental agencies involved in the planning and practice of development.

Research can, and ultimately should, be empowering for both the fieldworker and participants (at the very least, this should be an objective built into the research design). A number of examples of empowerment of research participants have been provided in this book. Examples of empowerment have not been provided, however, in an attempt to deny the potential for exploitation in the research process: empowering methodologies alone will not dissolve the power relations which exist between researcher and participants. However, the examples should show that it is simplistic to see cross-cultural research in the Third World as being an inherently uni-directional, exploitative process. Indeed, it should be acknowledged that in general: 'Locals remember researchers and "learn" from them through their personal relationships – not their monographs' (Wilson, 1992:189). Genuine respect for local people and customs, a sense of humour, and a willingness to share one's own experiences and knowledge with research participants, are all critical if cross-cultural understanding is to be enhanced through the research process.

Note

1. In this light we would like to encourage readers who are currently engaged in, or planning, fieldwork to consider sharing their experiences in the website we have set up for this purpose: www.fieldwork.massey.ac.nz

Bibliography

Abbott, D. (1995) Methodological dilemmas of researching women's poverty in third world settings: Reflections on a study carried out in Bombay. *Journal of Social Studies* 27: 87–113

Acker, J., Barry, K. and Esseveld, J. (1991) Objectivity and truth: problems in doing feminist research. In M. Fonow and J. Cook (eds) *Beyond Methodology: Feminist Scholarship as Lived Research* Indiana University Press, Bloomington, pp. 133–53.

Adams, W. M. and Megaw, C. C. (1997) Researchers and the rural poor: asking questions in the Third World. *Journal of Geography in Higher Education* 21(2): 215–29.

Agar, M. H. (1980) *The Professional Stranger: An Informal Introduction to Ethnography* Academic Press, New York.

Altheide, D. (1980) Leaving the newsroom. In W. Shaffir, R. Stebbins and A. Turowetz (eds) *Fieldwork Experience: Qualitative Approaches to Social Relations* St. Martins Press, New York, pp. 301–10.

Amadiume, I. (1993) The mouth that spoke a falsehood will later speak the truth: going home to the field in Eastern Nigeria. In D. Bell, P. Caplan, and W.K. Jarim (eds) *Gendered Fields: Women, Men and Ethnography* Routledge, London, pp. 182–98.

American Anthropological Association (1998) Statement of Ethics: Principles of Professional Responsibility. Retrieved 21 January, 2002 from: www.aaanet.org/stmts/ethstmny.htm

American Sociological Association (1997) Code of Ethics. Retrieved 22 January 2002 from: www.asanet.org/members/ecostand2.html

Amit, V. (2000) Introduction: constructing the field. In V. Amit (ed.) *Constructing the Field: Ethnographic Fieldwork in the Contemporary World* Routledge, London, pp. 1–18.

Babbie, E. (ed.) (2001) *The Practice of Social Research* Wadsworth, Belmont, CA.

Back, L. (1993). Gendered participation: masculinity and fieldwork in a South London adolescent community. In D. Bell, P. Caplan, and W. J. Karim (eds) *Gendered Fields: Women, Men and Ethnography* Routledge, London and New York, pp. 199–214.

Bailey, C.A. (1996) *A Guide to Field Research* Sage, Thousand Oaks.

Bailey, K.D. (1987) *Methods of Social Research* The Free Press, New York.

Barley, N. (1983) *The Innocent Anthropologist. Notes from a Mud Hut* Penguin, London.

Beinart, W. (2000) African history and environmental history. *African Affairs* 99: 269–302.

Belenky, M.F., Clinchy, B. M., Goldberger, N. R. and Tarule, J. M. (1986) *Women's Ways of Knowing: the Development of Self, Voice, and Mind* Basic Books Inc, New York.

Bender, B. (1998) *Stonehenge: Making Space* Berg Publishers, Oxford.

Berg, L. and Mansvelt, J. (2000) Writing in, speaking out: Communicating qualitative research findings. In I. Hay (ed.) *Qualitative Research Methods for Geographers* Oxford University Press, Melbourne, pp.161–82.

Bevan, P. (2000) Who's a goody? Demythologising the PRA agenda. *Journal of International Development* 12: 751–59.

Bishop, J. and Scoones, I. (1994) *Beer and Baskets: the Economies of Women's Livelihoods in Ngamiland, Botswana* International Institute for Environment and Development, London.

Blackwood, E. (1995) Falling in love with an-other lesbian: reflections on identity in field-work. In D. Kulick and M. Wilson (eds) *Taboo: Sex, Identity and Erotic Subjectivity in Anthropological Fieldwork* Routledge, London, pp. 51–75.

Blaxter, L., Hughes, C. and Tight, M. (1996) *How to Research* Open University Press, Buckingham.

Bleek (1979) Envy and inequality in fieldwork: an example from Ghana. *Human Organisation* 38(2):200–05.

Boddy, J. (1989) *Wombs and Alien Spirits: Women, Men and the Zãr Cult in Northern Sudan* University of Wisconsin Press, Madison.

Boesveld, M. (1986) *Towards Autonomy for Women: Research and Action to Support a Development Process* RAWOO (Advisory Council for Scientific Research in Development Problems).

Bogdan, R.C. and Biklin, S.K. (1998) *Qualitative Research for Education: An Introduction to Theory and Methods* Allyn and Bacon, Boston, MA.

Bollig, M. and Mbunguha, T.J. (1997) *When War Came the Cattle Slept...Himba Oral Traditions* Rüdigger, Köppe Verlag, Cologne.

Bolton, R. (1995) Tricks, friends, and lovers: erotic encounters in the field. In D. Kulick and M. Willson (eds) *Taboo: Sex, Identity, and Erotic Subjectivity in Anthropological Fieldwork* Routledge, London and New York, pp.140–67.

Bondi, L. (1997) In whose words? On gender identities, knowledge and writing practices. *Transactions of the Institute of British Geographers* 22(2):245–58.

Bourgois, P. (1995) *In Search of Respect. Selling Crack in El Barrio* Cambridge University Press, Cambridge.

Bowden, R. (1998) Children, power and participatory research in Uganda. In V. Johnson, E. Ivan-Smith, G. Gordon, P. Pridmore and P. Scott (eds) *Stepping Forward: Children and Young People's Participation in the Development Process* Intermediate Technology Publications, London, pp.281–83.

Boyden, J. and Ennew, J. (1997) *Children in Focus: A Manual for Participatory Research with Children* Radda Barnen, Swedish Save the Children, Stockholm.

Boyle, P. (1997) Writing up – some suggestions. In R. Flowerdew and D. Martin (eds) *Methods in Human Geography* Harlow, Longman, pp.235-53.

Bradburd, D. (1998) *Being There: The Necessity of Fieldwork* Smithsonian Institute Press, Washington, DC.

Brinkman, I. and Fleisch, A. (1999) Grandmother's Footsteps: Oral Tradition and South-East Angolan Narratives on the Colonial Encounter Rüdigger, Köppe Verlag, Cologne.

Broch-Due, V. and Anderson, D.M. (1999) Poverty and the pastoralist: deconstructing myths, reconstructing realities. In D.M. Anderson and V. Broch-Due (eds) *The Poor are Not Us. Poverty and Pastoralism* James Currey, Oxford, pp. 3–19.

Brockington, D. (1998) Land loss and livelihoods. The effects of eviction on pastoralists moved from the Mkomazi Game Reserve, Tanzania. Unpublished PhD thesis, University College London, London.

Brockington, D. (2001) Communal property and degradation narratives. Debating the Sukuma immigration into Rukwa region, Tanzania. *Cahiers d'Afrique* 20: 1–22.

Brohman, J. (1995) Universalism, eurocentrism, and ideological bias in development studies: from modernisation to neoliberalism. *Third World Quarterly* 16(1): 121–40.

Bryman, A. and Burgess, R. G. (1999) *Qualitative Research* Sage Publications, London.

Bryman, A. and Cramer, D. (1995) *Quantitative Data Analysis for Social Scientists* Routledge, London.

Bulmer, M. (1984) *The Chicago School of Sociology* University of Chicago Press, Chicago.

Bulmer, M. (1993a) General introduction. In M. Bulmer and D.P. Warwick (eds) *Social Research in Developing Countries* UCL Press, London, pp.3–24.

Bulmer, M. (1993b) Sampling. In M. Bulmer and D.P. Warwick (eds) *Social Research in Developing Countries* UCL Press, London, pp.91–9.

Bulmer, M. and Warwick, D. P. (eds) (1993) *Social Research in Developing Countries* UCL Press, London.

Burgess, R. G. (ed.) (1982) *Field Research: A Sourcebook and Field Manual* George Allen and Unwin, London.

Butler, B. and Turner, D. (eds) (1987) *Children and Anthropological Research* Plenum Press, New York.

Butler, R. (2001) From where I write: The place of positionality in qualitative writing. In M. Limb and C. Dwyer (eds) *Qualitative Methodologies for Geographers: Issues and Debates* Arnold, London, pp.264–78.

Cannon, J. (2002) Men at Work: Expatriation in the International Mining Industry. Unpublished PhD thesis, Monash University, Melbourne.

Caputo, V. (2000) At 'home' and 'away': reconfiguring the field for late twentieth-century anthropology. In V. Amit (ed.) *Constructing the Field: Ethnographic Fieldwork in the Contemporary World* Routledge, London, pp.19–31.

Casey, C. (2001) Ethics committees, institutions and organisations: subjectivity, consent and risk. In M. Tolich (ed.) *Research Ethics in Aotearoa New Zealand: Concepts, Practice, Critique* Longman, Harlow, pp.127–40.

Cassell, J. (1987) 'Conclusion'. In J. Cassell (ed.) *Children in the Field: Anthropological Experiences* Temple University Press, Philadelphia, pp. 257–70.

Cassell, J. (ed.) (1987) *Children in the Field: Anthropological Experiences* Temple University, Philadelphia.

Cassell, J. and Jacobs, S. (eds) (1987) *Handbook on Ethical Issues in Anthropology*. Special publication of the American Anthropological Association, number 23, American Anthropological Association, Washington, DC.

Caws, P. (1989) The law of quality and quantity, or what numbers can and can't describe. In B. Glassner and J.D. Moreno (eds) *The Qualitative–Quantitative Distinction in the Social Sciences* Kluwer, Dordrecht, pp.13–28.

Cernea, M. (1982) Indigenous anthropologists and development-oriented research. In H. Famim (ed.) *Indigenous Anthropology in Non-Western Countries* Caroline Academic Press, Durham, pp.121–37.

Chambers, R. (1983) *Rural Development: Putting the Last First* Longman, Harlow.

Chambers, R. (1997) *Whose Reality Counts? Putting the First Last* Intermediate Technology Publications, London.

Childs, G. (2001) Intimate knowledge of the Nubri Valley. *ANU Reporter* 32(6):2.

Chung, M. (1991) Politics, tradition and structural change: Fijian fertility in the twentieth century. Unpublished PhD thesis, Australian National University, Canberra.

Clarke, M. (1975) Survival in the field: implications of personal experience in the field. *Theory and Society* 2: 95–123.

Clifford, J. (1986) Introduction: partial truths. In J. Clifford and G. E. Marcus, (eds) *Writing Culture: the Poetics and Politics of Ethnography* University of California Press, London, pp. 1–26., London, pp.143–75.

Clifford, J. (1988) *The Predicament of Culture. Twentieth Century Ethnography, Literature and Art* Harvard University Press, Cambridge, MA.

Clifford, J. (1997) *Routes: Travel and Translation in the Late Twentieth Century* Harvard University Press, Cambridge.

Clifford, J. and Marcus, G. E. (eds) (1986) *Writing Culture. The Poetics and Politics of Ethnography* University of California Press, Berkeley.

Cloke, P., Philo, C. and Sadler, D. (1991) *Approaching Human Geography* Paul Chapman Publishing, London.

Cohen-Mitchell, J. B. (2000) Disabled women in El Salvador reframing themselves: an economic development program for women. In C. Truman, D.M. Mertens and B. Humphries (eds) *Research and Inequality* UCL Press

Cook, I. (2001) You want to be careful you don't end up like Ian. He's all over the place: autobiography of/in an expanded field. In P. Moss (ed.) *Placing Autobiography in Geography* Syracuse University Press, Syracuse, pp.99–120.

Cooke, B. and Kothari, U. (2001) The case for tyranny as participation. In B. Cooke and U. Kothari, (eds*) Participation: the New Tyranny?* Zed Books, London, pp. 1–15.

Corbridge, S. (1998) Development ethics: distance, difference, plausibility. *Ethics, Place and Environment* 1(1): 35–53.

Corbridge, S. (2000) Development geographies. In P. Cloke, P, Crang, and M. Goodwin (eds) *Introducing Human Geographies* Arnold, London, pp. 67–75.

Corbridge, S. and Mawdsley, E. (2003) Special issue: fieldwork in the 'tropics': power, knowledge and practice. *Singapore Journal of Tropical Geography.*

Cormode, L. and Hughes, A. (eds) (1999) The economic geographer as situated researcher of elites, Special issue of *Geoforum* 30: 299–300.

Cotterill, P. (1992) Interviewing women: issues of friendship, vulnerability, and power. *Women's Studies International Forum* 10 (5&6): 593–606.

Cotton, C. M. (1996) *Ethnobotany: Principles and Applications* John Wiley and Sons, Chichester.

Counts, A. M. (1996) *Give us Credit: How Small Loans Today can Shape our Tomorrow* Research Press, New Delhi.

Counts, D. (1990) Too many bananas, not enough pineapples, and no watermelon at all: three object lessons in living with reciprocity. In P. DeVita (ed.) *The Humbled Anthropologist* Wadsworth, Belmont, CA, pp. 18–24.

Couto, R. (2002) 'Free Trade' or Fair Trade? How Changes in the Current International Trade System Could Act as a Development Tool for Third World Countries: The Brazilian Case. Unpublished Masters Thesis, Massey University, Palmerston North.

Crang, M, (1997) Analysing qualitative materials. In R. Flowerdew, and D. Martin, (eds) *Methods in Human Geography* Longman, Harlow, pp. 183–96.

Crang, M. and Cook, I. (1994) *Doing Ethnographies* University of East Anglia, Norwich.

Crick, M. (1989) Shifting identities in the research process: an essay in personal anthropology. In J. Perry (ed.) *Doing Fieldwork* Deakin University Press, Geelong.

Crick, M. (1993) 'Introduction' In M Crick and B Geddes (eds) *Research Methods in the Field: Ten Anthropological Accounts* Deakin University Press, Geelong, pp.3–8.

Cross, N. and Barker, R. (1992) *At the Desert's Edge: Oral Histories from the Sahel* Panos Publications, London.

Crouch, D. (2001) Spatialities and the feeling of doing. *Social and Cultural Geography* 2(1): 61–75.

Csordas, T. J. (1999) Embodiment and cultural phenomenology. In G. Weiss and H.F. Haber, (eds) *Perspectives on Embodiment. The Intersections of Nature and Culture* Routledge, London: 143–62.

Cupples, J. (2002) Disrupting discourses and (re)formulating identities: The politics of single motherhood in post-revolutionary Nicaragua. PhD dissertation, Canterbury University, Christchurch.

Cupples, J. (2002) Disrupting discourses and (re)formulating identities: the politics of single motherhood in post-revolutionary Nicaragua. Unpublished doctoral thesis, Canterbury University, Christchurch.

da Corta, L. and Venkateshwarlu, D. (1992) Field methods for economic mobility. In S. Devereux and J. Hoddinott. (eds) *Fieldwork in Developing Countries* Harvester Wheatsheaf, New York, pp.102–23.

de Laine, M. (2000) *Fieldwork, Participation and Practice: Ethics and Dilemmas in Qualitative Research* Sage, Thousand Oaks, California.

De Vaus, D.A. (ed.) (1991) *Surveys in Social Research* Allen and Unwin,

Dear, M. J. (1988) The postmodern challenge: reconstructing human geography. *Transactions of the Institute of British Geographers* 13: 262–74.

Denzin, N. K.(1997) *Interpretive Ethnography: Ethnographic Practices for the 21st Century* Sage, Thousand Oaks, California.

Devereux, S. (1992) 'Observers are worried': learning the language and counting the people in northeast Ghana. In S.Devereux and J.Hoddinott (eds) *Fieldwork in Developing Countries* Harvester Wheatsheaf, New York, pp. 43–56.

Devereux, S. and Hoddinott, J. (1992) The context of fieldwork. In S. Devereux and J. Hoddinott (eds) *Fieldwork in Developing Countries* Harvester Wheatsheaf, New York, pp. 3–24.

Devereux, S. and Hoddinott, J. (eds) (1992) *Fieldwork in Developing Countries* Harvester Wheatsheaf, New York.

DeVita, P. R. (ed.) (1990) *The Humbled Anthropologist* Wadsworth, Belmont, CA.

DeVita, P. R. (ed.) (2000) *Stumbling Toward Truth: Anthropologists at Work* Waveland Press, Prospect Heights, IL.

Dockery, G. (2000) Participatory research: whose roles, whose responsibilities? In C. Truman, D.M. Mertens and B. Humphries (eds) *Research and Inequality* UCL Press, London, pp.95–125.

Dos Santos, T. (1970) *Dependencia y Cambio Social* Centro de Estudios Socio-Economicos, Universidad de Chile, Santiago.

Dowling, R. (2000) Power, subjectivity and ethics in qualitative rsearch. In I. Hay (ed.) *Qualitative Research Methods in Human Geography* Oxford University Press, Melbourne, pp.23–36.

Dumont, J.-P. (1978) *The Headman and I: Ambiguity and ambivalence in the fieldwork experience* University of Texas Press, Austin.

Edwards, M. (1989) The irrelevance of Development Studies. *Third World Quarterly* 11(1): 116–35.

Ellen, R. F. (1984) *Ethnographic Research: A guide to general conduct* Academic Press, London.

Endfield, G. and O'Connor, P.W. (1997) Flexibility, funding and foresight: tips for the physical geographer in developing areas research. In. E. Robson and K. Willis (eds) *Postgraduate Fieldwork in Developing Areas: A Rough Guide.* Monograph No. 9, Developing Areas Research Group (RGS-IBG), London. pp.38–50.

England, K. (1994) Getting personal: Reflexivity positionality, and feminist research. *Professional Geographer* 46 (1): 80–9.

Escobar, A. (1995) *Encountering Development: The Making and Unmaking of the Third World* Princeton University Press, Princeton, N.J.

Escobar, A. (1996) Constructing Nature. Elements for a poststructural political ecology. In R. Peet and M. Watts, (eds) *Liberation Ecologies. Environment, Development and Social Movements* Routledge, London and New York, pp. 46–67.

Esteva, G. (1992) Development. In W. Sachs (ed.), *The Development Dictionary: A Guide to Knowledge as Power* Zed Books, London, pp. 6–25.

Fabian, J. (1983) *Time and the Other: How Anthropology Makes Its Object* Columbia University Press, New York.

Falconer Al-Hindi, K. (2001) Do you get it? Feminism and quantitative geography. *Environment and Planning D: Society and Space* 19: 505–13.

Flinn, J. (1990) Reflections of a shy ethnographer: foot-in-the-mouth is not fatal. In P. DeVita (ed.) *The Humbled Anthropologist* Wadsworth, Belmont, pp. 46–52.

Flinn, J., Marshall, L. and Armstrong, J. (eds) (1998) *Fieldwork and Families: Constructing New Models for Ethnographic Research* University of Hawaii Press, Honolulu.

Foucault, M. (1977) *Discipline and Punish. The Birth of the Prison* Penguin, London.

Foucault, M. (1990) *Madness and Civilisation: A History of Iinsanity in the Age of Reason* Routledge, London.

Fowler, R. (1991) *Language in the News: Discourse and Ideology in the Press* Routledge, London.

Francis, E. (1992) Qualitative research: collecting life histories. In S. Devereux and J. Hoddinott (eds) *Fieldwork in Developing Countries* Lynne Rienner, Boulder, Colorado. pp. 86–101.

Frank, A. G. (1967 Philosophies underlying human geography research. In R. Flowerdew and D. Martin, (eds) *Methods in Human Geography) Capitalism and Underdevelopment in Latin America: Historical Studies of Chile and Brazil* Monthly Review Press, New York.

Frankfort-Nachmias, C. and Nachmias, D. (1992) *Research Methods in the Social Sciences* Edward Arnold, London.

Friere, P. (1972) *Pedagogy of the Oppressed* (translated by Myra Bergman) Penguin, Harmonsworth.

Gade, D. W. (2001) The languages of foreign fieldwork. *Geographical Review* 91(1–2): 370–79.

Gallmeier, C. (1991) Leaving, revisiting and staying in touch: Neglected issues in field research. In W. Shaffir and R. Stebbins (eds) *Experiencing Fieldwork: An Inside View of Qualitative Research* Sage, Newbury Park, pp. 224–31.

Gaskell, J. and Eichler, M. (2001) White women as burden: on playing the role of feminist "experts" in China. *Women's Studies International Forum*, Vol. 24 (6): 637–51.

Gearing, J. (1995) Fear and loving in the West Indies: research from the heart (as well as the head). In D. Kulick and M. Willson (eds) *Taboo: Sex, Identity, and Erotic Subjectivity in Anthropological Fieldwork* Routledge, London and New York, pp. 186–218.

Geertz, C. (1973) *The Interpretation of Cultures* Basic Books, New York.

Geertz, C. (1988) *Works and Lives: The Anthropologist as Author* Polity Press, Cambridge.

Giddens, A. (1984) *The Constitution of Society* Polity Press, Cambridge.

Glaser, B. and Strauss, A. (1968) *Time for Dying* Aldine, Chicago.

Goin, P. (2001) Visual literacy. *Geographical Review* 91(1–2): 363–69.

Goodman, M.J. (1985) Introduction. In M.J. Goodman (ed.) *Women in Asia and the Pacific: Towards an East–West Dialogue* Women's Studies Program, University of Hawaii, pp. 1–18.

Gordon, G. (1998) Introduction. In V. Johnson, E. Ivan-Smith, G. Gordon, P. Pridmore and P. Scott (eds) *Stepping Forward: Children and Young People's Participation in the Development Process* Intermediate Technology Publications, London, pp. 66–9.

Gordon, R. J. (2000) The stat(u)s of Namibian anthropology: a review. *Cimbebasia* 16: 1–12.

Goward. N. (1984) Publications on fieldwork experience. In R.F. Ellen (ed.), *Ethnographic Research: A Guide to General Conduct* Academic Press, London, pp. 88–100.

Graham, E. (1997) Philosophies underlying human geography research. In R. Flowerdew and D. Martin, (eds) *Methods in Human Geography* Longman, Harlow, pp. 6–30.

Green, L. (1995) Living in a state of fear. In C. Nordstrom and A.C.G.M. Robben (eds)

Fieldwork Under Fire: Contemporary Studies of Violence and Survival University of California Press, Berkeley, pp. 105–27.

Grills, S. (1998) An Invitation to the Field: Fieldwork and the Pragmatists' Lesson. In S. Grills (ed.) *Doing Ethnographic Research: Fieldwork Settings* Sage, Thousand Oaks, pp. 3–18.

Guèye, B. (1999) *Whither participation? Experience from francophone West Africa.* Drylands Programme Issue Paper 87, International Institute for Environment and Development, London.

Gupta, A. and Ferguson, J. (1997) Discipline and practice: 'the field' as site, method, and location in anthropology. In A. Gupta and J. Ferguson (eds) *Anthropological Locations: Boundaries and Grounds of a Field Science* University of California Press, Berkeley, pp. 1–46.

Haas, J. and Shaffir, W. (1980) Fieldworkers' mistakes at work: Problems in maintaining relations and research bargains. In W. Shaffir, R. Stebbins and A. Turowetz (eds) *Fieldwork Experience: Qualitative Approaches to Social Relations* St. Martins Press, New York, pp. 244–55.

Habermas, J. (1978) *Knowledge and Human Interests* Heinemann, London.

Hadjor, K. (1993) *The Penguin Dictionary of Third World Terms* Penguin, Harmondsworth.

Hahn, E. (1990) Raising a few eyebrows in Tonga. In P. DeVita (ed.) *The Humbled Anthropologist* Wadsworth, Belmont, pp. 69–76.

Hammersley, M. (1992) *What's Wrong with Ethnography? Methodological Explorations* Routledge, London.

Hammond, J. (1990) Cultural Baggage. In P. DeVita (ed.) *The Humbled Anthropologist* Wadsworth, Belmont, pp. 61–8.

Haque, M. (1998) Understanding with children: coping with floods in Bangladesh. In V. Johnson, E. Ivan–Smith, G. Gordon, P. Pridmore and P. Scott (eds) *Stepping Forward: Children and Young People's Participation in the Development Process* Intermediate Technology Publications, London, pp. 76–8

Hart, K. (1982) *The Political Economy of West African Agriculture* Cambridge University Press, Cambridge.

Hau'ofa, E. (1982) Anthropology at home: a South Pacific Islands experience. In H. Fahim (ed.) *Indigenous Anthropology in Non–Western Countries* Carolina Academic Press, Durham, pp. 213–22.

Hays–Mitchell, M. (2001) Danger, fulfilment and responsibility in a violence plagued society. *Geographical Review* 91(1–2): 311–21.

Healy, M. J. and Rawlinson M. B. (1993) Interviewing business owners and managers; A review of methods and techniques. *Geoforum* 24: 339–55.

Heggenhougen, K. (2000) The inseperability of reason and emotion in the anthropological perspective: perceptions upon leaving 'the field'. In P. R. DeVita (ed.) *Stumbling Toward Truth: Anthropologists at Work* Waveland Press, Prospect Heights, Illinois, pp. 264–72.

Heidegger, M. (1962) *Being and Time* Blackwell, Oxford.

Herod, A. (1999) Reflections on interviewing foreign elites: praxis, positionality, validity and the cult of the insider. *Geoforum* 30: 313–27.

Hershfield, A. F., Rohling, N. G., Kerr, G. B. and Hursh-Cesar, G. (1983) Fieldwork in Rural Areas. In M. Bulmer and D.P. Warwick (eds) *Social Research in Developing Countries* John Wiley and Sons, London, pp. 241–52

Hertz, R. and Imber, J. B. (1993) *Fieldwork in elite settings*, special issue, *Journal of Contemporary Ethnography* 22:3–6.

Heyer, J. (1992) Contrasts in village-level fieldwork: Kenya and India. In S. Devereux and J. Hoddinott, J. (eds) *Fieldwork in Developing Countries* Harvester Wheatsheaf, Hemel Hempstead, pp. 200–16.

Hitchcock, P. (1987) 'Our Ulleri child'. In J. Cassell (ed.) *Children in the Field: Anthropological Experiences* Temple University Press, Philadelphia, pp.173–83.

Hobart, M. (1996) Ethnography as a practice, or the unimportance of Penguins. Europæa 11: 3–36.

Hobbs, J .J. (2001) Exploration and discovery with the Bedouin of Egypt. *Geographical Review* 91(1–2): 285–94.

Hoddinott, J. and Devereux, S. (eds) (1992) *Fieldwork in Developing Countries* Harvester Wheatsheaf, Hemel Hempstead.

Hoddinott, J. (1993) Fieldwork under time constraints. In S. Devereux and J. Hoddinott (eds) *Fieldwork in Developing Countries* Lynne Rienner, Boulder, Colorado, pp.73–85.

Hodgson, D.L. and Schroeder, R.A. (2002) Dilemmas of counter-mapping community resources in Tanzania. *Development and Change* 33: 79–100.

Hoksbergen, R. (1986) Approaches to evaluation of development interventions: The importance of world and life views. *World Development* 14(2): 283–300.

hooks, b. (1990) *Talking Back: Thinking Feminist, Thinking Black* South End, Boston.

Hot Spring Working Group, (1995) *Local-level Economic Valuation of Savanna Woodland Resources: Village Cases from Zimbabwe* International Institute for Environment and Development, London.

Howell, N. (1990) *Surviving Fieldwork: A Report If the Advisory Panel on Health and Safety in Fieldwork.* A Special Report of American Anthropological Association, number 26 , American Anthropological Association, Washington, D.C.

Hugh-Jones, C. (1987) Children in the Amazon. In J. Cassell (ed.) *Children in the Field: Anthropological Experiences* Temple University Press, Philadelphia, pp.27–63.

Humphries, B., Mertens, D. M. and Truman, C. (2000) Arguments for an 'emancipatory' research paradigm. In C. Truman, D. M. Mertens and B. Humphries (eds) *Research and Inequality* UCL Press, London, pp.3–23.

Hutchinson, S.E. (1996) *Nuer Dilemmas. Coping with Money, War and the State* University of California Press, Berkeley.

Hye, H. (1993) *Co-operatives: Comilla and After.* Bangladesh Academy for Rural Development, Comilla.

Hyndman, J. (2001) The field as here and now, not there and then. *Geographical Review* 91(1–2): 262–72.

Ingold, T. (2000) *The Perception of the Environment: Essays in Livelihood, Dwelling and Skill* Routledge, London.

Iti, U. (1997) Home, abroad, home: the challenges of postgraduate fieldwork at home. In E. Robson and K. Willis (eds) *Postgraduate Fieldwork in Developing Countries* Monograph No.9, Developing Areas Research Group (RGS-IBG), London, pp.75–84.

Ivan-Smith, E. (1998) Introduction. In V. Johnson, E. Ivan-Smith, G. Gordon, P. Pridmore and P. Scott (eds) *Stepping Forward: Children and Young People's Participation in the Development Process* Intermediate Technology Publications, London, 259–62.

Jackson, P. (2001) Making sense of qualitative data. In M. Limb and C. Dwyer (eds) *Qualitative Methodologies for Geographers: Issues and Debates* Arnold, London, pp.199–214.

Jipson, A. and Litton, C (2000) Body, career and community: the implications of researching dangerous groups. In G. Lee-Treweek and S. Linkogle (eds) *Danger In the Field: Risk and Ethics in Social Research* Routledge, London, pp. 147–67.

Johnston, R. J. (1997) *Geography and Geographers* 5th ed, Edward Arnold, London.

Jolly, M. and Macintyre, M. (eds) (1989). *Family and Gender in the Pacific: Domestic Contradictions and the Colonial Impact* Cambridge University Press, Cambridge.

Jones, E.L. (1983) The courtesy bias in South-east Asian surveys. In M. Bulmer and D.P. Warwick (eds) *Social Research in Developing Countries* John Wiley and Sons, London, pp. 253–59.

Katz, C. (1992) All the world is staged: Intellectuals and the projects of ethnography. *Environment and Planning D: Society and Space* 10: 495–510.

Katz, C. (1994) Playing the field: questions of fieldwork in geography *Professional Geographer* 46(1): 65–72.

Keesing, R. (1985) Kwaio women speak: the micropolitics of autobiography in a Solomon Islands society. *American Anthropologist* 87(1): 27–39.

Keough, N. (1998) Participatory principles and practice: reflections of a Western development worker. *Community Development Journal* 33, 187–96.

Keyes, C. (1983) The observer observed: Changing identities of fieldworkers in a Northeastern Thai village. In R. Lawless, V. H. Sutlive Jr and M. D. Zamora (eds) *Fieldwork: The Human Experience* Gordon and Breach, New York, pp.169–94.

Killick, A.P. (1995) The penetrating intellect: on being white, straight, and male in Korea. In D. Kulick and M. Willson (eds) *Taboo: Sex, Identity, and Erotic Subjectivity in Anthropological Fieldwork* Routledge, London and New York, pp.76–106.

Kishwar, M. (1998) Learning to take people seriously. In M. Thapan (ed.) *Anthropological Journeys: Reflections on Fieldwork* Sangam Books, London, pp. 293–311.

Kitchen, R. and Tate, N. (2000) *Conducting Research into Human Geography* Prentice Hall, Harlow.

Kleinman, S., Copp, M. A. and Henderson, K. (1992) Qualitatively Different: Teaching Fieldwork to Graduate Students. Manuscript submitted for publication.

Kleinmann, S. and Copp, M. A. (1993) *Emotions and Fieldwork* Sage, Newbury Park.

Kobayashi, A. (1994) Coloring the field: gender, 'race', and the politics of fieldwork. *Professional Geographer* 46(1): 73–80.

Kondo, D. (1990) *Crafting Selves: Power, Gender and Discourses of Identity in a Japanese Workplace* University of Chicago Press, Chicago.

Krimerman, L. (2001) Participatory Action Research: should social inquiry be conducted democratically? *Philosophy of the Social Sciences* 31(1): 60–83.

Kuhn, T. S. (1970) *The Structure of Scientific Revolutions* 2nd ed. University of Chicago Press, Chicago.

Kulick, D. (1995) Introduction – the sexual life of anthropologists: erotic subjectivity and ethnographic work. In D. Kulick and M. Willson (eds) *Taboo: Sex, Identity, and Erotic Subjectivity in Anthropological Fieldwork* Routledge, London and New York, pp.1–28.

Kulick, D. and Willson, M. (eds) (1995) *Taboo: Sex, Identity, and Erotic Subjectivity in Anthropological Fieldwork* Routledge, London and New York.

Kuper, A. (1983) *Anthropology and Anthropologists. The Modern British School* Routledge and Kegan Paul, London and New York.

Lagisa, L. (1997) The Impacts of a Major Development Project on Women's Lives: A Case Study of Mining in Lihir, Papua New Guinea. Unpublished Masters thesis, Massey University, Palmerston North.

Lakatos, I. and Musgrave, A. (eds) (1970) *Criticism and the Growth of Knowledge* Cambridge University Press, Cambridge.

Lanigan, C. and Wheeler, M. (2002) *Lonely Planet: Travel with Children* Lonely Planet, Hawthorn.

Lareau, A. (1996) Common problems in fieldwork: a personal essay. In A. Lareau and J. Shultz (eds) *Journeys through Ethnography* Westview Press, Boulder, pp. 196–236.

Lather, P. (1988) Feminist perspectives on empowering research methodologies. *Women's Studies International Forum* 11(6), 569–81.

Latour, B. (1993) *We Have Never Been Modern* Harvester Wheatsheaf, Hemel Hempstead.

Lawless, R., Sutlive Jr, V .H. and Zamora, M. D. (1983) Introduction: Human variations in fieldwork. In R. Lawless, V. H. Sutlive Jr and M. D. Zamora (eds) *Fieldwork: The Human*

Experience Gordon and Breach, New York, pp.xi–xxi.

Leach, M. and Mearns, R. (1996) *The Lie of the Land. Challenging Received Wisdom on the African Environment* James Currey, Oxford.

Lee, R. (1995) *Dangerous Fieldwork*, Sage, Thousand Oaks, CA.

Lee-Treweek, G. and Linkogle, S. (eds) (2000) *Danger in the Field: Risk and Ethics in Social Research* Routledge, London.

Leslie, H. and McAllister, M. (2002) The benefits of being a nurse in critical social research practice. *Qualitative Health Research*.12 (5):700–12.

Leslie, H.M. (1999) Gendering Trauma and Healing in a Post–Conflict Context: Las Dignas, Mental Health, and the Empowerment of Salvadoran Women El Salvador. Unpublished PhD Thesis, Massey University, Palmerston North.

Letkemann, P. (1980) Crime as work: Leaving the field. In W. Shaffir, R. Stebbins and A. Turowetz (eds) *Fieldwork Experience: Qualitative Approaches to Social Relations* St. Martins Press, New York, pp.292–301.

Lewis, D. J. (1991) The "off-stage miracle: Carrying out and writing up field research in Bangladesh. *Journal of Social Studies*, 52:44–68.

Lewis, W. A. (1954) Economic development with unlimited supplies of labour. *Manchester School* 22(2) May.

Lockwood, M. (1992) Facts or fictions? Fieldwork relationships and the nature of data. In S. Devereux and J. Hoddinott (eds) *Fieldwork in Developing Countries* Harvester Wheatsheaf, New York, pp.164–78.

Loveridge, D. (2001) The Good Governance Agenda and Urban Governance: The case of Dhaka, Bangladesh. MPhil Thesis, Massey University.

Lyotard, J. F. (1984) *The Postmodern Condition: A Report on Knowledge* Manchester University Press, Manchester.

Macintyre, M. (1993) Fictive kinship or mistaken identity: fieldwork on Tubetube Island, Papua New Guinea.. In In D. Bell, P. Caplan, and W. K. Jarim (eds) *Gendered Fields: Women, Men and Ethnography* Routledge, London, pp.44–62.

Madan, T. N. (1982) Anthropology as the mutual interpretation of cultures: Indian perspectives. In H. Fahim (ed.) *Indigenous Anthropology in Non-Western Countries* Carolina Academic Press, Durham, pp.4–18.

Madge, C. (1993) Boundary disputes: Comments on Sidaway (1992) *Area,* 25(3): 294–99.

Madge, C. (1997) The ethics of research in the 'Third World'. In E. Robson and K. Willis (eds) *Postgraduate Fieldwork in Developing Areas: A Rough Guide* Monograph No.9, Developing Areas Research Group, Royal Geographical Society, and Institute of British Geographers, London, pp.113–24.

Madge, C., Raghuram, P., Skelton, T., Willis, K. and Williams, J. (1997) Methods and methodologies in feminist geographies: politics, practice and power. In Women and Geography Study Group (eds) *Feminist Geographies: Explorations in Diversity and Difference* Longman, Harlow, pp.86–111.

Maines, D., Shaffir, W. and Turowetz, A. (1980) Leaving the field in ethnographic research. Reflections on the entrance-exit hypothesis. In W. Shaffir, R. Stebbins and A. Turowetz (eds) *Fieldwork Experience: Qualitative Approaches to Social Relations* St. Martins Press, New York, pp.261–81.

Malinowski, N. (1967) *A Diary in the Strict Sense of the Term* Routledge and Kegan Paul, London.

Manning, C. and van Diermen, P. (eds) (2000) *Indonesia in Transition: Social Aspects of Reformasi and Crisis* Zed Books, Singapore.

Martin, G. J. (1995) *Ethnobotany: a Methods Manual* Chapman and Hall, London.

Martin, M. (2000) Critical education for participatory research. In C. Truman, D.M. Mertens and B. Humphries (eds) *Research and Inequality* UCL Press, London, pp.191–204.

Massey University Ethics Committee (2000) *Code of Ethical Conduct for Research and Teaching Involving Human Subjects* Massey University, Palmerston North.

Matthews, H. and Tucker, F. (2000) Consulting children. *Journal of Geography in Higher Education* 24(2): 299–310.

Matthews, H., Limb, M. and Taylor, M. (1998) The geography of children: some ethical and methodological considerations for project and dissertation work. *Journal of Geography in Higher Education* 22(3): 311–24.

May, T. (1997) *Social Research: Issues, Methods and Process* Open University Press, Buckingham.

Mazuchelli, S.A. (1995) Participatory methodologies for rapid urban environmental diagnoses. *Environment and Urbanisation.* 7: 219–26.

McClelland, D.C. (1970) The achievement motive in economic growth. In G. D. Ness (ed.) *The Sociology of Economic Development* Harper and Row, New York, pp.177–98.

McDowell, L (1992) Valid games? A response to Erica Schoenburger. *Professional Geographer* 44: 212–15.

McDowell, L. (1992) Doing gender: feminism, feminists and research methods in human geography. *Transactions of the Institute of British Geographers,* 17: 399–416.

McDowell, L. (1998) Elites in the city of London: some methodological considerations. *Environment and Planning A* 30(12): 213–16.

Medical Research Council of Canada, Natural Sciences and Engineering Council of Canada and Social Sciences and Humanities Research Council of Canada (1998) "Tri-County Policy Statement : Ethical Conduct for Research Involving Humans." Retrieved 20 January, 2002 from: http://www.sshrc.ca/english/programinfo/policies/ethics.htm

Merchant, C. (1980) *The Death of Nature: Women, Ecology and the Scientific Revolution* Harper and Row, New York.

Merleau-Ponty, M. (1962) *Phenomenology of Perception* London, Routledge.

Mies, M. (1983) Towards a methodology for feminist research. In G. Bowles and R. Duelli Klein (eds) *Theories of Women's Studies* Routledge and Kegan Paul, London and Boston, pp.117–39.

Mikkelson, B. (1995) *Methods for Development Work and Research: A Guide for Practitioners* Sage, New Delhi, Thousand Oaks and London.

Miller, B. and Humphreys, L. (1980) Keeping in touch: Maintaining contact with stigmatized subjects. In W. Shaffir, R. Stebbins and A. Turowetz. (eds) *Fieldwork Experience: Qualitative Approaches to Social Relations* St. Martins Press, New York, pp.212–23.

Mitlin, D. and Thompson, J. (1995) Participatory approaches in rural areas: Sstrengthening civil society or reinforcing the status quo. *Environment and Urbanisation* 7: 231–250.

Mohanty, C. T. (1988) Under Western eyes: feminist scholarship and colonial discourses. *Feminist Review* 30: 61–88.

Moreno, E. (1995) Rape in the field: reflections from a survivor. In D. Kulick and M. Willson (eds) *Taboo: Sex, Identity, and Erotic Subjectivity in Anthropological Fieldwork* Routledge, London and New York, pp.219–50.

Morton, H. (1995) My 'chastity belt': avoiding seduction in Tonga. In D. Kulick and M. Willson (eds) *Taboo: Sex, Identity, and Erotic Subjectivity in Anthropological Fieldwork* Routledge, London and New York, pp.168–85.

Mosse, D. (1994) Authority, gender and knowledge: theoretical reflections on the practice of participatory rural appraisal. *Development and Change* 25: 497–526.

Mowforth, M. and Munt, I. (1998) *Tourism and Sustainability: New Tourism in the Third World* Routledge, London.

Mullings, B. (1999) Insider or outsider, both or neither: some dilemmas of interviewing in a cross cultural setting. *Geoforum* (30): 337–50.

Munro, D. (1994) Who owns Pacific history? *Journal of Pacific History* 29(2):232–37.

Murray, W. E. (1997) Neo-liberalism, restructuring and non-traditional fruit exports in Chile: implications of export-orientation for small-scale farmers. PhD thesis, University of Birmingham, UK.

Nader, L. (1996) *Naked Science: Anthropological Inquiry into Boundaries, Power and Knowledge* Routledge, London.

Narayan, K. (1998) How native is a 'native' anthropologist? In M. Thapan (ed.) *Anthropological Journeys: Reflections on Fieldwork* Sangam Books, London, pp.163–87.

Nash, D. J. (2000) Doing independent overseas fieldwork 1: practicalities and pitfalls. *Journal of Geography in Higher Education* 24 (1):139–49.

Nash, D. J. (2000a) Doing independent overseas fieldwork 2: getting funding. *Journal of Geography in Higher Education* 24 (3):425–33.

Nash, J. (1976) Ethnology in a revolutionary setting. In M. Rynkiewich and J. Spradley (eds) *Ethics and Anthropology: Dilemmas in Fieldwork* John Wiley & Sons, New York, pp. 148–66

Nast, H. (1994) Opening remarks on "women in the field". *Professional Geographer* 46(1): 54–66.

Nichols, P. (1991) *Social Survey Methods: A Fieldguide for Development Workers* Oxfam, Oxford.

Nietschmann, B. Q. (2001) The Nietschmann syllabus: A vision of the field. *Geographical Review* 91(1–2):175–84.

Nordstrom, C and Robben, A. C. G. (1995) *Fieldwork Under Fire: Contemporary Studies of Violence and Survival* University of California Press, Berkeley, California.

Nowak, B.and Laird, P. (1998) Human rights, advocacy and the anthropologist's role:the truths behind the moral dilemma. In P. Cleave (ed.) *The Changing Field* Campus Press, Palmerston North, pp. 17–29.

Oakley, A. (1981) Interviewing women: a contradiction in terms. In H. Roberts (ed.) *Doing Feminist Research* Routledge and Kegan Paul, London, pp. 30–61.

Oglesby, E. (1995) Myrna Mack.In C. Nordstrom and A.C.G.M. Robben (eds) *Fieldwork Under Fire: Contemporary Studies of Violence and Survival* University of California Press, Berkeley, pp. 254–59.

Opie, A. (1992). Qualitative research, appropriation of the 'other' and empowerment. *Feminist Review* 40: 52–69.

Ott, J. Pharmacotheon enthaeogenic drugs: their plant sources and histories, 2nd edition. Kennewick: WA, Products Company Press.

Overton, J. D. (1983) Spatial differentiation in the colonial economy of Kenya:Africans, settlers and the state 1900–1920. Unpublished PhD thesis, University of Cambridge, Cambridge.

Overton, J. D. (1989) *Land and Differentiation in Rural Fiji* National Centre for Development Studies, Australian National University, Canberra.

Palys, T. and Lowman, J. Informed Consent, Confidentiality and the Law: Implications of the Tri-Council Policy Statement. A Submission to the Simon Fraser University Research Ethics Policy Revision Task Force. Retrieved 20 January, 2002 from: http://www.sfu.ca/~palys/Conf&Law.html

Passaro, J. (1997) You can't take the subway to the Field!: "village" epistemologies in the global village. In A. Gupta and J. Ferguson (eds) *Anthropological Locations: Boundaries and Grounds of a Field Science* University of California Press, Berkeley, pp.147–62.

Patai, D. (1991) US academics and Third World Women: Is ethical research possible? In S.B. Gluck and D. Patai (eds) *Women's Words: The Feminist Practice of Oral History* Routledge, London and New York, pp.137–54.

Peil, M. (1993) Situational variables. In M. Bulmer and D.P. Warwick (eds) *Social Research in Developing Countries* UCL Press, London, pp.71–88.

Peluso, N. (1995) Whose woods are these? Counter-mapping forest territories in Kalimantan, Indonesia. *Antipode* 27(4): 383–406.

Posner, J. (1980) Urban anthropology: Fieldwork in semifamiliar settings. In W. Shaffir, R. Stebbins and A. Turowetz (eds) *Fieldwork Experience: Qualitative Approaches to Social Relations* St. Martins Press, New York, pp.203–12.

Potter, R. (1993) Little England and little geography: Reflections on Third World teaching and research. *Area* 25(3): 291–94.

Pratt, B. and Loizos, P. (1992). *Choosing Research Methods: Data Collection for Development Workers* Oxfam, Oxford.

Prebisch, R. (1962) The economic development of Latin America: Its principal problems. *Economic Bulletin for Latin America* 7(1): 1–22.

Price, M. (2001) The kindness of strangers. *Geographical Review* 91(1–2):143–50.

Radcliffe, S. (1994) (Representing) post-colonial women: Authority, difference and feminisms. *Area:* 26 (1): 25–32.

Rahman, A. (1999) Micro-credit initiatives for equitable and sustainable development: Who pays? *World Development* 27(1): 67–82.

Rahnema, M. and Bawtree, V. (1997) *The Post-Development Reader* Zed, London.

Raybeck, D. (1996) *Mad Dogs, Englishmen, and the Errant Anthropologist: Fieldwork in Malaysia* Waveland Press, Prospect Heights, Illinois.

Razavi, S. (1992) Fieldwork in a familiar setting: the role of politics at the national, community and household levels. In S. Devereux and J. Hoddinott, (eds) *Fieldwork in Developing Countries* Harvester Wheatsheaf, Hemel Hempstead, pp.152–63.

Reinharz, S., with Davidman, L. (1992) *Feminist Methods in Social Research*. Oxford University Press, Oxford.

Richardson, L. (1994) Writing: A method of inquiry. In N.K. Denzin and S. Lincoln (eds) *Handbook of Qualitative Research* Sage, Thousand Oaks, pp.516–29.

Roadberg, A. (1980) Breaking relationships with research subjects: Some problems and suggestions. In W. Shaffir, R. Stebbins and A. Turowetz (eds) *Fieldwork Experience: Qualitative Approaches to Social Relations* St. Martins Press, New York, pp.281–91.

Robinson, G. (1998) *Methods and Techniques in Human Geography* Wiley, London.

Robson, C. (1993) *Real World Research* Blackwells, London.

Robson, E. (1997) From teacher to taxi driver: reflections on research roles in developing areas. In E. Robson and K. Willis (eds) *Postgraduate Fieldwork in Developing Countries* Monograph No.9, Developing Areas Research Group of the Royal Geographical Society, with the Institute of British Geographers, London, pp.51–74.

Robson, E. (2001) Interviews worth the tears? Exploring dilemmas of research with young carers in Zimbabwe. *Ethics, Place and Environment* 4(2): 135–42.

Robson, E. and Willis, K. (eds) (1997) *Postgraduate Fieldwork in Developing Areas: A Rough Guide* Monograph No.9, Developing Areas Research Group of the Royal Geographical Society, with the Institute of British Geographers, London.

Robson, E. and Willis, K. with Elmhirst, R.E. (1997) Practical tips In E. Robson and K. Willis (eds) *Postgraduate Fieldwork in Developing Countries* Monograph No.9, Developing Areas Research Group of the Royal Geographical Society, with the Institute of British Geographers, London, pp.135–62.

Roces, A. and Roces, G. (1985) *Culture Shock! Philippines* Times Books International, Singapore.

Rogers, S. (1978) Women's Place: a critical review of anthropological theory. *Comparative Studies in Society and History* 20: 123–62.

Rostow, W.W. (1960) *The Stages of Economic Growth: A Non-Communist Manifesto* Cambridge University Press, Cambridge.

Roth, R. (2001) A self-reflective exploration into development research. In P. Moss (ed.) *Placing Autobiography in Geography* Syracuse University Press, Syracuse, pp.121-37.

Said, E. (1978) *Orientalism* Pantheon, New York.

Sanders, C. (1998) Animal Passions: The Emotional Experience of Doing Ethnography in Animal-Human Interaction Settings. In S. Grills (ed.) *Doing Ethnographic Research: Fieldwork Settings* Sage, Thousand Oaks, pp. 184–98.

Sanders, R. (2001) Home and away: Bridging fieldwork and everyday life. *Geographical Review* 91(1–2):88–94.

Sangarasivam, Y. (2001) Researcher, informant, 'assassin', me. *Geographical Review* 91(1–2):95–104.

Sartre, J.-P. (1969) *Being and Nothingness* Routledge and Kegan Paul, London.

Sayer, A. (1988) *Method in Social Science – a Realist Approach* Routlege, London.

Sayer, A. and Storper, M. (1997) Guest editorial essay. *Environment and Planning D: Society and Space* 15: 1–17.

Scaglion, R. (1990) Ethnocentrism and the Abelam. In P. DeVita (ed.) *The Humbled Anthropologist* Wadsworth, Belmont, pp. 29–34.

Schenk-Sandbergen, L. (1998) Gender in field research: experiences in India. In M. Thapan (ed.) *Anthropological Journeys: Reflections on Fieldwork* Sangam Books, London, pp. 267–92.

Scheper-Hughes, N. (1992) *Death Without Weeping: The Violence of Everyday Life in Northwest Brazil* University of California Press, Berkeley, California.

Scheyvens, R. (1995) A Quiet Revolution: Strategies for the Empowerment and Development of Rural Women in the Solomon Islands. PhD thesis, Massey University, Palmerston North.

Scheyvens, R. and Leslie, H. (2000) Gender, ethics and empowerment: dilemmas of development fieldwork. *Women's Studies International Forum* 23(1): 119–30.

Schoenburger, E (1991) The corporate interview as a research method in economic geography. *Professional Geographer* 44: 1980–999

Schrijvers, J. (1993) Motherhood experienced and conceptualised: changing images in Sri Lanka and the Netherlands. In D. Bell, P. Caplan, and W. K. Jarim (eds) *Gendered Fields: Women, Men and Ethnography* Routledge, London, pp.143–58.

Schroeder, D.G. (1993) *Staying Healthy in Asia, Africa and Latin America* Moon Publications, Chico, CA.

Scott, J. C. (1985) *Weapons of the Weak. Everyday Forms of Peasant Resistance* Yale University Press, New Haven.

Seymour-Smith, C. (1986) *Macmillan Dictionary of Anthropology* Macmillan, London.

Shaffir, W. and Stebbins R. (eds) (1991) *Experiencing Fieldwork: An Inside View of Qualitative Research* Sage, Newbury Park.

Shaffir, W. and Stebbins, R. (1991) Leaving and keeping in touch. In W. Shaffir and R. Stebbins (eds) *Experiencing Fieldwork: An Inside View of Qualitative Research* Sage, Newbury Park, pp.207–10.

Shaffir, W., Stebbins, R. and. Turowetz, A. (eds) (1980) *Fieldwork Experience: Qualitative Approaches to Social Relations* St. Martins Press, New York.

Shaw, B. (1995) Contradictions between action and theory: Feminist participatory research in Goa, India. *Antipode* 27(1): 91–99.

Sidaway, J. D. (1992) In other worlds: On the politics of research by "First World" geographers in the "Third World". *Area* 24(4): 403–8.

Slim, H. and Thompson, P. (1993) *Listening for a Change: Oral Testimony and Development* Panos Publications Ltd, London.

Sluka, J. A.(1995) Reflections on managing danger in fieldwork: dangerous anthropology in Belfast. In C. Nordstrom and A. C. G. M.Robben (eds) *Fieldwork Under Fire:*

Contemporary Studies of Violence and Survival University of California Press, Berkeley, pp. 276–94.

Smith, L. T. (1999) *Decolonizing Methodologies: Research and Indigenous Peoples* Zed, London.

Smith, S. J. (1994) Qualitative methods. In R. J. Johnston, D. Gregory and D. M. Smith, (eds) *The Dictionary of Human Geography* Blackwells Publishers Ltd., Oxford, pp. 491–93.

Smith, S. E., Willms, D. G., with Johnson, N.A. (1997) *Nurtured by Knowledge: Learning to do Participatory Action-Research* International Development Research Centre, Ottawa.

Soja, E. W. (1968) *The Geography of Modernization in Kenya* Syracuse, University Press. Syracuse.

Soja, E. W. (1979) The geography of modernization: a radical reappraisal. In R.A. Obudho and D.R.F. Taylor (eds) *The Spatial Structure of Development: A Study of Kenya* Westview Press, Boulder, pp.28–45.

Sollis, P. and Moser, C. (1991) A methodological framework for analysing the social costs of adjustment at the micro-level: the case of Guayaquil, Ecuador. *IDS Bulletin* 22(1): 23–30.

Sörbö, G. M. (1982) Anthropology at home and abroad: a discussion of epistemological and ethical issues. In H. Famim (ed.) *Indigenous Anthropology in Non-Western Countries* Caroline Academic Press, Durham, pp.152–63.

Spender, D. (1980) *Man Made Language* Routledge and Kegan Paul Ltd, London.

Spivak, G. C. (1987) *In Other Worlds: Essays in Cultural Politics* Methuen, New York.

Staeheli, L. and Lawson, V. (1994) A discussion of "women in the field": The politics of feminist fieldwork. *Professional Geographer* 46(1): 96–102.

Stanley, D. (2000) *South Pacific Handbook* Moon Travel Handbooks, Emeryville, California.

Stebbins, R. (1991) Do we ever leave the field? Notes on secondary fieldwork involvements. In W. Shaffir and R. Stebbins (eds) *Experiencing Fieldwork: An Inside View of Qualitative Research* Sage, Newbury Park, pp.248–55.

Stevens, S. (2001) Fieldwork as commitment. *Geographical Review* 91(1–2):66–73.

Storey, D. (1997) 'Hey Joe! What are you doing?: Practicing participatory research in urban poor communities – lessons and experiences from the Philippines. Working Paper 97/2, Institute of Development Studies, Massey University.

Sullivan, S. (1998) People, plants and practice in drylands: socio-political and ecological dimensions of resource-use by Damara farmers in north-west Namibia. Unpublished PhD Dissertation. University College, London, London.

Sullivan, S. (2000) Gender, ethnographic myths and community-based conservation in a former Namibian 'homeland'. In D. Hodgson, (ed.) *Rethinking Pastoralism in Africa: Gender, Culture and the Myth of the Patriarchal Pastoralist* James Currey, Oxford, pp. 142–64.

Sullivan, S. (2001) On dance and difference: bodies, movement and experience in Khoesan trance-dancing – perceptions of 'a raver'. *Africa e Mediterraneo Cultura e Societa* 37: 15–22.

Sullivan, S. (2002) "'How can the rain fall in this chaos?' Myth and metaphor in representations of the north-west Namibian landscape." Anthropology in the African Renaissance. *Proceedings of the Anthropological Association of Southern Africa conference* Gamsberg MacMillan, Windhoek.

Taussig, M. (1987) *Shamanism, Colonialism and the Wild Man: A Study in Terror and Healing* University of Chicago Press, Chicago.

Taylor, P. (1992) Understanding global inequalities. *Geography* 77(11): 10–21.

Taylor, S. J. (1991) Leaving the field: Research, relationships and responsibilities. In W.B. Shaffir and R.A. Stebbins (eds) *Experiencing Fieldwork: An Inside View of Qualitative Research* Sage, Newbury Park, pp.238–47.

Teare, P. (1996) Grameen women blues. *Living Marxism*, 90.

Theis, J. (1998) Participatory research on child labour in Vietnam. In V. Johnson, E. Ivan-Smith, G. Gordon, P. Pridmore and P. Scott (eds) *Stepping Forward: Children and Young People's Participation in the Development Process* Intermediate Technology Publications, London, pp.81–5.

Thurston, W. (1998) The inadvertent acquisition of kinship during ethnographic fieldwork. In J. Flinn, L. Marshall and J. Armstrong (eds) *Fieldwork and Families: Constructing New Models For Ethnographic Research* University of Hawai'i Press, Honolulu.

Till, K. E. (2001) Returning home and to the field. *Geographical Review* 91(1–2):46–56.

Tilley, C. (1994) *A Phenomenology of Landscape: Places, Paths and Monuments* Oxford, Berg.

Todd, H. (1996) *Women at the Center: Grameen Bank Borrowers after One Decade* Westview Press, Boulder, Colorado.

Tomm, W. (1989) Introduction. In W. Tomm (ed.) *The Effects of Feminist Approaches on Research and Methodologies* Wilfrid Laurier University Press, Ontario, pp. 1–11.

Townsend, J. with Arrevillaga, U., Bain, J., Cancino, S., Frenk, S.F., Pacheco, S. and Perez, E. (1995) *Women's Voices From the Rainforest* Routledge, London and New York.

Truman, C., Mertens, D.M. and Humphries, B. (2000) *Research and Inequality* UCL Press, London.

Twyman, C., Morrison, J. and Sporton, D. (1999) The final fifth: autobiography, reflexivity and interpretation in cross-cultural research. *Area* 31(4): 313–25.

Valentine, G. (1999) Being seen and heard? The ethical complexities of working with children and young people at home and at school. *Ethics, Place and Environment* 2: 311–24.

Valentine, J. (1997) Tell me about...: using interviews as a research methodology. In R. Flowerdew and D. Martin (eds) *Methods in Human Geography* Longman, Harlow, pp.110–26.

van Binsbergen, W. (1979) Anthropological fieldwork: 'there and back again'. *Human Organisation* 38(2):205–9.

Van Maanan, J. (1988) *Tales of the Field: On Writing Ethnography* University of Chicago Press, Chicago and London, pp. 31–42.

Van Maanen, J. (1991) Playing Back the Tape: Early days in the field. In W. B.Shaffir and R. A.Stebbins (eds) *Experiencing Fieldwork: An inside View of Qualitative Research* Sage, Newbury Park.

Van Maanen, J. (1988) *Tales of the Field: On Writing Ethnography* University of Chicago Press, Chicago.

Veeck, G. (2001) Talk is cheap: cultural and linguistic fluency during field research. *The Geographical Review* 1/2:34–40.

Wagley, C. (1983) Learning Fieldwork: Guatemala. In R. Lawless, W. Sutlive and M. Zamora (eds) *Fieldwork: The Human Experience* Gordon and Breach, New York, pp.1–18.

Walcott, H. F. (1995) *The Art of Fieldwork.* AltaMira Press, Walnut Creek, CA.

Walsh, A. C. (1995) *Getting on Top of Your Thesis* Amokura Publishers, Suva.

Walsh, A. C. (1996) Ethnicity, gender and survey biases in Fiji. *The Journal of Pacific Studies* 19:145–58.

Walsh, A.C. (ed.) (1996) *Getting on Top of Your Thesis* (2nd ed) Suva, Fiji, Amokura Publications.

Ward, C., Bochner, S., and Furnham, A. (2001) *The Psychology of Culture Shock* (2nd ed.) Routledge, Hove.

Watson, S. D. (1993) Education as a social indicator and agricultural education in Papua New Guinea. Unpublished Masters thesis, Massey University, Palmerston North.

Wax, M. L. (1979) On the presentation of self in fieldwork: the dialectic of mutual deception and disclosure. *Humanity and Society* 3(4):248–59.

Wax, R. (1971) *Doing Fieldwork:Warnings and Advice* University of Chicago Press, Chicago and London.

Weaver, D. B. (1998) *Ecotourism in the Less Developed World* CAB International, Wallingford.

Weiss, G. and Haber, H. F. (1999) *Perspectives on Embodiment: the Intersections of Nature and Culture* Routledge, London

Werner, D., Thuman, C. and Maxwell, J. (1993) *Where there is no Doctor: A Village Health Care Guide* Macmillan, London.

Werner, O. and Schoepfle, G. M (1987) *Systemic Fieldwork. Volume 1: Foundations of Ethnography and Interviewing* Sage, Newbury Park, CA..

Weulker, G. (1983) Questionnaires in Asia. In M. Bulmer and D.P. Warwick (eds) *Social Research in Developing Countries* John Wiley and Sons, London, pp.161–66.

Whiteford, A. H. and Whiteford, M. S. (1987) Reciprocal relations: family contributions to anthropological field research—and vice versa. In B. Butler and D. Michalski Turner (eds) *Children and Anthropological Research* Plenum Press, New York, pp.115–36.

Wikan, U. (1996) *Tomorrow God Willing:Self-Made Destinies in Cairo* University of Chicago Press, Chicago and London.

Willis, P. (1977) *Learning to Labour. How Working Class Kids Get Working Class Jobs* Saxon House, Farnborough.

Willis, R. (1981) *A State in the Making. Myth, History and Social Transformation in Pre-colonial Ufipa* Indiana University Press, Bloomington, IN.

Wilson, K. (1993) Thinking about the ethics of fieldwork. In S. Devereux and J. Hoddinott (eds), *Fieldwork in Developing Countries* Harvester Wheatsheaf, New York, pp.179–99.

Wilson, K. (1993) Thinking about the ethics of fieldwork. In S.Devereux and J.Hoddinott (eds) *Fieldwork in Developing Countries* Lynne Rienner, Boulder, pp. 179–99.

Wolcott, H. (1995) *The Art of Fieldwork* AltaMira Walnut Creek.

Wolf, D. L. (1996) Situating feminist dilemmas in fieldwork. In D.L.Wolf (ed.) *Feminist Dilemmas in Fieldwork* Westview, Boulder, pp. 1–55.

Wolf, D. L. (1996) *Feminist Dilemmas in Fieldwork* Westview, Boulder.

Wolf, D. R. (1991) High-risk methodology: Reflections on leaving an outlaw society. In W.B. Shaffir and R. A. Stebbins (eds) *Experiencing Fieldwork: An Inside View of Qualitative Research* Sage, Newbury Park, pp.211–23.

Wolfe J. M. (1989) Theory, hypothesis, explanation and action. In A. Kobayshi, and S. Mackenzie (eds) *Remaking Human Geography* Unwin Hyman, London, pp.62–77.

Women and Geography Study Group of the Institute of British Geographers, (1984) *Geography and Gender* Hutchison, London.

Wood, G. D. (1994) *Bangladesh:Whose Ideas,Whose Interests?* University Press Ltd., Dhaka.

Wuelker, G. (1993) Questionnaires in Asia. In M. Bulmer and D.P. Warwick (eds) *Social Research in Developing Countries* UCL Press, London, pp.161–66.

Young, L. and Barrett, H. (2001) Adapting visual methods: action research with Kampala street children. *Area* 33(2): 141–52.

Zarkovich, S. S. (1993) Some problems of sampling work in underdeveloped countries. In M. Bulmer and D.P. Warwick (eds) *Social Research in Developing Countries* UCL Press, London, pp.101–08.

Index